HOCKEY'S
Greatest Stars

HOCKEY'S
Greatest Stars

Legends and Young Lions

Chris McDonell

FIREFLY BOOKS

A FIREFLY BOOK

Published by Firefly Books Ltd. 1999

First Printing 1999

Library of Congress Cataloging-in-Publication Data

McDonell, Chris
    Hockey's greatest stars : legends and young lions /
    Chris McDonell
1st ed.
[192] p. :   col. ill. ;   cm.
Includes index.
Includes each player's statistics.
ISBN 1-55209-332-8
1. Hockey. 2. Hockey players – Biography. I. Title.
796.962/092–dc21   1999   CIP

Published in the United States in 1999 by
Firefly Books (U.S.) Inc.
P.O. Box 1338, Ellicott Station
Buffalo, New York 14205

Produced by
Bookmakers Press Inc.
12 Pine Street
Kingston, Ontario K7K 1W1
(613) 549-4347
tcread@sympatico.ca

Design by
Andrew McLachlan, Kroma Design

Canadian Cataloguing in Publication Data

McDonell, Chris
    Hockey's greatest stars : legends and young lions

Includes index.
ISBN 1-55209-332-8

1. Hockey players – Biography. 2. National Hockey League –
Biography. I. Title.

GV848.5.A1M27 1999   796.962'092'2   C99-930383-X

Published in Canada in 1999 by
Firefly Books Ltd.
3680 Victoria Park Avenue
Willowdale, Ontario M2H 3K1

Printed and bound in Canada by
Friesens
Altona, Manitoba

Canadä

The Publisher acknowledges the financial support of the Government of Canada through the Book Publishing Industry Development Program for its publishing activities.

Contents

Philadelphia Flyers' captain Eric Lindros chases a loose puck while dodging a hook from Toronto's rear guard Bryan Berard.

Introduction

"I respected 'Rocket' Richard," Gordie Howe once said, "but I didn't like him. He was the man who led the way for the rest of us. He was my pacemaker—first for career points, then for career goals. Like I tell all of the kids, if you really want to learn the game of hockey, pick somebody you admire and emulate him. I picked 'The Rocket,' and he showed me a lot."

Howe, in turn, inspired another legend. "Growing up, my player role model was always Gordie," Wayne Gretzky has said, and "The Great One" himself has fired the dreams of

National Hockey League stars such as Paul Kariya and the players to emerge in coming generations.

In the same way, every hockey fan has a favorite player or two. This has always been true, but never more so than it is today. Fan loyalty to a team is harder to maintain in the face of the threat (occasionally carried out) of franchise moves, trades openly made more for the sake of "the business" than to acquire the best players and player free agency. Longtime devotees and new converts may find their personal heroes in

the following pages, but popularity was not an issue in deciding who would be included. *Hockey's Greatest Stars: Legends and Young Lions* comprises two lists: the "legends," the greatest players of all time; and the "young lions," the players who currently prowl NHL arenas. "Young" is a relative term, but for the purposes of this book, it means those born in 1970 or later. At the time of publication, the young players had not yet reached their thirtieth birthdays.

Compiling these two lists has been an arduous task. I consulted with various hockey sages, who were promised anonymity, and closely studied other lists, but nothing resembling a consensus ever resulted. The enjoyable debate lost some of its pleasure when it came time to limit the many worthy candidates to the prescribed numbers: 60 of the best ever and the top 20 young players. By organizing these lists according to position, however, certain names simply fell into place: at center, Wayne Gretzky; on wing, Gordie Howe; on defense, Bobby Orr; and in goal, Terry Sawchuk. Their achievements made them automatic and unarguable choices. Corresponding young stars such as Eric Lindros, Paul Kariya, Nicklas Lidstrom and Martin Brodeur were equally easy to include. Finalizing the latter half of each subsection was where the real work lay.

The number-one criterion for inclusion in *Hockey's Greatest Stars* was personal accomplishment. Looking at a player's statistics and accumulated awards was instructive, but it was not enough. Once asked what he liked best about Mario Lemieux, Howe quipped, "His paycheck." But more than player salaries have changed. Different eras cannot be compared in a completely straightforward manner. A second assist was rarely given on goals during Charlie Conacher's career in the 1930s; Georges Vezina, who died in 1926 and for whom the NHL's best goaltender award is named, never played a game in which the rules permitted a netminder to hold or smother the puck. It is an oft-repeated maxim that the best players would star in any era, yet as Nels Stewart allowed, even the renowned Howie Morenz would have had a difficult time in the NHL of the 1950s. The best ones sometimes find a way to overcome challenges, but I gave consideration to the question of how a player would fare in hockey as we now know it.

Another important ingredient in the makeup of a great hockey player is his contribution to team success. "Steve Yzerman is the best example," says winger Brendan Shanahan. "He's a guy whose image has gone back and forth so many times in the organization, and now he's considered one of the greatest captains to ever play. That's what winning does for all of us." Strong performance under playoff pressure lifted more than one player into *Hockey's Greatest Stars*, although the lack of a Stanley Cup ring was never a reason for exclusion.

"I have been able to maintain my scoring pace while guys like Guy Lafleur have tailed off," Marcel Dionne once remarked with a wistful smile. "I always get an extra two months of rest because we never make the playoffs." The list of legends here is sprinkled with others who never hoisted the Cup—goaltender Vladislav Tretiak didn't even compete in the NHL—and the young stars who have played on Stanley Cup winners are the exception rather than the rule.

Consistency and durability were weighted more heavily than meteoric exploits for the legends' roster, less so for the young lions. Thus a player such as 700-goal-scorer Mike Gartner is included, although he was never selected to an end-of-season All-Star Team, while 1972 Team Canada hero Paul Henderson is not. Several other players, too old to qualify as young lions, might have joined Gartner in this book had they put in more years as consistently as some contemporary players—defenseman Brian Leetch springs immediately to mind. Likewise, it was hard to exclude players such as goaltender Tony Esposito, a frequent All-Star during his lengthy Hall of Fame career with the Chicago Blackhawks. Yet when everything was factored in, center Phil is the only Esposito on this honor roll.

Beyond including players or not, I made no attempt to

rank them. In the end, it came down to singular decisions—this star or that?—and the answers were never easy.

"There will always be young hockey champions," wrote journalist Andy O'Brien in 1971. "Those of tomorrow could very well force the National Hockey League to change its name to the Global Hockey League." Considering that NHL players had yet to eat some humble pie in the 1972 Summit Series, O'Brien's prediction is almost eerily accurate. Hockey has evolved not only by drawing the world's best players into the NHL during this generation but also through the tremendous expansion of the league. Such rapid change invites risks—losing sight of tradition and, at times, looking back through rose-colored glasses. In winnowing down the lists for *Hockey's Greatest Stars*, I have tried to avoid sentimentality yet do justice to the athletes of yesteryear.

"One of the greatest parts of our game is the history," observed Gretzky at the 1999 All-Star Game. "I mean the Stanley Cup itself, the original six teams and the star players who created the NHL." He chatted with Maurice Richard, who unveiled the new Richard Trophy for the league's top goal scorer. "There are some guys who don't get as much recognition as they deserve for getting hockey to the level it is today," he continued. "I was telling 'Rocket' at center ice that the NHL was lucky to have him in the game."

As William Shakespeare once wrote, though: "What's past is prologue." While Richard's appearances provide a tangible link with a bygone era, so, too, does the veteran and recently retired Gretzky, as will, eventually, the young lions profiled here. These vignettes, although arranged by position rather than in chronological order, collectively serve as a snapshot of glorious hockey history—past, present and future.

The results of my difficult decisions are now before you. After perusing the table of contents, try to put aside your own arguments for a while. The portraits offered here, in words and pictures, sketch talented, gritty and inspiring men who represent all that is wonderful and exciting about the fabulous sport of hockey. The game itself has its own charm, but the players bring it to life. Enjoy their stories and the recollection of their exploits. And watch the greatest stars still playing. Game by game, new chapters continue to be written.

Left: Toronto's inspiring captain Syl Apps (center) gets behind the New York Rangers' defense and slips the puck past goalie Chuck Rayner. Facing page: In a classic confrontation, the Montreal Canadiens' elegant center Jean Beliveau matches wits with legendary netminder Terry Sawchuk of the Maple Leafs. Previous pages: In a tense moment for goaltender Dominik Hasek in the 1996 All-Star Game, page 8, Teemu Selanne takes aim while Mike Gartner (22) readies himself for a pass or a rebound. Jaromir Jagr, page 9, won his third Art Ross Trophy as the 1998-99 scoring champion, despite taking on a new leadership role with the Pittsburgh Penguins.

The Centers

Hockey's greatest players can be found at every position, but a team's best player is most often found at center. As the name implies, much of the game revolves around the centerman. At the opening face-off and after every stop in the action, two centers square off head-to-head. How they handle that play dictates the ensuing flow of the game. A strong face-off artist can give his team a tremendous advantage.

The drop of the puck, however, is only the beginning. A center's skills must be more varied than those of any other player. Legendary goal scorers such as Nels "Old Poison" Stewart and "Super Mario" Lemieux have been able to leave most defensive responsibilities to others, but an offensive star such as Steve Yzerman has a place in this book in part because of his evolution into a two-way player. With rare exceptions, the centerman must be skilled both on the attack—passing and shooting—and in checking.

The centers featured here include slightly built men such as Marcel Dionne and Henri Richard as well as behemoths like Eric Lindros and Phil Esposito. "Scoring is easy," said Esposito, whom most defensemen found immovable. "You stand in the slot, take your beating and shoot the puck in the net." At the opposite extreme, Richard speaks about using his diminutive size to scoot under a defenseman's reach and get in alone on the goalie.

But the greatest center of all time is physically unremarkable in any way. The 6-foot 175-pound Wayne Gretzky is arguably the greatest player ever to have laced on skates, yet myriad others have possessed a stronger shot, greater speed or superior strength. Appropriately, another sense of the word

"center" means "to concentrate and focus," and it is in this area that Gretzky proved to be without peer. Unique in his ability to "read" a play and dissect the possibilities, he regularly surprised everyone by executing the unexpected but clearly best option.

Obviously, there are different ways to approach the position, but it is no coincidence that of the 20 centers in this book, all but three have served as team captain. Exceptional physical skills are not enough to make an elite center. Brawn is an obvious asset, but the savvy of Stan Mikita, the fortitude of the diabetic Bobby Clarke and the ambassadorial presence of Jean Beliveau are traits that all of these centers possess to a high degree. As critical to their teams' success as their prodigious talents, these are also key ingredients of leadership.

Strength up the middle is a general prerequisite of a championship team. "The measure of Mark Messier's game is not in goals and assists," observed Gretzky. "The statistic he cares about is number of Stanley Cups won." But while Hall of Fame member Dionne didn't win a single title, he remains, a decade after retiring, third in NHL history in both career goals and points scored. Stanley Cup rings are not essential components of greatness, as some of the young centers featured here may eventually have to discover, but manifesting an unquenchable drive to win is characteristic of every center in this book.

New York Rangers center Wayne Gretzky, above, prepares to battle Buffalo's Mike Peca for control of the puck. Facing page: Philadelphia's Bobby Clarke pesters Montreal defenseman Guy Lapointe.

Syl Apps

Syl Apps combined Boy Scout virtue with exceptional athletic ability, the perfect profile for a hockey hero in what was once known as "Toronto the Good." Although Apps had only a 10-season career, he is still regarded by many as the greatest leader the Toronto Maple Leafs ever had. His minuscule 56 career penalty minutes attest to his sportsmanship, but his chiseled good looks, great physical strength and slick stick-handling, passing and scoring were equally important to the lasting image he created.

Apps helped the Maple Leafs win three Stanley Cups, captained the team after his World War II military service and quit the game while still at his peak. "I hope that Apps doesn't retire," Toronto netminder Turk Broda once commented. "He's been my meal ticket for 10 years. When things look rugged, Hap [Maple Leaf coach Hap Day] drops him over the boards, and the situation improves instantly."

An all-round athlete who excelled at hockey, football and track, Apps was the 1934 Commonwealth Games pole vault champion and delayed accepting Conn Smythe's invitation to join the Maple Leafs so that he could compete in the 1936 Olympics in Berlin. Apps finished sixth at the Olympics, and only then did he turn his full attention to hockey.

He went on to win the inaugural Calder Trophy in 1937, presented by NHL president Frank Calder to the league's best rookie, but the spring of 1942 provided his greatest excitement. "Nothing can compare," he said, "with the thrill of winning our fourth in a row over the Red Wings after they had won three straight." No other team has ever made such an amazing comeback in the Stanley Cup finals. "If you want to pin me down to not only my biggest night in hockey but also my biggest second," he told writer Trent Frayne in 1949, "I'll say it was the last tick of the clock that sounded the final bell. I'll never forget it."

Halfway through the 1942-43 season, Apps broke his leg and shocked owner Smythe when he tried to return part of his salary—he felt he hadn't earned his full pay. Once the leg healed, he volunteered for Canadian military service, missing two full NHL seasons at the height of his career. Although he was only 30 years old at the war's conclusion, Apps wasn't certain that the Leafs would want him back. His genuine humility further endeared him to Smythe and to the public.

Apps picked up right where he had left off. In 1947, Hall of Fame defenseman Bill Quackenbush, a league All-Star for Detroit at the time, claimed that Apps was the hardest player in the league to stop. "When he hits the defense," said Quackenbush, "he doesn't slow down, he digs in. That extra burst of speed makes him awful tough." Apps, however, believed he'd lost a step. He wanted to retire before he "slowed the team down," but he set one last target: 200 career goals.

Heading into the final weekend of play in the spring of 1948, Apps needed only three more goals to reach 200. He scored one on Saturday night. In Sunday's game against Detroit, he banged in another one after a goalmouth scramble in the second period. Later in the same period, Harry Watson of the Leafs had an excellent scoring opportunity, but instead of shooting, he slid a neat pass over to Apps, who buried goal 200 behind netminder Harry Lumley. "I just blasted it with everything I had," said Apps. The Detroit crowd gave him a noisy ovation, and Apps put the icing on the cake by completing a hat trick in the third period.

The press commented on how generous Watson had been in setting Apps up for the goal. "It was nice of him, all right," agreed Apps, "but you should have heard the yelling I was doing at him to pass it!" Apps hoisted the Stanley Cup for the second consecutive year, but when the Leafs "three-peated" the following season, it was without Apps in the lineup. The 33-year-old captain had retired and joined the business world.

"I was always keen about politics," explained Apps, when he answered yet another calling years later. Elected as a member of the governing Progressive Conservative Party in 1963, he later chaired the Select Committee on Youth as it grappled with the emerging issue of drugs and youth.

"He was convinced," fellow committee member (and Opposition Leader) Stephen Lewis once commented, "that the way to keep any boy out of trouble was to get him into a hockey league, preferably one sponsored by a church. I rather think that's been Syl through all his government career."

Apps later served as Minister of Corrections, and his rock-solid image was untarnished by 11 years in Ontario politics. True to form, he retired on his own terms in 1974.

Syl Apps buries one of his 201 career goals behind Boston netminder
Frank Brimsek, above. Apps, whose 10-year hockey career was interrupted by World War II service, helped the Toronto Maple Leafs to three
Stanley Cup victories in the 1940s. Facing page: Apps celebrates a win
flanked by Hap Day and Leafs owner/manager Conn Smythe.

Jean Beliveau

- -

No one meeting Jean Beliveau today would be surprised to hear that he has been offered an appointment to the Canadian Senate as well as the prestigious position of Governor General of Canada. And during his 20-year NHL hockey career, Beliveau was every bit as much the diplomat. Although he was never a recipient of the Lady Byng Trophy, Beliveau was hockey's greatest gentleman and a born leader. Upon Maurice "Rocket" Richard's retirement from the Montreal Canadiens in 1960, Beliveau won a literal vote of confidence from the players and quickly became the quintessential team captain.

James Christie of *The Globe and Mail* recorded Beliveau's own reflections on his approach to leadership: "To me, there are three things that a captain should do. First is what the fans see during a game. There is your play and the job you do as the man in the middle, the man between the coaches and the players and the referee. Second, there is the job every day in the dressing room. You have to listen to your teammates, even help them with their personal problems. I always tried to solve things right there in the dressing room, without going to management. Third, especially with the Canadiens, you act as a spokesman and representative wherever you go. But the most important of these is number two. You have to be ready to give time to your teammates in any situation." Both on and off the ice, Beliveau earned undying respect, and upon his retirement, he received a rare and lengthy standing ovation from the usually taciturn media.

Few players have entered the NHL with as much fanfare as did Beliveau. The Montreal Canadiens wooed him unsuccessfully for years, even though it was patently obvious to all that his eventual destiny lay with the Habs. Beliveau's patience paid off: By the time he signed with Montreal at age 22, he was one of the highest-paid players in the NHL. His first contract paid $105,000 over five years, plus bonuses—an astronomical sum in 1953. But Beliveau had been making similar money with the Quebec Aces in the Quebec Hockey League, and it took more than cash to get him into the NHL.

Beliveau played as a junior for two years in Quebec City with the Citadelles and was honored with his first "Jean Beliveau Night" in 1951. The whole city had embraced the 61-goal scorer (in a 43-game season), and he was presented

with the keys to a new maroon Nash Rambler in front of 15,000 fans. Although Montreal beckoned, Beliveau decided to stay in Quebec City. In an ostensibly amateur league, Beliveau earned a then enormous $15,000 a year for his "civic" loyalty, and he reciprocated with 45- and 50-goal seasons. Meanwhile, he had already signed a contract with Montreal stipulating that he would play for the Canadiens when he turned professional.

Beliveau had played two NHL games in the 1950-51 season, getting a goal and an assist, and he donned the famous *bleu, blanc et rouge* sweater for three games in the 1952-53 season, scoring five times. Still, he seemed quite happy to remain in Quebec. The Canadiens took drastic action: They bought the entire Quebec senior league and made it officially professional. Beliveau's hand was thus forced, and at the start of the 1953-54 season, he began his much-anticipated rookie campaign.

Unfortunately, Beliveau struggled at the outset, was injured and finished with an unimpressive 13 goals and 21 assists in 44 games. Montreal's perseverance was rewarded in his second season (37 goals, 36 assists); in the third season, even more so. "I used to wonder why 'Rocket' Richard would blow up when other players chopped at him," Beliveau said in 1956, "but I am beginning to understand." Responding to critics who urged him to use his size and strength to better advantage, Beliveau began to adopt a more belligerent style. His 143 penalty minutes in 1955-56 set a team record, but more important, his 47 goals and 41 assists led the league. He scored 12 more goals in Montreal's 10-game march to Stanley Cup victory, the first of five consecutive winning seasons.

Once he'd proved that he could play a rough game, Beliveau gradually settled into a style frequently described as elegant. "Beliveau," wrote novelist Hugh MacLennan, "is poetry in action." He continued to use his size to park himself in front of the enemy net, but his greatest physical assets were his long reach and tremendous stickhandling ability.

Although Beliveau failed to win another scoring title, the goals came regularly over the years. On February 11, 1971, during his final NHL season, he became only the fourth player to record 500 career goals. He capped his glorious career by hoisting the Stanley Cup for a tenth time.

Montreal captain Jean Beliveau tries to outmuscle Toronto Maple Leaf Johnny Bower and defenseman Larry Hillman, above, to put the puck in the goal. Facing page: A huge star in his home province well before he signed a contract with the Montreal Canadiens in 1953, Beliveau is pictured in his Quebec Aces uniform.

Bobby Clarke

Described as one of hockey's greatest leaders and one of its dirtiest players, Bobby Clarke has earned both tags. Each characterization was intrinsic to Clarke's role in the 1970s as captain of Philadelphia's infamous "Broad Street Bullies," a team that constantly tried to blur the line between aggression and violence. Red Kelly, then coach of the Toronto Maple Leafs, added an important nuance: "I don't think I'd call Clarke dirty—mean is a better word."

"Guys who complain about my being dirty," countered Clarke, "should go home with my body at night. I've eaten quite a few too"—sticks, that is. Clarke's toothless grin has become one of hockey's enduring images, and it is still used to sell beer and the game 25 years after he led Philadelphia to its first of two consecutive Stanley Cups in 1974.

Clarke showed early promise as a hockey player in the gritty mining town of Flin Flon, Manitoba, but at the age of 15, he'd arrived at a crossroads. Diagnosed with juvenile diabetes, Clarke began self-administering the daily insulin

injections necessary to stay alive. He also sought medical advice to confirm his conviction that his diabetes need not end his dream of playing professional hockey. His doctors concurred, and by the time Clarke was 17, he was starring for the Flin Flon Bombers in the junior Western Hockey League. Working in the mines a few hours each day further hardened his resolve to make hockey his career.

Clarke entered the 1969 NHL entry draft ranked the premier player in the WHL, but many questioned whether he could sustain the NHL pace. The Philadelphia Flyers took a chance on him with their second pick, seventeenth overall. It was the best move the franchise ever made.

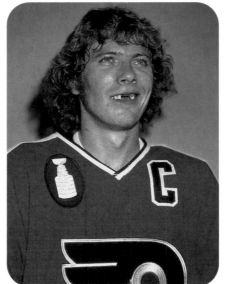

Clarke gave the Flyers cause for worry when he fainted after his first shift in training camp, but it was soon determined that his diet simply needed to be adjusted, and he had a decent 1969-70 rookie season. His growing success and perseverance were acknowledged when he won the Bill Masterton Trophy in 1972. Later that fall, Clarke played a big role in Team Canada's narrow victory over the Soviet Union, centering a line of two other unlikely heroes: Toronto's Paul Henderson and Ron Ellis.

Clarke's tenacious checking was invaluable, but his vicious two-handed slash on the ankle of Soviet star Valery Kharlamov is what is best remembered. The intentional foul, which took Kharlamov out of the critical last three games of the series, was slyly admired at home in the Cold War climate of 1972. "It's not something I'm

Philadelphia Flyers' captain Bobby Clarke wears a celebratory crest on his jersey, above, in honor of his team's 1974 Stanley Cup victory. Fearful that the crest would antagonize the opposition, Clarke removed the patch shortly after. Facing page: Combining talent with grit and a tireless work ethic, Clarke won the Hart Trophy as the NHL's most valuable player three times.

really proud of," Clarke recently noted, "but I honestly can't say I was ashamed to do it."

Off the ice, Clarke gained some notoriety as a "walking salary cap." It was rumored that he cut secret deals to augment his wages while allowing Philadelphia management to cite his contract when negotiating with its other stars. On the ice, Clarke was almost universally admired. In the 1970s, goalie Bernie Parent conceded, "Clarke is our leader. He works so hard himself that the other guys just have to work to keep up. He is the guy who makes us go." Philadelphia owner Ed Snider agreed. No matter how hard they tried, he said, his players could not emulate the talented Orrs and Lafleurs of the league, but they saw that they could have the success Clarke enjoyed if they put out as much effort.

Clarke was indeed visibly industrious, with his head bobbing as he raced about the ice, but he was also a gifted player. He controlled the puck a great deal of the time, then threaded passes to his teammates. Yet there were games when Clarke *did* seem to dig deeper than humanly possible, dragging his team up by the bootstraps to victory, particularly in the 1974 Stanley Cup finals.

Facing the powerful Boston Bruins, Clarke's Flyers were down 2–0 in game two after losing the series opener. Clarke scored once to narrow Boston's lead, then tied the game with only 52 seconds left in regulation time. With 12 minutes gone in overtime, Clarke concluded a magnificent evening's work by completing a hat trick and swinging all the momentum Philadelphia's way. The Bruins never fully recovered, and Clarke delivered the *coup de grâce* to Boston's hopes when he lured Bobby Orr into hauling him down with just over two minutes remaining in the deciding game. With Orr sitting in the penalty box, the Flyers won the game 1–0 and hoisted the Stanley Cup for the first time.

Clarke eventually lost his choirboy looks and evolved into "Bob" Clarke, the man who is well into his second term as Philadelphia's general manager. Using the same approach to model his club that was so successful to him as a player, he has consistently constructed big and tough Stanley Cup contenders. But it was his work on skates that earned Clarke the eternal gratitude of the City of Brotherly Love.

Marcel Dionne

On skates, he was as solid as a fire hydrant and not much bigger, but Marcel Dionne had quick acceleration and an aggressive run-and-gun style that put him in the spotlight at a young age. Family and hometown pressures in Quebec were so great during his teenage years that the scoring sensation opted to play in Ontario's junior league, where, in spite of the culture shock he experienced, he won two consecutive scoring championships.

Even when fully grown, Dionne stood just under five-foot-eight, but NHL scouts ranked him with Guy Lafleur, his perennial rival in Quebec. After some dithering, the Montreal Canadiens selected Lafleur as the number-one pick in the 1971 NHL entry draft, and the Detroit Red Wings quickly snapped up Dionne with the second pick.

Dionne had an auspicious rookie year, with 28 goals and 49 assists, but he found himself on a team in turmoil. Problems at the top of the Red Wings organization seemed to trickle down to the players. Dionne was suspended from the team twice for arguing with his coach. "You have to find a way to survive," maintained Dionne in the face of criticism for selfishness. He racked up 366 points in four seasons with the Wings and moved into the rarefied atmosphere at the top of the league's scoring race, finishing behind only Bobby Orr and Phil Esposito in the 1974-75 season. But Dionne and the Red Wings never got a hint of playoff action together.

Discouraged by the losing atmosphere in the Motor City, Dionne became the first high-profile player to test the new free-agent market. In the summer of 1975, the Los Angeles Kings made a generous offer, and Dionne jumped at the chance to play for a team that had been rising consistently in the standings. Unfortunately, Dionne soon found himself in a situation similar to the one he had just left. While the Kings enjoyed little success during the almost 12 seasons he spent in Los Angeles, Dionne remained an offensive force. In his second season in L.A.'s purple and gold, he broke the 50-goal plateau for the first of six times in seven years.

His clean play was twice rewarded with the Lady Byng Trophy; he also won the Art Ross Trophy, by the narrowest of margins. Dionne entered the final month of the 1979-80 season 17 points ahead of Wayne Gretzky, but he had to come up

with 2 assists in the final game of the season to match Gretzky's surge to 137 points. Dionne got the title because of his 53 goals versus Gretzky's 51.

Dionne appreciated his trophies, but he valued none so much as the Pearson Award as the league's most valuable player, which he collected in 1979 and 1980. That honor is voted for by the players. Dionne had lost respect for the hockey writers when they voted him center for the First All-Star Team for the 1976-77 season. "I played the right wing in the Canada Cup that September," he explained. "I went back to Los Angeles, played the whole year at right wing, and they voted for me at center." His success that season notwithstanding, Dionne was soon back at home in the pivot position, where his freewheeling style gave defensemen nightmares. Dave Taylor and Charlie Simmer joined him at his flanks, and although they were playing in hockey's hinterland, the "Triple Crown Line" quickly gathered notice as one of the NHL's best.

Ostensibly for a better shot at a Stanley Cup, Dionne demanded a move at the 1986-87 trading deadline, although he later claimed that his request was a bluff, a contract-negotiation ploy. To his dismay, he became a New York Ranger. "My heart is still with the Kings," the always outspoken star admitted with controversial candor two weeks later, "but my body is with the Rangers."

Although Dionne adjusted to the move, the Stanley Cup ring he genuinely coveted never materialized. He did pass Phil Esposito as a Blueshirt, moving into third place in career goals scored, but as his always-churning legs started to slow, the goals came further and further apart. "Because you love the game so much," said Dionne, "you think it will never end." He spent nine games in the minors before retiring in 1989.

The little man had left a big mark: He retired as second in NHL career goals and points, and a year later, the Kings retired his number-16 jersey, making him only the second player in L.A. history to be so honored.

Marcel Dionne scored 550 of his 730 career goals with the L.A. Kings. Above: He battles for the puck in his determined fashion with Larry Patey of the St. Louis Blues. Facing page: Dionne broke into the NHL as a Detroit Red Wing, posting four excellent seasons with the club.

Phil Esposito

Phil Esposito was blessed with many skills as a hockey player, but it was his passion that set him apart. He shattered the single-season scoring record, won five scoring championships and helped lead his team to two Stanley Cup victories. Yet his emotional nature had its greatest impact when Esposito gave a tongue-lashing to Canada at the midpoint of the historic 1972 Summit Series.

The roundly favored Canadians had just suffered their second defeat to the Soviets, concluding their home half of the series with a win, a tie and two losses. An angry Vancouver crowd rained down boos on Team Canada. In a televised interview, an exhausted and heavily perspiring Esposito spoke from the heart, insisting that the Canadian players had their hands full but were giving their all. He couldn't believe that they weren't getting the fan support they needed. Few watching were unmoved. The nation rallied behind the team, which eked out a slim and miraculous series victory on Soviet ice. Paul Henderson's winning goals in the last three games are forever etched into the Canadian consciousness, but Esposito's leadership and effectiveness on the ice—he led the series in scoring—were arguably even more crucial.

If Esposito had a weakness, it was his skating. He hadn't taken up skating until he was a teenager, although he had started to hone his shooting ability at an early age, practicing with his younger brother Tony—a future Hall of Fame goalie. But Esposito was a hulking bear of a man who became an immovable object when he parked himself in front of the net. At the age of 19, he finally caught on with St. Catharines, a junior team affiliated with the Chicago Blackhawks.

After a decent season, Esposito served a three-year minor-league apprenticeship, and when he finally earned a permanent spot in the NHL for the 1964-65 season, it was a golden one. He centered a line with Bobby Hull on his left. With Esposito feeding him, Hull enjoyed seasons of 39, 54 and 52 goals. Esposito put the puck in the net too, although his detractors claimed that many of them were "garbage" goals, a charge he faced throughout his career. In truth, Esposito had a sure touch close to the net, a talent that didn't fully blossom until he left Chicago.

Despite his success, "Espo" was sent to the Boston Bruins

in 1967 in one of the most lopsided trades in NHL history. He joined Ken Hodge and Fred Stanfield in Boston, while Pit Martin, Gilles Marotte and goalie Jack Norris went to Chicago. Hodge and Stanfield became key elements in a powerhouse Boston club, and Esposito achieved even greater heights.

He won the Art Ross Trophy in his second season in Beantown, after finishing second to Chicago's Stan Mikita the previous year. He earned runner-up status again in 1970 (to Bobby Orr), but he erupted the next season with a 76-goal 76-assist campaign, eclipsing Bobby Hull's 58-goal record, set the previous year. In fact, Esposito had raised the bar so high that it would be 11 years before his record fell to a young player named Wayne Gretzky.

Esposito dominated the dressing room as well as the scoring race with his gregarious manner and a penchant for superstition. His locker was festooned with good-luck charms, and he made sure that no one left hockey sticks crossed on the floor, for fear they would cause bad luck. Suffering from a cold one game night, Esposito wore a black shirt with the collar backwards to keep his throat warm. He had such good results during the game that the "lucky" black shirt became a permanent part of his on-ice attire.

When Esposito tripped and fell flat on his face during his introduction at the first 1972 Canada-Soviet game in Moscow, the tension was high—it was surely a bad omen. But any premonitions of doom were immediately wiped away when the ever confident Esposito rose to one knee, delivered a sweeping bow to the crowd and stood up to the thunderous applause and laughter of the appreciative Soviets. The great players make their own luck.

Esposito and Orr were the linchpins of the Bruins' success and two Stanley Cup victories, but when the team began

to falter in 1975, Boston's general manager Harry Sinden felt that a shake-up was needed. Esposito and Carol Vadnais went to their archrival, the New York Rangers, in return for Brad Park, Jean Ratelle and Joe Zanussi. The heart on Esposito's sleeve was broken, but while he never challenged for the scoring title again, he won legions of fans in the Big Apple and took the Rangers to the Stanley Cup finals in 1979. He retired in 1981, second only to Gordie Howe in NHL career goals and points scored. Esposito moved into management ranks with the Rangers in 1986 before helping secure a franchise for Tampa Bay in 1990. He served as president and general manager of the Lightning for most of the 1990s.

Phil Esposito established himself as a superstar in Boston, shattering the single-season scoring record in 1970-71, with 76 goals and 76 assists. Above: He finds the net behind Toronto's Bernie Parent. Facing page: Esposito was acquired by the Rangers in a blockbuster trade in 1975.

Wayne Gretzky

Although Wayne Gretzky's assault on the NHL record books is over, statisticians were kept busy appending his records right until the end. Gretzky, already owner of most significant single-season and career scoring records, decided to retire after the 1998-99 season, before he slipped out of the NHL elite.

Like Abe Lincoln's log cabin in America, the Gretzky back-yard rink has become a part of Canadian folklore. Even as a youngster, Gretzky was the center of national attention: At age 10, he scored 378 goals in a 69-game season, and in 1978, at the age of 17, he signed his first professional contract with the Indianapolis Racers of the WHA. Gretzky's contract was soon sold to Peter Pocklington, owner of the Edmonton Oilers, a season prior to the NHL's buying out the WHA.

"The pace seems a little faster in this league," commented Edmonton's franchise player when his team joined the NHL, "but the WHA was a good league. I feel I did well for my first year. I will do my best and hope it's good enough." A "merger" rule disqualified Gretzky from Calder Trophy voting, and he suffered a further disappointment when his 51-goal 86-assist 1979-80 season left him tied with Marcel Dionne for total points. Dionne was awarded the scoring crown based on his 53 goals. "I was always taught that an assist is as good as a goal," stated Gretzky tersely, but for the next seven years, he beat his closest rival by an average of 66 points.

"Wayne kind of sneaks up on you," Edmonton coach and general manager Glen Sather once remarked. "He doesn't have Bobby Hull's power or Bobby Orr's speed, but he has the same magic."

Orr himself was amazed. "You figure a guy has Gretzky trapped. Next thing you know, Gretzky has given the puck to somebody you figure he couldn't even see."

Writer Peter Gzowski attempted to explain the origins of that "magic," postulating that Gretzky's brain might just oper-ate a little differently from most, allowing him to process visual information in great detail even while the game is moving at breakneck speed. While admitting to often "sensing" where his teammates were, Gretzky believes his celebrated vision was honed by fear. He had always played against boys older, bigger and stronger and, later, as a boy against men. "I couldn't beat people with my strength," the still slightly built superstar has

said. "I don't have a hard shot. I'm not the quickest skater. My eyes and my mind have to do most of the work."

While his natural gifts are awesome, Gretzky has always been a hard worker. "First, you have to have a passion and a love for the sport," he has explained. "Second, you have to have a dedication to it." He dominated the NHL during the regular season, most notably with his 92-goal 120-assist 1981-82 campaign and his 52-goal 163-assist 1985-86 year, but Gretzky also enjoyed postseason success. "Kids grow up dreaming about holding up the Stanley Cup," he once said. "That dream fuels you in the playoffs."

But after leading Edmonton to four Stanley Cups, "The Great One" was sold to the Los Angeles Kings in the summer of 1988.

His "trade" was seen by many Canadians as a national disaster, but his presence invigorated the L.A. fran-chise and stimulated NHL growth throughout the southern United States. Gretzky won three more scor-ing championships in Los Angeles, but he requested a trade to a con-tender in 1995-96. After a short stay in St. Louis, he headed for Broadway and the New York Rangers.

His passion for the game was always evident, but the image of Gretzky sitting alone on the bench, tears streaming down his cheeks, while the Czech Republic celebrated its shoot-out victory over Canada for the right to compete for the 1998 Olympic gold medal was one of the most poignant of the Nagano Games. "It's devastating, the worst feeling I've ever had in hockey," said Gretzky. "I knew when I lost my first Stanley Cup, I'd get another chance. When we lost [here], that was it for me."

Even more tears were shed when "The Great One" for-mally announced his retirement the day before playing his final game in Madison Square Garden in April 1999. Gretzky notched one last assist, but the highlights happened before and after the game. Amid an abundance of ovations and accolades, the NHL announced the most fitting tribute of all: No player on any team will ever wear Gretzky's sweater number 99 again.

Wayne Gretzky, above, led the NHL in assists 16 times, including twice as a New York Ranger. Facing page: As a member of the Oilers, "The Great One" shattered dozens of scoring records. He tallied more than 200 points—a threshold no other player has ever crossed—four times.

Mario Lemieux

Mario Lemieux scored on the first shift of his first NHL game with his first shot on net. No other player has ever made quite so auspicious a debut, and it was all the more remarkable because no one had entered the NHL with such high expectations since Wayne Gretzky was a rookie. The Pittsburgh Penguins selected Lemieux with the first pick in the 1984 NHL entry draft, refusing tempting offers for proven NHL players.

Lemieux didn't disappoint them and was grateful to play a little out of the limelight he'd basked in as a prodigy in Quebec. "All the media attention and fan pressure demand so much of your time," he explained. "I don't think I would have lasted too long in Montreal. The less people know about me, the better."

The highly touted junior—he scored 282 points in his last junior season—stepped right into the NHL and won the Calder Trophy with his first of ten 100-point seasons, notching 43 goals. Disbelievers tagged Lemieux as a floater, accusing him of neglecting his defensive responsibilities, but the Penguins were looking for offense, and Lemieux delivered. Halfway through his rookie year, when he earned a spot in the 1985 NHL All-Star Game by leading his club in scoring (22 goals and 38 assists), many of the doubters fell silent.

The celebrity tilt offered Lemieux the perfect stage. He scored twice and had one helper in leading the Wales Conference to victory and was named the game's most valuable player, an honor that would come to him twice more in the following five years. Yet the Penguins continued to languish near the league's cellar.

Lemieux played brilliantly for Canada in the 1987 Canada Cup tournament, and with 168 points, he dethroned Gretzky as league-scoring champion in the 1987-88 season. He retained the title with an amazing 199 points the following year, his fifth season. When the Penguins made the playoffs that year, Lemieux had fulfilled one of his primary goals.

The team slipped in 1989-90, however, and failed to qualify for postseason action (Lemieux missed 21 games because of a herniated disk in his back but still managed to amass 123 points), and Lemieux's detractors were vocal once more. There was only one way for Lemieux to silence his critics.

Unfortunately, after Lemieux's back surgery that summer, a deep infection set in, and the center missed the first 50 games of the regular season. But he came back, tallied 45 regular-season points in 26 games and almost matched that total with 16 goals and 28 assists in the playoffs. Lemieux dominated almost every game, and after raising the Stanley Cup in victory, he was awarded the Conn Smythe Trophy.

Lemieux punctuated that glorious achievement with another scoring title in 1991-92, despite missing 20 games with intermittent back pain. He followed up with his second Conn Smythe Trophy (even after missing six playoff games when his wrist was slashed and broken) and a second Stanley Cup. He will be best remembered, however, for his courage the following year.

Well on his way to yet another scoring crown, Lemieux was diagnosed with Hodgkin's disease when a suspicious lump was found during a routine physical examination. He underwent two months of radiation treatment, a fatiguing and intense process. When his doctors cleared him to play, Lemieux rejoined the Penguins. Buffalo's Pat Lafontaine was enjoying a career year and had a substantial lead in the scoring race, but Lemieux blew past Lafontaine, winning his fourth Art Ross Trophy by a 12-point margin. The Penguins finished atop the league, and although they failed to win the Cup again, Lemieux's courage earned him unanimous respect and his second Hart Trophy (MVP), his third Pearson Award (players' choice for MVP) and the Bill Masterton Trophy (for his perseverance and dedication to the game).

The next season, Lemieux missed 58 games due to complications from further back surgery. Still anemic from the radiation therapy, an exhausted Lemieux sat out the entire 1994-95 season to recuperate. His career in jeopardy once more, Lemieux made a reassuring pronouncement: "I'm not

Even after being knocked down, Mario Lemieux manages to put the puck in the net. Here, he celebrates a goal against St. Louis Blues netminder Jon Casey, above. Facing page: Lemieux dances nimbly around defenseman Alexei Zhitnik and heads toward the Buffalo Sabres goal.

coming back to be an average player." He proved his point by winning the scoring championship the next two seasons.

Yet Lemieux was not happy. He had always avoided the role of hockey's goodwill ambassador, and he was outspoken about the state of the game. He began to talk of retirement, citing both a desire to spend more time with his young family and a distaste for the game of clutching, hooking and grabbing that the NHL tolerated.

True to his word, the 31-year-old hung up his skates after the 1996-97 season. As a tribute to his genius and the range of his accomplishments, the Hockey Hall of Fame inducted Lemieux immediately, waiving the requisite three-year waiting period.

Mark Messier

"I can never shrug off a defeat," Mark Messier has said. "I can remember a friend of mine—a rookie and a real competitor—on a team that hadn't done well for years. He'd be upset after a loss, and the veterans would say, 'Listen, don't worry about it. There's nothing you can do.' That's why some teams never get turned around. They accept losing." Only Messier has captained two different teams to the Stanley Cup, and few have earned their championship rings in such dramatic fashion.

Messier was 17 years old when he turned professional with the WHA Indianapolis Racers in 1979—ironically, he was brought in to replace Wayne Gretzky, who had been traded to Edmonton. Although he scored only one goal that year, Messier was drafted by the Edmonton Oilers when the NHL swallowed the rival league that summer.

Mean, with a fierce glare, "Moose" Messier learned to use his speed and aggression to record his first and only 50-goal season in 1981-82, at the same time making the First All-Star Team. He broke the 100-point barrier the following season and had 15 playoff goals before being injured prior to the final round. Postseason success, however, was where his destiny lay.

Messier was at his healthy best when the young and dynamic Oilers faced the veteran New York Islanders in the Stanley Cup finals for the second consecutive time. In the third game of the series, he scored a dramatic goal, and the Islanders didn't recover. Messier was named the Conn Smythe Trophy winner as the playoffs' most valuable player. He continued to earn All-Star status and was a huge part of Edmonton's first four Stanley Cups, always scoring at least 25 playoff points. But it took a separation from Gretzky to bring Messier to his greatest heights.

Messier became captain of the Edmonton Oilers in 1988, when Gretzky was sold to the Los Angeles Kings. After an adjustment year—when, as everyone predicted, the Oilers sagged—Messier hit a career high with 129 points in 1990 and won both the Hart Trophy and the Pearson Award as the league's most valuable player. Messier then led all playoff scorers by contributing 22 assists toward Edmonton's fifth Stanley Cup win. "I don't think we could have pulled it off without Mark," said teammate Craig Simpson. "He held us all together."

Continuing to sell off its assets, Edmonton sent Messier to the Rangers just before the 1991-92 season got under way. He stormed Manhattan and earned the Hart Trophy and the Pearson Award again. "The players talk about what it would be like to skate around Madison Square Garden with the Cup," said Messier, not one to rest on his laurels. "And we talk about what it would be like to have a parade down Broadway. You've got to visualize these things if you want to make them happen." When the team didn't even qualify for the playoffs the next season, though, the New York fans and media screamed their displeasure. "I think that kind of pressure is good, because winning a Stanley Cup doesn't just happen," Messier commented. "Putting a little fear into the players sometimes brings out the best in them."

Messier had learned a lot about motivation, but he took a great risk in the playoffs the following year. Down three games to two against the New Jersey Devils in the 1994 Stanley Cup semifinals, Messier offered a guarantee. "We know we are going to go in there and win game six and bring it back to the Garden," he announced to a crowd of reporters. When the Rangers had their backs against the wall, trailing 2–1 after two periods, Messier took over and notched a third-period hat trick to secure the promised win. A seventh game went into overtime before the Rangers prevailed. They met Vancouver in the finals, and Messier won his sixth Stanley Cup ring.

"There aren't any motives for me other than wanting to compete and win," said free-agent Messier when he signed a five-year $30 million contract with the Canucks in the summer of 1997. "It begins and ends with that." Vancouver fans were hopeful that the legendary "Greatest Leader in NHL History" would lead their team to the promised land. "When I hear that legend talk, I actually feel a little guilty, a little embarrassed," remarked Messier. "One player, no matter how good a leader on and off the ice, does not win the Stanley Cup. Your teammates have to have the same burning desire as you."

As an Edmonton Oiler, Mark Messier reached All-Star status at left wing three times before switching positions, above, and he won the same honor at center before being dealt to the New York Rangers. Facing page: Messier joined the Vancouver Canucks as a free agent in 1997.

Stan Mikita

Many of the meanest men on the ice turn into the most kindly once they step off it. But Stan Mikita took that character transformation in a different direction. Confirming his reputation as one of the smartest players in the game, Mikita drastically reduced his time in the penalty box while remaining the league's top playmaker. His metamorphosis was complete when this once chippy, frequently penalized scoring whiz was awarded the Lady Byng Trophy (most gentlemanly player), the Art Ross Trophy (most scoring points) and the Hart Trophy (most valuable player) at the end of the 1966-67 *and* 1967-68 seasons. No one else has ever won that triumvirate of awards in one season, let alone two.

Mikita's on-ice change in demeanor pales in comparison with the one he had undergone some 20 years earlier. On May 20, 1940, he was born Stanislav Guoth in Sokolce, Czechoslovakia. Reflecting on their poverty and uncertain future behind the new Iron Curtain, his parents decided in 1948 that it would be in their son's best interest to join his aunt and uncle, who had immigrated to Canada some years earlier. The Mikitas of St. Catharines, Ontario, adopted Stan as their son, and he soon discovered hockey.

He excelled at the game, and hockey served as an excellent vehicle for him to avenge the taunts he faced because of his strongly accented English. "I wasn't going to be pushed around or laughed at," Mikita explained. "That egged me on, made me perform better. I said I was going to be better than those guys." Small but fiery, Mikita carried a chip on his shoulder for years.

That all changed when Mikita married and became a father. Asked innocently by his young daughter why he had to sit by himself so often (in the penalty box) rather than joining his teammates on the bench, Mikita was embarrassed by his own answer. He determined to curb his anger and work harder, while sacrificing nothing on the score sheet.

Mikita won only one Stanley Cup, in 1961, and he led all playoff scorers that season. His most productive years were still to come, though, and the "Scooter Line" (Mikita between Doug Mohns and Ken Wharram) gave opposition goalies trouble for five years in the 1960s. Red Kelly, who faced Mikita on defense, at center and behind the bench, paid tribute when he stated: "Mikita would fool you, because he

could always pull something extra out of the hat. He was tricky, a good stickhandler and one of the best face-off men in the business."

Mikita's constant tinkering led to his accidental discovery of the benefits of the curved stick in 1961. While a slight curve was not unheard of (Hall-of-Famer Andy Bathgate had used one for years), Mikita noticed how the puck behaved unpredictably when he fired a shot in frustration with a stick blade cracked into a severe hook. After further experimentation, the "banana blade" was born—and eventually banned. Mikita was

also one of the first players to wear a helmet as a preventive measure rather than as a result of injury. Soon, his own improved helmet design was on the market.

Despite Mikita's many achievements, he remained in the shadow of his teammate Bobby Hull for most of his long career. (In fact, Mikita's greatest notoriety came years after his retirement, when the movie *Wayne's World* featured scenes in "Stan Mikita's Donuts.") Mikita and Hull first played together in high school, then in junior hockey and finally with the Chicago Blackhawks. Hull's explosive power, beaming *smile* and legendary public relations skills contrasted sharply with Mikita's sometimes abrasive personality, his acerbic wit and his use of finesse rather than brawn. Mikita, who always denied feeling any resentment toward Hull, once explained, "I played hard and got the job done. But I didn't lift fans out of their seats doing it, and Bobby did."

Still, when he scored his 500th career goal in Chicago Stadium on February 27, 1977, the crowd's roar was ear-splitting, even compared with that arena's usual deafening volume. Mikita's number 21 was officially retired by the Blackhawks in 1981, the season after he hung up his skates—he was the first player to be so honored in that franchise's history. And fittingly, although Hull and Mikita separated when Hull joined the new World Hockey Association's Winnipeg Jets in 1972, the two entered the Hockey Hall of Fame together in 1983.

Stan Mikita sits with the Hart (MVP), the Art Ross (scoring leader) and the Lady Byng (sportsmanship), above, all trophies he won in both the 1966-67 and 1967-68 seasons. Facing page: Mikita tallied 541 goals over 22 seasons with the Chicago Blackhawks.

Howie Morenz

It was a funeral unlike any ever seen before in Canada. On March 11, 1937, Howie Morenz's body lay in state at center ice in the Montreal Forum. "As I walked below the north end [of the Forum]," reported Andy O'Brien in *Weekend Magazine*, "profound silence left an impression of emptiness, but at the promenade, I stopped in breathless awe. The rink was jammed to the rafters with fans standing motionless with heads bared." In three hours, more than 50,000 mourners filed past Morenz's casket. An estimated 250,000 people lined the route of his funeral procession, many weeping openly. Hockey had lost one of its greatest stars.

Morenz earned the nickname of "Mitchell Meteor" with his Ontario hometown Mitchell Juveniles, his first organized team. After Morenz let in 21 goals in one game as a goaltender, the coach wisely moved him to rover—a position that was soon eliminated from the game. Morenz's next team, in nearby Stratford, won a provincial title in 1921, and the "Stratford Streak" caught the attention of the Montreal Canadiens.

After reluctantly agreeing to play for Montreal two years later, a homesick Morenz tried to break his contract and headed back to Mitchell during his first training camp. Cecil Hart of the Canadiens went after him, and when he placed $850 cash—Morenz's signing bonus—on the kitchen table, he convinced the whole Morenz family that Howie should return to Montreal.

Morenz quickly became famous for his blazing rushes and reckless style of hockey. Seemingly able to accelerate to top speed in a single stride, he helped establish Montreal's growing reputation for "fire wagon" hockey. By the end of his rookie NHL year of 1923-24, Morenz had tied for eighth in league scoring and had helped Montreal win its first Stanley Cup since 1916, when the team competed in the National Hockey Association. Morenz eventually won two scoring crowns and was named the most valuable player in the league three times.

"He could adjust to any situation," recalled his contemporary King Clancy in 1964. "He could barge [through] a defense, or he could poke a puck between your legs, then wheel around you and pick it up. His shot was just like a bullet, and he didn't fool around looking for an opening, he just let it go."

A fierce competitor, Morenz accumulated his share of penalty minutes, but he was admired by his opponents and teammates alike. In his second NHL season, in a game against the New York Rangers, he knocked out four of Bun Cook's front teeth with the butt end of his stick while digging for the puck. Morenz immediately dropped his stick and helped Cook off the ice. "It was just an accident," explained Cook after the game. "Howie wouldn't pull anything like that intentionally."

Cook's feelings were later echoed by Boston's notorious Eddie Shore, whose nastiness seemed indiscriminate. "Everybody likes Howie," said Shore. "He's the one player who doesn't deserve any rough treatment."

Yet years of success and admiration didn't stop the Canadiens from trading Morenz to the Chicago Blackhawks in the summer of 1934. He had started to slow down the previous season, and the fans had begun to boo him. Leo Dandurand, general manager of the Canadiens, lent a little dignity to the situation when he announced that no Montreal player would ever again wear Morenz's number 7. Morenz sadly accepted his fate, but he hated Chicago. Halfway through his second mediocre season with the Blackhawks, he was traded again, this time to the New York Rangers. He finished out the 1935-36 season as a Ranger, but when his old admirer Cecil Hart was installed as Montreal's new general manager that summer, Morenz became a Hab again.

His return to Montreal seemed to be a tonic for Morenz, and he began to show signs of his old magic. Then tragedy struck. In a game on January 7, 1937, Morenz was knocked down and slid into the boards with Chicago's Earl Seibert on top of him. Morenz's skate jammed into the boards, and his leg snapped. Five fractures above the ankle forced him to spend weeks convalescing in hospital, with constant visitors—

many arriving with bottles—and frequent parties in his room.

With his dapper wardrobe, Morenz had cultivated a prosperous image, but the truth was that he hadn't saved much money and had a wife and three young children to support. Despite putting on a brave public face, Morenz suffered a nervous breakdown.

On March 8, at the age of 34, he died in his sleep of a coronary embolism. More than 60 years later, Howie Morenz Jr. disclosed a nurse's long-held confession—a doctor had postponed until morning treatment for blood clots that had been detected in his leg the night of his death. A romantic legend was debunked: "When he realized that he would never play again, he couldn't live with it," Morenz's teammate Aurèle Joliat had claimed. "I think Howie died of a broken heart."

Howie Morenz battles for the puck, above, with Rangers goalie Andy Aitkenhead and defenseman "Duke" Dutkowski. Facing page: Morenz won two scoring races as a Montreal Canadien. Hundreds of thousands of fans lined the route of his funeral procession from the Montreal Forum to pay their final respects after his tragic death in 1937.

Henri Richard

"I was just mad. I didn't really mean it," claimed Henri Richard, although he had gone on record as proclaiming that Al MacNeil was the worst coach he'd ever played for. In his first term at the helm, MacNeil had benched Richard for the fifth game of the 1971 Stanley Cup finals, which had made the veteran center livid, although he was embarrassed that his outburst made headlines when it was interpreted as a French-English feud.

Richard went on to tie the deciding seventh game, then potted the winner to defeat the Chicago Blackhawks 3–2 and thereby earn his tenth Stanley Cup ring. "I could have been a bum," Richard admitted, for the Canadiens were one game away from defeat, "and instead, I was a hero." He was also gracious enough to admit that MacNeil might have successfully inspired him to greater feats than he would otherwise have accomplished, but MacNeil resigned his position anyway.

Although he was never as dynamic as his brother Maurice "The Rocket," who had already been an NHL star for 13 years when his little brother joined him on the Canadiens in 1955, Henri made his own mark on the game. Even after his successful junior career, many thought that the Canadiens were merely placating his brother when they signed Henri, for he never grew bigger than five-foot-seven and 160 pounds. "He's a little small yet," Montreal coach Toe Blake said in the autumn of 1955, "but with his speed, we keep telling him not to try to go through the big opposition defensemen, just go around them."

"Once you are alone with a goaler," Richard eventually answered his critics, "size doesn't matter," but the shy, soft-spoken rookie let his first season's 19 goals do most of his talking. A tireless skater, Richard turned his perceived liability into an asset. "Sometimes I think my size was an advantage," he noted, after heeding Blake's advice, "especially when I developed a crouching style. A big defenseman was often at a disadvantage. He'd even tumble over me if he tried to use his body rather than his stick."

Richard had long dreamed of playing for the Canadiens, but centering a line with Maurice on his wing—at "The Rocket's" request—was an unexpected surprise. With Dickie Moore on left wing, the potent line made a major contribu-

tion to the five consecutive Stanley Cup victories Richard enjoyed in his first five NHL campaigns. He fed his wingers brilliantly and led the league in assists in 1957-58, earning a spot on the First All-Star Team.

Moore won two scoring championships, and many felt that Richard's presence made Maurice a more complete player. From Maurice's point of view, his brother extended his career a year or two longer than would have been possible without him. "The Pocket Rocket" worked so hard, he made Maurice's job easier. In the spring of 1960, Maurice retired and took his turn at watching his brother from the sidelines. Although Richard was never the goal scorer that Maurice had been—few were—he eventually set the family records for assists, points and seasons.

Richard excelled at both ends of the rink and was particularly effective in keeping the opposition off balance with his tenacious forechecking. Blake was one of his biggest boosters. "He's smart enough to be where the puck is all the time," the legendary coach said in 1957. "He sizes up how a play is going to go, and then he gets there. And sometimes when he doesn't have things figured out in advance, he's so fast that he gets there first anyway."

Richard played with doggedness and was immune to intimidation, never betraying the slightest feelings of fear despite getting into scraps with some of the biggest and most aggressive players in the NHL. Moore expressed a sentiment shared by many: "Henri Richard might have been the toughest competitor I played with."

As goalie Gump Worsley noted, "Henri would get bounced around and always come back for more, stronger and faster than ever."

When Jean Beliveau retired in 1971, Richard assumed the team captaincy and hoisted the Stanley Cup for the last time two seasons later. Silver-haired by then, Richard continued for two more years and entered his twentieth NHL campaign. But after a broken ankle was slow to heal, he decided that he'd "better quit before it's too late," although he still had a year on his contract and the Canadiens were willing to extend it further. Montreal won the Cup for four consecutive years after he retired, but Richard had no regrets. His 11 Stanley Cup rings stand as a record that will never be broken.

*Henri "The Pocket Rocket" Richard circles the net, above, hounded by
Boston defenseman Bobby Orr. Richard's speed and tireless skating more
than compensated for his small stature. He was on 11 Stanley Cup-
winning teams in Montreal. Facing page: Richard fires one of his 358
career goals past Toronto Maple Leaf Johnny Bower.*

Milt Schmidt

The Bruins' "Kraut Line"—hard-nosed center Milt Schmidt between elegant right-winger Bobby Bauer and the tenacious Woody Dumart—was at the height of its power when World War II interrupted the trio's NHL careers. "It was our last game before we went into service [for three years]," said Schmidt, looking back fondly at a game on February 10, 1942, "and we had a fine night against the Canadiens at the Garden. I think we racked up 10 or 11 scoring points, and when the game was over, the other players on both teams picked us up on their shoulders and skated us off the ice while the crowd gave us an ovation."

Although Schmidt was a member of two Stanley Cup championship teams and won the Hart Trophy in 1951, that evening in 1942 remained a personal highlight. "A man could never forget a thing like that," he reminisced.

Originally known as the "Sauerkraut Line," all three Kitchener-born players shared a German heritage and an uncommon bond. "We clicked first as personalities," said Schmidt, "then as hockey players," although several years separated them in age. It was Dumart and Bauer who convinced the Boston Bruins to give their young friend Schmidt a shot at an NHL career. Their loyalty was rewarded when their line became the NHL's first to finish 1-2-3 in the scoring race. Schmidt won the Art Ross Trophy, with 52 points over the 48-game 1939-40 season, and Dumart and Bauer followed with 43 points apiece.

All three returned to the NHL from the armed services, with Schmidt hitting his personal high of 62 points in the 1946-47 season. But the "Kraut Line" broke up when Bauer retired at the end of that season. Schmidt and Dumart were honored together with a "Schmidt/Dumart Night" on March 18, 1952. The fans had a treat in store: Bauer suited up for the evening. Although heavier and slower, he scored a goal on a pass from Schmidt, and both Bauer and Dumart assisted on Schmidt's 200th NHL goal.

"[Schmidt] was tough," recalled Montreal defenseman Butch Bouchard, "a big guy, and he was one of the best skaters I ever saw. He gave me a big shift one night in my first year. When I went to the bench, Dick Irvin [Montreal's coach] asked me if I had caught a cold because of the breeze that Schmidt made when he went by me." Schmidt also

served as the team "policeman" and waged a personal war with Detroit's "Black" Jack Stewart, one of the meanest defensemen in the NHL.

"Oh, we had some dandies," Schmidt laughed years later, "but we both finally wised up. We still had to earn a living!" For Schmidt was not invulnerable to injury, although he missed few games. "I never backed away from anyone. I never let up while I was on the ice," Schmidt recalled at the end of his playing career, when he moved immediately into coaching. "I expect my players to be that way too."

"Milt will be a good coach," said Schmidt's former teammate Lynn Patrick, who stepped into the position of general manager when Schmidt replaced him as coach during the 1954-55 season, "but he'll lack one thing that has made me successful [as a coach]. When things get really tough for him, he won't be able to get out of the jam just by looking down the bench and yelling, 'OK, Milt, get out there.' "

The Bruins enjoyed some great years under Schmidt's guidance, but the bloom was beginning to fade by the 1960s. "This is a government secret," Schmidt joked, when U.S. Space Agency experts hooked up an electronic device to him in 1963 to record his physical symptoms of stress. "I don't even want to know the results. I'm liable to stay home in an easy chair instead of doing this if I were to find out." It was as Boston's general manager, however, that Schmidt achieved his greatest success off the ice. In 1967, he engineered the deal that brought Phil Esposito, Ken Hodge and Fred Stanfield to Boston from Chicago, and the trade represented a turning point for the Bruins which led to Stanley Cup victories in 1970 and 1972.

When the Washington Capitals asked him to manage their inaugural squad in 1974, Schmidt took a brief hiatus from the Bruins organization. While he had felt pressure in Beantown, it paled in comparison with his experience in Washington. He fired two coaches and ensconced himself behind the bench, but his team lost 95 times in 116 games. Schmidt resigned just after Christmas in 1975. Fittingly, he eventually returned to work for the Bruins, who had retired his number 15 in 1955 so that his distinguished accomplishments would always be remembered.

Milt Schmidt, above, was appointed captain of the Boston Bruins in the 1950-51 season, an honor he held until his retirement in 1955. Facing page: Schmidt (center) was the youngest member of the high-scoring "Kraut Line," which featured Bobby Bauer (left), at right wing, and Woody Dumart (right), who skated on the left.

Nels Stewart

Nels Stewart was known as "Old Poison," for the quick and deadly way he put the puck in the net. On January 3, 1931, he set a record that still stands, scoring two goals four seconds apart, but by then, Stewart had already established his reputation. After spending five seasons with Cleveland in the old U.S. Amateur Hockey Association, Stewart burst into the NHL with the Montreal Maroons in 1925-26. His 34 goals in the 36-game campaign led the league, as did his 42 scoring points. The Maroons won the Stanley Cup after Stewart scored the winning goal in each of his team's victories over the Victoria Cougars in a best-of-five series (the last season a non-NHL club vied for the Stanley Cup).

"In some ways, 1925 was the high spot in my career, which had only started," recalled Stewart. "I won the rookie award and the Hart Trophy. I showed I could take it and dish it out too." His 119 penalty minutes were only two fewer than league leader Bert Corbeau, and the following year, Stewart was the NHL's most penalized player, with 133 minutes.

Early in the 1927-28 season, he found the ideal wingers, and the "S-Line" became one of the league's most potent. "Hooley Smith and Babe Siebert did most of the work," Stewart said humbly. "They knew I was out there waiting, and if they freed the puck, I'd do the rest." Using his 200 pounds and six-foot-one frame to advantage in battling for position, Stewart also had a deft scoring touch.

"Goalmouth scrambles were my forte," he maintained. "I scored three-quarters of my goals by drifting in front of the goalmouth until the proper moment occurred. There's a trick in this, and I used every trick in the book." Stewart's stick had about half the average angle between shaft and blade. "I always used a lie-12, which stood almost straight up and down," he explained, "so I could control the puck close to my skates."

Back-checking was an activity that Stewart pretty much left to others. "I was a lazy daisy who hung around the goal waiting for passes," he said, but an economy of movement was critical when a player was on the ice for 45 to 50 minutes of every game, as Stewart was. "I always figured someone else could stymie the opposition," he admitted. "My job was to score goals."

In 1929-30, Stewart hit his career high of 39 goals and 55 points and earned a second Hart Trophy. His consistent scoring and aggressive play weren't enough to help the Maroons to a Stanley Cup victory, however, and he was traded to the Boston Bruins in 1932. He placed in the top 10 among NHL scoring leaders for three consecutive seasons before the New York Americans acquired him in 1935.

Stewart tied for the NHL lead with 23 tallies in the 1936-37 season, a noteworthy campaign that not only saw him traded back to Boston and returned to the Americans after just 10 games but also saw him pass Howie Morenz to become the league's career leader in goals scored. Stewart held that distinction for 16 years. He became the first NHL player to score 300 goals, but the end was in sight. "My reflexes were slower," he said. "I lacked that extra step, and I hit the post instead of the net."

Stewart retired after the 1938-39 season, having eclipsed Morenz's career-points record, but the Americans persuaded him to come back for one more year when they lost their first six games the next autumn. After 7 more goals, 7 assists and an almost saintly six penalty minutes in 35 games, "Old Poison" retired for good in 1940.

Stewart had retired with 324 career goals, and he made a sporting trip to the Montreal Forum in 1952 when Canadien Maurice Richard was expected to score his record-breaking 325th goal. "I figured I was a jinx," said Stewart, when "The Rocket" was shut out, so he went home and waited for the inevitable. "Congratulations on breaking the record," read the telegram Stewart sent the day after Richard set the new mark. "Hope it will hold for many seasons." Stewart did, however, remain the highest-scoring NHL centerman for 30 years, until another Canadien, Jean Beliveau, bettered that mark in 1964.

Stewart was a regular visitor to Maple Leaf Gardens for years. "When I see that loose puck in front of the cage," he said in 1953, "my heart still jumps. That was the moment I always waited for." Stewart died suddenly in 1957 at the age of 55. He was elected to the Hockey Hall of Fame five years later.

The Montreal Maroons won their first Stanley Cup in 1925-26, thanks in part to the addition of Nels Stewart, above, who won the Hart Trophy that season and again in 1929-30. Facing page: Stewart was the NHL's first 300-goal scorer.

Bryan Trottier

Over the past 20 years, Bryan Trottier has had as intimate a relationship with the Stanley Cup as any player—and then some. His six Stanley Cup rings bear testimony to his triumphs, and after one of his victories with the New York Islanders, he and his wife actually slept with the Cup—"just to know what it was like." That unusual act was characteristic of Trottier, who immersed himself fully in all that he did.

After several distinguished seasons as a junior in western Canada, Trottier was selected by the Islanders in the 1974 entry draft as an underage player. Trottier played a final year of junior hockey and responded with his best season ever, prodding a lucrative offer from the Cincinnati Stingers of the WHA. But Trottier had eyes only for the NHL. As he told writer Roy MacGregor during his rookie season with the Islanders, "The dream has not come true. I am *living* the dream. And that's better." The three-year-old Islanders franchise was a team on the rise, and Trottier quickly became an integral part of its success. In his first NHL campaign, Trottier tallied 98 points and won rookie-of-the-year honors and serious consideration for the Lady Byng Trophy.

While only five-foot-ten, Trottier displayed a tenacity and single-mindedness that more than compensated for his size, and as his penalty minutes grew, a nastier side emerged. "Trottier's hidden talent," said Pittsburgh coach Johnny Wilson, "is that he looks like an altar boy and hits like a monster."

When the Islanders drafted sharpshooter Mike Bossy in the 1977 entry draft, Trottier received the perfect winger and entered the NHL stratosphere in only his third season. He led the league in assists, with 77, and finished second in points behind Guy Lafleur, earning a First All-Star Team selection. He followed up with an even more sensational year, adding the Art Ross and Hart trophies to his list of accomplishments. Meanwhile, his team led the league during the 1978-79 regular season and was fine-tuning its squad to challenge for the Stanley Cup.

The next season, Trottier dropped to sixth place in regular-season scoring but led the playoffs with 12 goals and 29 points and was awarded the Conn Smythe Trophy. The Islanders won the first of four consecutive Stanley Cups, and Trottier was an important contributor each time. He notched his first and only 50-goal campaign in the 1980-81 season and led the playoffs in scoring again that spring, eclipsing Bobby Orr's playoff assist record by notching 23.

But that proved to be the last time Trottier would take a scoring race. After winning their third and fourth Stanley Cups in four-game sweeps, Trottier and the Islanders slipped back into the pack during the regular 1983-84 season. They clawed their way to the Stanley Cup finals for the fifth consecutive time, but Wayne Gretzky and his Edmonton Oilers finally dethroned the Islanders in five games.

When Trottier decided to compete for the United States at the Canada Cup tournament that autumn, he entered controversial waters. He had played for Canada in the 1981 tourney, but in 1984, he decided to invoke his North American Indian status, which, in effect, gave him dual citizenship. "I want to give something back," Trottier claimed, noting that the United States had allowed him to make a good living. Years later, he took out American citizenship.

Trottier continued to rack up respectable point totals over the years, but he had also established himself as one of the game's premier checkers with his gritty play. "I'm vocal when I think my opinion will accomplish something advantageous," he said with respect to his leadership role, and he enjoyed his place in the game. When asked, "Is hockey still fun?" he once answered, "It's love. It's made me what I am today."

On February 13, 1990, Trottier scored his 500th career goal, but he was stunned later that spring when the Islanders exercised a contractual option and bought out the last two years of his contract. The terms, unfavorable to Trottier, sent his off-ice business interests into a downward spiral. He fell into a clinical depression and financial ruin, but he rebounded fully after receiving therapy and declaring bankruptcy. The Pittsburgh Penguins added him to their roster, and Trottier played a key role in assisting them to Stanley Cup victories in 1991 and 1992.

In 1986, Trottier described how he wanted to be remembered: "As a consistently hard worker who gave his all on every shift; as a guy who, if he missed a check, kept coming back and gave that second and third effort; as a guy who just didn't quit." Bryan Trottier has received his wish.

Bryan Trottier, above, was rookie of the year in the 1975-76 season with the New York Islanders and centered the team's top line during four consecutive Stanley Cup triumphs in the early 1980s. Facing page: Trottier brought his leadership skills to the Pittsburgh Penguins in 1990-91 and enjoyed two more Stanley Cup wins.

Steve Yzerman

Having led the Detroit Red Wings to commanding first-place finishes during the previous two regular seasons, Steve Yzerman had seen his team swept in the finals by New Jersey in 1995 and vanquished in the 1996 semifinals by the underdog Colorado Avalanche. Yzerman's critics again cited his lack of a championship ring, a knock heard against "Stevie Y" for years, but he refused to be burdened by the pressure and remained undaunted. "My approach is to have fun," he said in the fall of 1996. "My desire to win the Cup hasn't changed at all, but I'm not consumed by it now.

"I want to experience the celebration of winning the Cup, of getting to carry it around the ice," he added with enthusiasm. "I've dreamed about it since I was a kid." Yzerman finally fulfilled his wish in the spring of 1997. "You hold your dreams out there and wonder if you're ever going to get there," he said after the Wings won. "I've never been this happy in my life." When the Wings took their second consecutive Stanley Cup in 1998, Yzerman was awarded the Conn Smythe Trophy as the most valuable playoff performer.

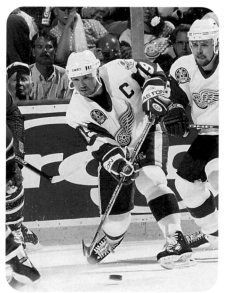

Yzerman has won legions of fans, including some of hockey's greatest stars. "He's a credit to his parents and a credit to himself," said retired Detroit legend Ted Lindsay in 1998.

Asked whether he had a favorite player in the league today, a typically reserved Maurice "Rocket" Richard answered, "I like Steve Yzerman. He's good to watch."

Yzerman made his first mark on the game through his prodigious offensive skills. His 39 goals and 87 points as an 18-year-old rookie earned him an invitation to the 1984 All-Star Game.

While his sniping skills waned temporarily over the next three years, Yzerman had already revealed enough of his character that he was made team captain in 1986, at the tender age of 21. Yzerman embraced the role as seriously then as he does today and blossomed with the added responsibility. He scored 18 points in 16 playoff games the following spring, guiding the Wings further into the Stanley Cup showdown than they had been in more than 20 years.

Yzerman hit the magic 50-goal-season plateau in 1987-88 and topped 100 points for the first of six consecutive seasons. The following season, he peaked offensively, with 65 goals and

155 points. Only Wayne Gretzky and Mario Lemieux have ever posted higher numbers, which they did that year, but the NHL players voted "Stevie Wonder" the Pearson Award as the league's outstanding player. That peer recognition and All-Star Game appearances were the only honors bestowed on Yzerman by the league for his first 14 seasons.

Detroit's lack of playoff success fueled constant speculation about whether Yzerman should be traded. "That's like asking me if I'd trade my son Jason for the kid next door," claimed Detroit's coach Jacques Demers. Although Yzerman tallied 62 goals in the 1989-90 season, the Wings missed the playoffs, and it was Demers who got the pink slip. The rumors that had Detroit's captain on the trading block ended soon after Scotty Bowman stepped behind the bench in 1993.

Yzerman was already a strong two-way player, but Bowman's insistence on more consistent attention to team defense meant that the Wings' captain would have to change his approach somewhat. Taking his game up another level, Yzerman sacrificed the possibility of scoring championships while still remaining an offensive threat. His inspirational shot blocking and ferocious back-checking set the tone, and within three years, his team became the league's stingiest defensively, setting an NHL record with 62 regular-season victories in 1995-96. A quiet man in the dressing room, Yzerman spoke volumes with his actions on the ice, his eyes blazing with competitive fire.

"I had set a goal of 20 years that I'd like to play," he said recently. "That is not necessarily set in stone, but I'd like to continue to play for as long as I feel I am an effective player and getting things done on the ice. But 20 would be great—something I'd like to reach."

Yzerman attains new milestones every year. Early in the 1998-99 season, he notched his 1,426th point, passing his boyhood hero Bryan Trottier and moving into tenth place on the NHL career-point list. "Bryan Trottier was my favorite player," said Yzerman, who intentionally wears the number 19, which Trottier had used. "We all have role models, and he's mine. I followed his entire career as soon as he came into the league. In some ways, I tried to play like he did. In my mind, he is one of the best players ever." Countless young hockey players today are obviously saying the same thing about Yzerman.

Steve Yzerman, above, remains a potent scorer with the Detroit Red
Wings, although he peaked offensively in 1988-89, with 65 goals and
90 assists. Facing page: Captain of the Red Wings since the 1986-87
season, Yzerman was the 1998 Conn Smythe Trophy winner for his
strong two-way play in Detroit's defense of the Stanley Cup.

Peter Forsberg

By scoring a dramatic goal against Canada in an overtime shootout during the 1994 Olympic Games, Peter Forsberg won the Olympic gold medal for Sweden and earned his nation's gratitude—he was subsequently immortalized on a Swedish postage stamp. The goal also distinguished his name among casual hockey fans. Although he was one of eight players (and $15 million cash) traded to the Quebec Nordiques for Eric Lindros in 1992, Forsberg toiled in the relative obscurity of the Swedish professional league for almost three more years. Staying home to polish his skills, however, paid off in a big way.

Once the 1994-95 NHL lockout ended, Forsberg stepped right into the Nordiques lineup. Discussing his adjustment to NHL action, he explained: "I played more physical back home, more dirty. I played on a lousy team, and we were always behind in games. I would get crazy and run at guys. On this team, we have four good lines, and we're usually ahead by a couple of goals. I don't get as angry."

Forsberg's chippy side, an important aspect of his game, grew more evident as his rookie year progressed. What immediately impressed observers, though, was his smooth stickhandling and speed. He helped his team to first place in the Eastern Conference, finishing second in team scoring and first among NHL rookies, a contribution recognized by his being awarded the Calder Trophy.

Although Forsberg carried the distinction of being rookie of the year into the 1995-96 season, he had to make another big adjustment that year. "It's sad when teams have to move," he said shortly after the Quebec Nordiques became the Colorado Avalanche. "Don't get me wrong, we're having a great time in Denver, but I find it sad that Canada is losing teams. I liked it in Quebec, and I wanted to play there. It was just like my hometown—not too big, lots of snow, and everybody liked hockey." But Forsberg surpassed his rookie point totals only 29 games into his sophomore season, battling through checks relentlessly.

"Forsberg's ability to handle himself in traffic and the fact that he has no fear of playing his way through a crowd allow him to make some incredible plays," notes ESPN analyst Brian Engblom. "He will go right through a couple of people to get to a hole on the other side. That's a tremendous talent, and it's a tribute to his tenacity as well as his ability."

Forsberg came fifth in league scoring, with 30 goals and 86 assists, notching four five-point games. More important, he got his first NHL hat trick in the Stanley Cup finals against the Florida Panthers, and his 21 playoff points and strong two-way play were critical elements of Colorado's 1996 Stanley Cup victory.

When he triumphantly returned to Sweden the following summer, Forsberg became the first NHL player to take the Cup overseas. The autumn of 1996 provided him with another opportunity to play both for his country and for his father. Kent Forsberg was behind his son's bench for the 1996 World Cup, as he had been for most of the years that Forsberg was making a name for himself in Sweden. The two have developed a professional relationship, but when Kent talks about his son, a father's pride still emerges. Kent recalled that at the age of 8, Peter came home in tears after his team lost 8–7. "Did you score any of the goals?" he asked his son empathetically.

"Yes, seven," Peter quietly replied.

"But he was crying," Kent beamed, "because they lost the game!"

Over the 1996-97 season, Forsberg led the Avalanche in scoring despite missing six weeks of action due to a deep thigh bruise. He finished as runner-up to Buffalo's Mike Peca in Frank Selke Trophy voting as the league's best defensive forward. The Avalanche rewarded him with a three-year contract extension in February, an offer Forsberg could likely have jacked up by waiting for his free-agency eligibility to kick in that summer. But he was happy to sign.

A poll conducted during the 1997-98 season by *The Hockey News* determined that 11 of 15 NHL general managers would choose Forsberg over Eric Lindros in a one-for-one trade. The Swedish superstar finished behind only Jaromir Jagr in league scoring and was a force in the playoffs. Unfortunately, Forsberg's 6 goals and 5 assists in the first four games of the quarter-finals against Edmonton were all he could muster for that series. Netminder Curtis Joseph allowed only one more goal in the next three games, and Colorado was eliminated.

The Avalanche continued its struggle to score goals early in the 1998-99 campaign, prompting rookie coach Bob

Hartley to move Forsberg from his customary center position onto team captain Joe Sakic's left wing. "In my business, we have to do experiments every day," explained Hartley. "At the time we decided to put Peter and Joe together, we wanted to create a spark." The switch helped turn the team's fortunes around, adding "adaptable" and "versatile" to Forsberg's extensive list of star qualities.

Facing page: Peter Forsberg tallied 50 points in 47 games to win the 1995 Calder Trophy as top rookie before helping Colorado win the Stanley Cup the following season. Right: Combining speed and skill with rugged tenacity, Forsberg led all Avalanche scorers for the third straight season in 1998-99, with 30 goals and 67 assists.

Eric Lindros

Hailed as "The Next One" since he was a teenager, Eric Lindros has resisted embracing the role of NHL hockey ambassador, the role that Wayne Gretzky, "The Great One," played for so many years. The pressure in Philadelphia is enough. Openly accusing Lindros of "choking" in clutch games, Philadelphia Flyers general manager Bob Clarke told Lindros in the summer of 1998, "If you want to be the highest-paid player in the game or close to it, you've got to play that way. It's time."

Responding to Clarke's challenge, Lindros said: "I talked to Steve Yzerman and Mario

Lemieux. They told me the same thing—just play." As sound as that advice is, Clarke's message hit home. Anything but immediately leading his team to Stanley Cup victory will be seen as a failure. "I know I have to win the Cup," admitted Lindros. "I want to finish what I started here."

Lindros isn't opposed to challenges; indeed, he's made several of his own. He bucked the draft systems in both Canadian junior hockey and the NHL to force trades to teams that met with his approval. Lindros made some enemies, but that, in turn, fuels his game. "I get pumped up," said Lindros in explaining how hostile crowds motivate him. "I get possessed with the fear of losing." In the summer of 1992, Philadelphia gave up $15 million and eight players—including soon-to-emerge superstar Peter Forsberg—for Lindros, seriously depleting the squad. It would be three years before the player Philadelphia had coveted would lead the Flyers into the playoffs.

Lindros's initial attempts at being a one-man wrecking crew were futile but exciting. He scored an impressive 41 goals and 75 points during his rookie year but missed 23 games due to injury, a pattern that has continued. "There was a time when I thought I could throw my body around and not be injured," acknowledged Lindros, who missed almost one-quarter of his team's games in his first six seasons. "Now I know there's a time to shy away from that."

The promising hockey career of Lindros's younger brother

Brett was snuffed out due to recurring concussions after only 51 NHL games, but "The Big E" hasn't dramatically changed his style as a result. "There's no one else in the league," observed rugged NHL journeyman Shawn Antoski, "who's capable of scoring 50 goals and using you as a speed bump."

Lindros had 97 points as a sophomore, but when six-foot-three John LeClair joined the Flyers in February 1995, the "Legion of Doom" line was soon formed. At age 21, Lindros had already been given the captain's "C," and with hulks LeClair and six-foot-two Mikael Renberg for wingers, it seemed that Lindros might have the right support to fulfill his destiny. On the final day of the 1994-95 season, Jaromir Jagr edged him out of a scoring championship by virtue of having more goals but identical points. Still, Lindros took home the Hart Trophy, the Pearson Award and a First All-Star Team berth. "I certainly do not want to become satisfied with what I've done," he maintained. "I've got a lot of improving to do."

Lindros posted a career-high 115 points in 1995-96, and it looked as if he would finally have the torch passed to him the following year. "It's your time," Mario Lemieux told Lindros after Lemieux's final game in the spring of 1997, when Philadelphia knocked off the Pittsburgh Penguins.

Lindros's hero, Mark Messier, said much the same. "I told him, 'Go get it,'" Messier said of his conversation with the Philadelphia captain after the Flyers eliminated Messier's New York Rangers. "He had a great series—he was a factor in every game."

Only the Detroit Red Wings remained to be vanquished. Lindros led all playoff scorers, with 26 points, but the Wings countered the "Legion of Doom" with finesse defensemen Larry Murphy and Nicklas Lidstrom and threw the line off its game entirely. Lindros looked bewildered; his team was swept in four straight matches.

Lindros's first chance for personal redemption came when Bob Clarke, as manager of the Canadian Olympic Team, selected him as team captain for the 1998 Olympic Games. But for a goalpost, the story might have gone as scripted. In the qualifying game for the gold medal, Lindros bore down on Czech goalie Dominik Hasek in a tie-breaking shootout. Lindros deked out the almost invincible Hasek and had him going the wrong way, but his shot caromed off the pipe and went wide. No other Canadian shooter came even that close to scoring, and Hasek and company went on to Olympic gold.

The following spring, back in the NHL, Hasek and his Buffalo Sabres knocked Philadelphia off in the first round of the playoffs, but the setback did not deter Lindros from his mission.

"I've dreamed of what I'd do with the Stanley Cup," he said recently, "what it would be like in the dressing room, what it would be like on the ice."

Unfortunately, Lindros has proved again that even giants can be felled. A lung puncture suffered late in the 1998-99 season went undetected for hours, bringing the Flyers captain frighteningly close to death. Lindros was still out of the lineup, recovering from a massive loss of blood, when Philadelphia lost the opening round of the playoffs to Toronto. He'll have to wait at least another year to realize his dream, although few would bet against his getting there eventually.

"I've never seen a big guy do the things he does," says Bobby Orr, agreeing that Lindros today is the best hockey player in the world. "He's a brute force."

Facing page: The most highly touted player in years, Eric Lindros joined the Philadelphia Flyers as a teenager and became team captain at age 21. Right: Lindros parks himself at the edge of the crease in front of his two-time nemesis in 1998, Buffalo goaltender Dominik Hasek.

Mike Modano

Although he left a lot of friends behind, Mike Modano had little difficulty making the transition from being a Minnesota North Star to becoming a Dallas Star. "It was pretty easy," he joked. "It was just me and my clothes and my golf clubs." More seriously, he also pondered the effect on the club when it relocated from Minnesota to Texas in 1993. "It was as if the entire team had been traded," he noted. Modano led his team in scoring for the third consecutive season, joining the elite 50-goal club for the first and last time. "All we knew was each other. The move had a lot to do with my 50-goal season."

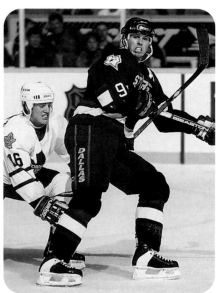

In the 1988 NHL entry draft, Modano was the North Stars' first pick. The 18-year-old Detroit-area native was unable to come to contract terms, however, and returned to his junior team in Prince Albert, Saskatchewan. On schedule to shatter his personal best of 127 junior points that year, he suffered a season-ending broken wrist instead. The North Stars called him up, more or less just to observe, but Modano dressed for two NHL playoff games with a cast on. In his rookie year, fully healed, he tallied 29 goals and 46 assists, finishing behind only Soviet veteran Sergei Makarov in Calder Trophy voting.

Modano carried himself particularly well during Minnesota's startling run for the 1991 Stanley Cup. With 27 wins and 39 losses in the regular season, the North Stars seemed oblivious to their underdog status, and Modano chipped in 20 playoff points. Unfortunately, Mario Lemieux and the Pittsburgh Penguins defeated Minnesota in six games, but Modano emerged as his team's scoring leader in 1991-92 and in the following two seasons.

Despite his scoring prowess, Modano started to get some painful prodding from within the Dallas organization. Bob Gainey, one of the NHL's best defensive forwards for most of his 16-season Hall of Fame career, was trying to implement a team orientation to defense. To that end, Gainey relinquished his coaching duties to Ken Hitchcock midway through the 1995-96 season, while remaining general manager. Although

Modano led the team with 36 goals and 45 assists, the Stars didn't make the playoffs.

The pressure to win fell most heavily on Modano. "It has always been directed or deflected in my direction," he says. "If I play well, the team seems to play well. I accept that's the way it is and will always be." His high-energy contribution helped Team USA to victory in the 1996 World Cup, but Modano also carved out new ground for himself in the NHL.

Fourth at season's end in Frank Selke Trophy voting—an award many felt was created 20 years earlier specifically to honor Gainey—Modano still notched 83 points and had a hand in 51 percent of the team's tying or winning goals in 1996-97. Dallas won its division, on average lopping one goal off the opposition's scoring every game. Unfortunately, the Stars bowed out of the playoffs in the first round.

Although Modano missed 30 games in the 1997-98 season due to a knee injury and a separated shoulder, he led Dallas with a plus-25 scoring differential while on the ice and helped his team to the Western Conference finals before the Stars fell to the eventual Stanley Cup champions, the Detroit Red Wings. Yet Modano continues to refine his game.

"I've changed my direction on things I'm doing away from the ice," he says. "I was going more off the ice than I was on." Early in the 1998-99 season, Modano announced that he had hired new financial advisers and would cut back on endorsements. "It's like a weight off my shoulders. You try as much as you can not to bring that to the rink, but it's difficult."

The difference has been noticed. "He's becoming his own person, his own personality," says Hitchcock. "The nice thing about working with Mo is, he's willing to look himself in the mirror and say, 'I've got some areas to deal with.' I've been impressed with how he's dealt with it. He was up front with myself and Bob [Gainey]. He dealt with those areas and moved on." Modano's focus has become narrower and narrower.

To those critics still unconvinced of his heart and commitment, Modano's 1999 Stanley Cup playoff performance was answer enough. Although he sustained a broken wrist in the finals, Modano donned a special cast and did not miss a single game. His 23 points were tops in his club, and through tears of joy and relief, Modano raised the Cup over his head in victory, having finally led his team to the promised land.

Facing page: Mike Modano led the Dallas Stars with 81 points in the 1998-99 season, moving into second place behind Neal Broten in franchise career scoring. Looking for a pass near the Toronto goal, above left, Modano battles past Darby Hendrickson.

Mats Sundin

"I'm very happy and proud to be wearing the 'C' for the Maple Leafs," said Mats Sundin. "It puts a smile on my face every day." Sundin was asked by the Leafs to take on the prestigious leadership role over the summer of 1997. But before accepting the honor, Sundin approached former Toronto defenseman Borje Salming, a fellow Swede.

"It's something you'll carry with you for the rest of your life," said Salming, advising his friend to say yes right away.

"He was asked to be captain," explained Sundin, "said no and regretted it." On September 30, 1997, Sundin was named the sixteenth Leaf captain in the franchise's history.

Sundin played a variety of sports before focusing on hockey at the age of 17. By then, the possibility of crossing the ocean to play professional hockey had become a reality. But when Sundin was named the number-one pick by the Quebec Nordiques in the 1989 NHL entry draft, it wasn't something he had even dared to dream about. Having become the first European ever to have been picked first overall, Sundin spent another season in Sweden before posting fine NHL rookie numbers, with 23 goals and 36 assists, while acclimatizing to a different style of play.

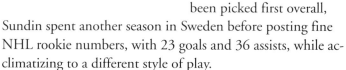

"In terms of my game, I'm more comfortable playing North American hockey," he says today. "I enjoy playing on the smaller ice surface. There's a faster pace to the game." Nevertheless, there was an adjustment period. Continually coaxed by his coaches to shoot more often, Sundin had a 33-goal 43-assist sophomore campaign before hitting a career peak in 1992-93, with 47 goals and 114 points. He'd arrived as an NHL star, but when his totals dipped substantially and the Nordiques failed to qualify for the playoffs the following year, he became one of the key figures in an eight-player trade with Toronto.

The Leafs gave up their team captain to land Sundin. "Wendel Clark was a star—a legend. He was the soul of the team," Sundin noted when he was traded. "I'm not looking to replace him. That's impossible. We're different types of players. I'll just try to contribute the best way I can."

Clark's first game back in Toronto didn't come for over a year, and by then, the former Leaf captain was a New York Islander. He got a noisy cheer from the crowd, but Sundin put in an emotionally charged effort. He tallied 2 goals and 2 assists and celebrated with an intensity he had rarely shown. The fans roared their approval, offering evidence that Sundin had won them over completely. Clark rejoined Toronto in 1996, and while he was welcomed back unanimously, Sundin was, by then, clearly a crowd favorite.

The Leafs' number 13 has led his team in total points every year he's played in Toronto. A fast skater, Sundin is also strong and has a long reach—a deadly combination for opposing goalies and defensemen. Using the NHL's maximum-length stick (63 inches), he's able to sweep around the net for the wraparound, but he's crafty enough to feed a teammate from down low as well. Sundin may have the league's best backhand in going top-shelf from close range.

Unfortunately, opposing teams were frequently able to neutralize Sundin because he represented most of Toronto's offensive weaponry. At the 1997 All-Star Game, Sundin commented: "It takes a game like this to remind you hockey is supposed to be fun. There has been a lot of pressure in Toronto. This was a nice diversion." That spring, the Leafs missed the playoffs, and although Sundin bought into coach Mike Murphy's defensive system the following year, he saw his scoring totals slip, and the team continued to falter. International play gave the big Swede a better chance to shine. Considered by many to have been the best individual player at the 1996 World Cup tournament, Sundin led Sweden to a World Championship in 1998.

Coach Pat Quinn, hired for the start of the 1998-99 campaign, has introduced a system that takes better advantage of the Maple Leaf squad's speed. New goaltender Curtis Joseph has taken some of the load off Sundin's shoulders, and sniper Steve Thomas has been a welcome addition on the captain's wing. Despite the distraction caused by the closing of Maple Leaf Gardens in February 1999, Sundin and the Leafs played better and generated more excitement than Toronto had seen in years.

"This is a club with history," Sundin noted in 1996. "It's great to play in a city where hockey means so much." The team's recent revival has made him even more enchanted. "If the Maple Leafs want me for the rest of my career, they can probably have me," he said in 1998. "I can't see any reason why not."

Mats Sundin uses his strength in traffic to launch a shot at the opposition net, above. Facing page: Team captain Sundin—the sixteenth captain in the history of the Maple Leafs' franchise—celebrates a goal during Toronto's impressive 1998-99 season as defenseman Alexander Karpovtsev comes in to congratulate him.

Alexei Yashin

For once, "The Million Dollar Man" was *not* the headline for a story about a player's new contract. Alexei Yashin's generous donation to the National Arts Centre in Ottawa in 1997 was national news and distinguished Yashin as a cultural hero, a "Renaissance Man" whose love of theater, dance and symphonic music had moved him to share some of his good fortune. A quiet man who generally deflects attention, Yashin even joined the NAC Symphony on stage at a gala celebratory performance, briefly waving the conductor's baton. Unfortunately, when the NAC announced a year later that

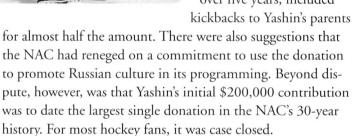

Yashin had withdrawn the bulk of his donation "for personal reasons," the fallout was even bigger news.

Yashin, who had made huge strides in building up a positive image, elicited a surprising amount of sympathy during the NAC fiasco, even from broadcaster Don Cherry, who routinely denigrates European players. There were allegations that the million-dollar donation, to be made in equal payments over five years, included kickbacks to Yashin's parents for almost half the amount. There were also suggestions that the NAC had reneged on a commitment to use the donation to promote Russian culture in its programming. Beyond dispute, however, was that Yashin's initial $200,000 contribution was to date the largest single donation in the NAC's 30-year history. For most hockey fans, it was case closed.

Despite being the first-ever draft pick of the Ottawa Senators in 1992, Yashin entered the league without much fanfare. He spent another year with the Moscow Dynamo club before joining the Senators for the 1993-94 season, so his rookie year coincided with the arrival of highly touted— and richly rewarded—Alexander Daigle, Ottawa's 1993 draft pick, who signed a $12.5 million rookie contract. While Daigle proved to be at best a mediocre player, Yashin impressed immediately. He was the only rookie invited to the 1994 All-Star Game, and he potted two goals, including the game-winner. "It was all luck," Yashin said in his typically humble fashion, but not everyone else agreed.

"He's a tremendous talent," noted Wayne Gretzky. "I see a lot of Mario [Lemieux] in him. He's got good puck sense and Mario's size."

Yashin finished his rookie season first in team scoring, with a 28-point bulge over second-place Daigle, and felt he deserved a raise. Discussions were held, but when the NHL lockout ended in January 1995, Yashin didn't show up for training camp. His holdout won him a minor concession: If certain standards were met that season, the team would renegotiate his contract.

When Yashin fell a single point shy of the agreed-upon target, he believed he'd met the spirit of the agreement. The Senators saw things differently. Once again, when training camp opened, Yashin stayed home. He didn't rejoin the club until midway through the 1995-96 season, but when he did, he was a wealthier man. Yashin's situation, symptomatic of a larger problem, had triggered a major management shake-up, and making the team's best player happy became the first order of business. Yashin reciprocated with a strong second half, finishing second in team scoring despite playing only 46 games.

Yashin took his more customary position at the top of the Ottawa scoring charts the following year, a position he shows no sign of relinquishing. "I know people expect me to score goals," he said, "but that shouldn't always be what says whether you're a good player or not. Yes, it's nice to get the points, but it's better for us to get the wins. I'll do whatever I can to help us have success." In 1996-97, the Senators made the playoffs for the first time, and the following campaign went even better, when the Senators knocked off top-ranked New Jersey in the first round of the postseason. Fans had occasion to see Yashin sporting the captain's "C" whenever Randy Cunneyworth was out of the lineup, and the honor became permanent in the fall of 1998.

"Alexei is doing everything we've expected and asked him to do," said coach Jacques Martin. "He's been a leader on the ice for the past few seasons. It was a natural progression for him to become captain and become our leader off the ice too." Yashin impressed his coach by asking for the added responsibility of penalty killing. "That's the way he shows leadership on this team," said Martin. "He's not the type of guy who is going to be a big talker in the dressing room. He leads with a different style."

Having earned a black belt in combat karate, Yashin uses that discipline to enhance his play and his approach to life. "There are so many things to work on," he says, "foot speed, reaction, concentration. You have to be very focused to do this stuff. It's great for my energy level." He seems able to take all things in stride, including his role with the team. "I'm still adjusting," he admits. "I'm young and still learning how to play in the NHL. There is a lot of pressure in being a captain, especially as a Russian on a Canadian team. People really watch you." So far, they like what they see.

Alexei Yashin, right, moved into the NHL's top-10 scoring leaders with an excellent 1998-99 season, notching 44 goals and 50 assists. Facing page: Ottawa captain Yashin, seen here grappling with Toronto defenseman Yannick Tremblay, has become accustomed to constant attention from the opposition.

The Wingers

Above all else, hockey's top wingers do one thing well: put the puck in the net. Defense is not to be ignored, but without disparaging the Frank Selke Trophy—established in 1977 to recognize the year's best defensive forward in the NHL—none of these players was ever awarded this trophy.

Winning hearts and scoring titles from the flank position is a long tradition, represented in these pages by such players as Charlie Conacher in the 1930s right up to Jaromir Jagr in today's game. But all the wingers featured in *Hockey's Greatest Stars* have demonstrated strong talent and creativity in finding the net, as witnessed by their impressive personal statistics.

Toughness among these players is certainly not lacking. Maurice "The Rocket" Richard's ferocity, especially from the blue line to the net, earned him not only suspensions but general acknowledgment as hockey's greatest clutch performer. Detroit's "Terrible Ted" Lindsay lined up on left wing directly opposite Montreal's Richard for most of his career. His adage "hit 'em first" sums up the aggressive approach that helped make him a nine-time All-Star. "In this game, you have to be mean, or you're going to get pushed around," said Lindsay. "I keep telling myself to be mean. Be mean."

Lindsay's advice was taken to heart by the slightly junior "Mr. Hockey"—Gordie Howe. "If you find you can push someone around," said Howe, "then you push him around." Howe's elbows and the damage he inflicted with them are as legendary as any other aspect of his storied career.

Yet Keith Tkachuk is the only young winger here who has brought a nasty streak to his game.

Paul Kariya, a two-time winner of the Lady Byng Trophy (awarded for skill and sportsmanship), personifies the type of All-Star who follows more in the footsteps of wingers such as Jari Kurri and Mike Bossy, Hall of Fame snipers with a penchant for staying out of the penalty box. Their kind of toughness involves *absorbing* physical punishment rather than dishing it out, exacting their retribution on the score sheet.

Unfortunately, Kariya has stated that he may have to spare some of his temperance for self-protection. But even if he does, he will remain in good company. Hard-hitting "Big, Bad Bruin" Johnny Bucyk won the Byng twice, albeit over a 23-season NHL career. Father-son duo Bobby and Brett Hull both collected the Byng, although "The Golden Jet" often went through, rather than around, his opponents, and the outspoken "Golden Brett" could never be described as temperate, despite his clean play.

Jagr's consistent artistry and years of accomplishments place him solidly on the all-time-greatest list, yet his youth also qualifies him as one of the best young wingers in the game today. Although the task is herculean, the other young wingers featured here may eventually join Jagr in the more prestigious group. They will be assisted most by the pressure and payoffs found in playoff action, which they have rarely partaken in so far. Without a doubt, the potential is there.

Above: Toronto's Frank Mahovlich lifts a backhand goal over Detroit netminder Roger Crozier. Facing page: Jaromir Jagr gets to the net but is foiled by Felix Potvin at the 1996 NHL All-Star Game.

Mike Bossy

A goal scorer's paradise, the Quebec junior leagues are notorious for sacrificing defense in favor of offense. Nevertheless, it was astonishing that Mike Bossy had averaged 77 goals a year over four seasons with the Laval Nationals. More surprising was that Bossy was still available in the 1977 NHL entry draft when the up-and-coming New York Islanders made their first selection.

That Bossy went 15th that year did nothing to diminish his confidence. After signing his first NHL contract, he predicted a 50-goal rookie season. Islanders management obviously liked Bossy, but since Buffalo's Rick Martin had set the rookie scoring record six years earlier with 44 goals, Bossy's prediction sounded like a naive boast. He admitted later that even *he* was surprised when he shattered the record with a 53-goal campaign. He won not only the Calder Trophy but a prestigious Second All-Star Team selection at right wing as well.

An extraordinary goal scorer, Bossy was perhaps the greatest sniper in league history. He had an incredibly quick release with his wrist shot and could score from anywhere in the offensive zone. His accuracy was uncanny at even the toughest angles, but he was most deadly in the slot. Bossy became an integral part of the young and increasingly successful Islanders franchise, combining with center Bryan Trottier and left-winger Clark Gillies (two other judicious Islanders draft picks) on a powerhouse line right from the beginning. Bossy followed up his rookie year with 69 goals, a career high but no fluke. His 10 NHL seasons were remarkable for his accomplishments and his consistency, and he had five 60-plus seasons. Only in his last year, when the ailing back that forced his early retirement in 1987 hobbled him for most of the season, did he fail to score at least 50 goals (he still tallied 38).

While he remained a dedicated team player, Bossy set himself a lofty personal goal at the start of the 1980-81 season: He set out to score 50 goals in 50 games, an achievement matched only by the legendary Maurice "Rocket" Richard in 1944-45. Bossy had come fairly close two years earlier, notching number 50 in game 58, and he started the season in fine form. His target seemed within reach when he needed only two more goals in his 50th game, at home against the Quebec Nordiques. Quebec managed to keep him off the scoreboard

until, with just over four minutes remaining, the mighty Islanders power play took the ice. Bossy banged in a goal after a scramble in the crease, and the air of anticipation that had marked the night became almost electric.

Bossy got one more miraculous chance when Trottier found him unguarded and snapped a pass over with a minute and a half left in the game. Bossy rifled in goal 50. He, his teammates and the entire Nassau County Coliseum went wild in celebration. Bossy finished the season with 68 goals and a First All-Star Team selection, his first. He then led all playoff goal scorers on his way to his second Stanley Cup. In all, he won four Cups with the Islanders, making a significant contribution with 61 playoff markers in those four consecutive years, including the final winning goals both in 1982, when he won the Conn Smythe Trophy, and in 1983.

Because of his elegant play and commitment to a nonviolent approach to the game, Bossy was also a perennial candidate for the Lady Byng Trophy over the course of his career. He won the award three times and was runner-up once, a tribute to his great discipline. Although he suffered a high degree of abuse, he refused to retaliate. An outspoken critic of fighting and the use of intimidation, he refused to drop his gloves even when goaded. (Of course, the presense of his linemate, Gillies, offered him a measure of protection.) Despite the machismo prevalent in the NHL, Bossy suffered little criticism for his convictions, and he always played his own style, exacting his revenge on the power play. Even while being fouled or apparently hopelessly tied up, he could launch the puck with zip and accuracy.

What bothered Bossy most was being hit from behind. In attempting to dissuade him from hovering anywhere near the net, many defensemen resorted to a cross-check to his back as a method of moving him away or slowing him down. Although never the fastest of skaters, Bossy was nimble enough on his feet to avoid most hits, but an illegal attack from the rear couldn't be guarded against. Such cheap shots took their toll. Bossy never made categorical claims that they were the source of his subsequent back problems, but upon his retirement, he worked on a public campaign to educate minor-hockey players about the danger of hitting from behind.

Above: Mike Bossy, a three-time winner of the Lady Byng Trophy, remains the top goal scorer in New York Islanders' history, having notched better than 50 goals in nine consecutive seasons. Facing page: Bossy played in three Canada Cup tournaments, scoring an overtime winner against the Soviet Union in 1984.

Johnny Bucyk

"It breaks your heart when a club lets your buddies go," said Johnny Bucyk late in his career, "but you can't be soft about it. It's a hard game and a hard life, and you do the best you can. It's been a good life for me." Bucyk patrolled left wing for 21 seasons in Boston, setting club records for scoring and longevity along the way. He arrived when the Bruins were serious contenders for the Stanley Cup in the 1950s; he survived the club's eight-year era of futility in the 1960s; and he was a team mainstay in the glory years of the 1970s. Even after his retirement, Bucyk has remained an active and visible Bruins employee for an additional 20-some years. It's difficult to picture him with any other organization, yet Bucyk played his first two NHL seasons with the Detroit Red Wings.

Bucyk grew up in Detroit's farm system, and the Red Wings thought enough of the promising winger to give him a Stanley Cup ring as a member of their 1955 championship team, even though he didn't actually dress for a game. He saw limited action in his rookie year the following winter, scoring only a single goal, nor did he distinguish himself greatly the next season. Meanwhile, Detroit general manager Jack Adams decided to bring goalie Terry Sawchuk—a former All-Star and Vezina Trophy winner—back from Boston.

"Being traded for [Sawchuk] made me feel good," said Bucyk, "and it was the biggest break in my career. I wanted to play hockey more than anything, and knowing that I'd be getting regular ice time had me excited to get to Boston." Even better, Bucyk was reunited with former junior linemates Bronco Horvath and Vic Stasiuk, and the "Uke Line"—named for the Ukrainian heritage all three men shared—skated together for four productive seasons.

One of the heaviest forwards in the league for most of his career, Bucyk packed 220 pounds on his six-foot frame and used his bulk to advantage, banging into the corners and parking himself at the opposition net. "I never knew anyone who could hit a guy harder," noted Bobby Orr, "especially with a hip check."

Bucyk was an integral part of the "Big, Bad Bruins," but unlike some of his teammates, he confined his aggressiveness to legal hits. "I know the Lady Byng isn't a popular trophy with the Boston fans," he said in 1970, after finishing as

runner-up for the award for the second time, "but I'd sure like to win it." Bucyk's wish came true when he combined a career-high 51 goals and 65 assists with a meager eight minutes in penalties the following season. He took the league's award for sportsmanship again in 1974 and finished just behind Marcel Dionne in 1975.

Bucyk earned his nickname "Chief" because some fans thought he looked like a native American, but others may have assumed that the title referred to his leadership position on the club. Bucyk was first named team captain in the fall of 1966, but he found his off-ice responsibilities too time-consuming and suggested that he share the load. Bucyk traded his "C" for an "A." The captainless Bruins competed for six years with as many as four alternates, but when the team won the Stanley Cup in 1970 and 1972, there was no doubt about who would raise the victory mug first. Bucyk assumed formal captaincy again in 1973, until relinquishing the title in his retirement season to Wayne Cashman.

While Bucyk hit the 50-goal plateau only once (just the fifth player at the time to do so), he was a consistent scorer. "If you're going to get goals," he explained, "you've got to get in where the action is." His hard-nosed style wasn't flashy, but he joined the 500-goal club in 1975. "I've hit more posts than nets," he said, "but the numbers are nice. I've thought of myself as a spear-carrier, not a star, really. I've just gone along getting what I could out of every game, and it's added up."

Over the years, Bucyk learned an economy of movement ("doing the most I can with the least effort"), which he claimed was the key to being able to play at 42 years of age. "I'm old enough to be a father to some of these kids," he said in 1977, "but if they call me 'Pop,' I'll lay one on them." He never had to. Bucyk's number 9 jersey was officially retired by the Bruins when he retired in 1978. "All my records eventually will fall," Bucyk noted, "so I'm thankful that a tribute to my accomplishments will survive."

When Johnny Bucyk, above, retired after 21 seasons with the Boston Bruins, his sweater number 9 was also retired. Facing page: A heavy hitter but a determinedly clean player, Bucyk hip-checks Toronto's Murray Oliver off the puck behind the net.

Charlie Conacher

Although some decried Toronto's Jesse Ketchum Park as a breeding ground for juvenile delinquents, hockey scouts kept a close eye on the ice rinks there. Amid a plethora of card and crap games, there was always at least one hockey game in progress, and the neighborhood hangout spawned a number of NHL players, Charlie Conacher among them. The poverty that surrounded him fueled Conacher's desire to make a career of professional hockey. "It represented money," he said. "We didn't have a pretzel. We didn't have enough money to buy toothpaste." The Maple Leafs signed Conacher into their organization in 1929, having seen his potential and bloodlines. Conacher's brother Lionel, nine years his senior, was already beginning to establish the family name as one of the greatest in Canada's sporting history.

Lionel "Big Train" Conacher was voted Canada's Best Athlete of the Half-Century in 1950, but he was a hero in his brother's eyes long before that. Following in Lionel's footsteps, Charlie excelled at every sport he tried, particularly football, baseball, lacrosse and hockey. When Charlie saw his brother make the professional hockey ranks, he made sure his skating was top-notch. By the time Charlie had worked his way up to the Toronto Marlboros in junior hockey, Lionel had already played two NHL seasons for the Pittsburgh Pirates and was on his way to New York to play for the Americans. Although Charlie became a junior sensation, he couldn't imagine attaining NHL All-Star status before his brother.

When the younger Conacher graduated to the Maple Leafs in 1929, he scored 20 goals in his rookie year. One of the NHL's heftiest players, at six-foot-one and just under 200 pounds, Conacher was a sharpshooter with heavy ammunition. "It felt like somebody had turned a blowtorch on me," said Ottawa defenseman King Clancy after blocking one of Conacher's wrist shots. "I couldn't sit down for a week." Conacher led the league in goals in his second season, a feat he accomplished four more times in the next five years. Charlie "The Big Bomber" Conacher had earned his own nickname and a chance to replace Ace Bailey on Toronto's best line.

When coach Conn Smythe united Conacher with "Gentleman Joe" Primeau and Harvey "Busher" Jackson (the term busher referred to a go-getter), Toronto's original "Kid Line" was born. The combination was dynamite: Conacher scored the most goals again in the 1931-32 season; Primeau, the Lady Byng winner, had the most assists for the second consecutive year; Jackson won the scoring crown with the most points. Their line maintained a torrid pace through the playoffs, vanquishing Lionel Conacher and his Montreal Maroons in the semifinals. "The Big Bomber" continued to hit the target and led his team in goals and points—assisting on the clinching tally— to help the Leafs defeat the New York Rangers and win their first Stanley Cup in Maple Leaf Gardens.

Conacher made the Second All-Star Team a year before his defenseman brother Lionel shared that honor with him in the 1932-33 season. They both made the First Team the subsequent year. Charlie won his first scoring title, with 32 goals and 20 assists, while Lionel was steering the Chicago Blackhawks to a Stanley Cup victory. The two met head-to-head in the league finals for the first and last time in the spring of 1935, both in pursuit of their second Stanley Cup championship. Charlie had already won the scoring race again, and Lionel was back with the Montreal Maroons, who swept the Leafs in three straight games.

Conacher had one more All-Star season just ahead of him, but injuries took their toll thereafter. He played only 34 games over the next two regular seasons—and even then, he was but a shadow of his former self. The Leafs sold him to the Detroit Red Wings shortly after he notched his 200th career goal. Although Conacher starred for the Wings in the 1939 playoffs, he was traded that summer to the New York Americans, where he put in two undistinguished years before retiring in 1941 at the age of 31.

After coaching junior hockey for several years, Conacher was hired to coach the Chicago Blackhawks in 1947. His younger brother Roy was his best player and won the Art Ross Trophy as scoring champion in 1949. Conacher retired again a year before his son Pete, the next member of hockey's "royal family," made it to the NHL in 1951.

Toronto's "Kid Line" of the 1930s, above: Right-winger Charlie Conacher (left), "Gentleman Joe" Primeau (center) and left-winger Harvey "Busher" Jackson (right). Facing page: "The Big Bomber" Conacher led the NHL in scoring for five out of six seasons in the early 1930s.

Mike Gartner

Filling in for injured teammate Mark Messier at the 1993 All-Star Game, Mike Gartner not only won the skating race in the NHL Skills Competition but took away a car as the prize for being named the game's most valuable player. Opening the scoring with two goals only 22 seconds apart on his way to a first-period hat trick, Gartner contributed a fourth goal in the second period, helping the Wales Conference set an All-Star Game scoring record in a 16–6 blowout. "I'll give Mark a big handshake," he laughed when asked whether he owed Messier anything, "but not the car!"

Gartner has been the quietest member of a select group. On December 15, 1997, he became only the fifth NHL player to register 700 goals in a career. Like Gordie Howe, another "700 Club" member, Gartner never erupted for a 60- or 70-goal season, but he did hit the prestigious 50-goal mark in the last game of the 1984-85 season. The key to Gartner's success was consistency. He holds the NHL record with 17 seasons of 30 or more goals, with 15 of those seasons in succession. The lockout-shortened 1994-95 season interrupted his unprecedented streak, but trades never broke his stride. Gartner is the only player who has scored 30 or more goals for five different teams.

In 1978, Gartner made a bold move when he signed as an underage free agent with the World Hockey Association's Cincinnati Stingers. When the NHL swallowed the WHA the next year, the Washington Capitals made Gartner the league's number-four draft pick. Generous amounts of ice time on a weak Washington team translated into more goals than even Gartner knew he was capable of scoring. Although convinced that his strength lay in his two-way play, Gartner found his niche as a fleet sniper. "My speed was a God-given thing," said Gartner. "I worked on it, but for the most part, it was there from the very beginning, when I was a kid." He established franchise records for career goals and points that still stand, but after 10 years with the Capitals, Gartner was traded for the first time in March 1989 to Minnesota.

Although Gartner tallied more than a point a game for the North Stars, he was sent to the New York Rangers a year later. He had three consecutive 40-goal years in Manhattan. The 1991-92 season was an especially auspicious one: He recorded his 500th goal, 500th assist and 1,000th point and played in his 1,000th NHL game. All cylinders were firing as the Rangers headed toward their first Stanley Cup victory in over 40 years, but at the 1994 trading deadline, Gartner was dealt to the Toronto Maple Leafs for Glenn Anderson, the rights to another player and a draft pick.

The knock against Gartner was that he didn't perform well in postseason action, but his 43 goals and 50 assists in 122 playoff games suggest otherwise. He had even contributed 8 goals and 8 assists in 13 games in 1991-92, the last time the Rangers were in the playoffs. Unfortunately for Gartner, though, Anderson got his sixth championship ring with the Rangers in 1994. Gartner himself never played on a Stanley Cup winner.

Gartner, NHLPA president from 1993 to 1998, completed two solid seasons for the Leafs before they made a move to younger players and sent him to Phoenix. While Gartner's age was a factor in others' eyes, the 36-year-old proved that he still had wings when he won the NHL skating race for the third time at the 1996 All-Star Game. "You knew if you got him the puck, he could make things happen," said Larry Murphy, who played with Gartner in Washington, Minnesota and Toronto. "When you played against him, you had to respect his speed. You had to back off him, or he'd burn you." But Gartner had his worst season in 1997-98, battling injuries for the first time in his career. His age and seven-figure salary prompted Phoenix to place him on waivers. There were no takers.

While Gartner was capable of signing a free-agent contract with anyone, he determined, instead, to honor a commitment he had made to his wife and children to be settled at that point in their lives. "Maybe I'm leaving something on the table," he said in announcing his retirement, after failing to strike a deal with one of a select few teams for which he was willing to play, "but 20 years from now, will it matter if I scored 780 goals instead of 708? Will it matter if I played 22 years instead of 19?" Gartner bowed out gracefully, one of the classiest men ever to play in the NHL.

New York Ranger Mike Gartner, above, tries to get the puck past Leafs defenseman Jamie Macoun. Facing page: Gartner joined Toronto in March 1994; the following year, a lockout ended his 15-season streak of 30-plus goals. In 1997-98, he became the NHL's fifth 700-goal scorer.

Bernie Geoffrion

Bernie Geoffrion invented the slap shot in his youth, and when he brought it to the big leagues, it was unlike anything the NHL had ever seen. "It's definitely harder than anything [Charlie] Conacher shot," claimed Toronto coach Hap Day, who played with Conacher in the 1930s. "I watched Geoffrion closely on one play. I saw him draw the stick back, but I didn't see the puck until it bounced off the goalpost."

Geoffrion's nickname "Boom-Boom" referred to the sound of the puck reverberating off the end boards, but he hit twine often enough that the Montreal Canadiens were clamoring for his services while he was still a teenager. He had joined Montreal's junior team at the age of 14 and more than held his own, and he continued to improve his entire game while paying particular attention to the shot that would make him famous. Geoffrion held out until there were only 18 games left in the Canadiens' 1950-51 season, potting eight goals but still preserving his rookie status for the following year. Then, in his official rookie season, he won the Calder Trophy he coveted, with 30 goals and 24 assists.

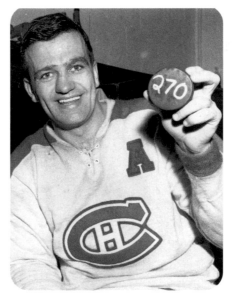

Geoffrion had a glorious career with the Canadiens; his name went on the Stanley Cup six times. He battled through numerous injuries, earning a deserved reputation as a dedicated and fiery competitor. Most times jovial off the ice, he showed a darker side when things weren't going his way. "When Maurice [Richard] doesn't score, he's not happy and he doesn't want to speak to anyone," explained Geoffrion. "I'm the same way." But Geoffrion scored more than 20 goals in a season a dozen times for Montreal—when that total really meant something in the NHL.

Unfortunately, Richard (who also patrolled right wing for Montreal), Detroit's Gordie Howe and Andy Bathgate of the Rangers were such outstanding players that it was difficult for Geoffrion to gain league-wide recognition of his considerable talents. Even after Geoffrion won the scoring championship in the 1954-55 season, Richard was named to the First All-Star Team. Geoffrion's resulting anger, however, was nothing compared with that of the fans in the Montreal Forum when Richard was suspended for the last few games of the season, after a violent outburst, and Geoffrion passed him by a single point to earn the scoring title.

"I couldn't deliberately *not* score," complained Geoffrion,

but the boos and catcalls rained down on him regardless. "I was sick of the whole thing," an emotional Geoffrion later confessed. "Even thinking about hockey made me throw up. I wanted to get away from hockey. But [Jean] Beliveau and [Maurice] Richard visited me. They urged me to stay in the game."

Even after Richard retired in 1960 and Geoffrion won his second Art Ross Trophy in 1960-61, with only the second 50-goal campaign in NHL history, some fans continued to harbor resentment that "Boom-Boom" had again entered Richard's territory. But it all ended happily: Most of those in the Forum gave Geoffrion a standing ovation, he made the First All-Star Team, and he added the Hart Trophy as the league's most valuable player.

Finally admitting that his numerous injuries had gotten the better of him and noting the arrival of a young and promising speedster named Yvan Cournoyer, Geoffrion called it quits after the 1963-64 season. He then turned his attention to coaching for the Canadiens organization in the minor leagues and spent two years there. When the step up the ladder that he believed he had been promised didn't materialize, he severed his long relationship with Montreal.

Geoffrion arrived in New York in 1966, although not as coach. He made a remarkable comeback that proved his exit had been premature and reentered the NHL ranks as a player with the Rangers. He helped the team into the playoffs twice—he never missed the playoffs over 16 seasons in total—before deciding to retire for good in 1968.

He briefly coached the Rangers, but his nerves and personality weren't truly suited for that position. Fortunately, the Big Apple offered different opportunities. His sense of humor, combined with a thick French accent and gravelly voice, had made him an immensely popular figure. Geoffrion parlayed his appeal into employment as a pitchman for

numerous companies, work that keeps him busy to this day.

While Geoffrion coached the Atlanta Flames for their first few seasons in the early 1970s, the pressure of coaching eventually made him too ill to continue. Yet he made a celebrated return to Montreal to coach his old club in 1979. "I am the new, improved Bernard Geoffrion," he said during a serious moment in a joke-filled press conference. "I can handle this. I am serious, and I am going to prove it to you." But several months later, he quit, claiming that the players would not listen to him and did not care. He returned to his home in Atlanta and eventually helped his adopted hometown regain an NHL franchise that begins play in 1999-2000. If the Atlanta Thrashers have learned anything from their association with Geoffrion, we should be entertained.

Bernie "Boom-Boom" Geoffrion, above, corrals a loose puck on the back-check. "Someday," the sniper told his bride, the daughter of Howie Morenz, "I'll score more goals than your father did." Facing page: Geoffrion fulfilled his promise on December 7, 1960, with goals 270 and 271.

Gordie Howe

Affectionately known as "Mr. Hockey," Gordie Howe is the most durable and consistent star ever to lace on skates. Not only did he play 26 NHL seasons, but he dominated the league for most of that time. In his 23rd NHL season, he reached his highest point total of 103. For 20 consecutive years, he finished among the top five scorers in the league, and he garnered 21 All-Star Team selections. In today's game, he would be regarded as a "power forward," but his team-mates simply called him "The Power."

On the ice, Howe deferred to no one. Detroit general manager Jack Adams had to pull him aside after his first three NHL seasons and point out that he needn't have a punch-out with every player in the league. Howe curbed his fighting, which seemed to translate directly into more goals, but he remained one of the nastiest players in the game. He was just more subtle about it.

Howe had a rare ambidextrous shooting ability, but he also possessed the "sharpest" elbows in the league. "We had very poor equipment and I have very sloping shoulders," he has explained. "It was almost a necessity to get my elbow out." But Howe also wasn't averse to stickwork, and he used his awesome strength in surprising ways. "When a guy was a little faster than me and we were going behind the net," he once laughed, "I'd swing a little wide to give him the inside spot, then squeeze him off so he'd run into the net. A lot of guys have told me, 'Oh, I knew when I was halfway through there, I was in trouble.' "

While Howe notched only seven goals as a rookie, he impressed the Red Wings enough to be placed on a line with the proven veterans Sid Abel and Ted Lindsay in his second season. Before long, the "Production Line" was tearing up the league. After losing in the Stanley Cup finals two years in succession, Howe tried to ram Toronto captain Ted Kennedy into the boards in the first game of the 1950 playoffs. Kennedy ducked, and Howe crashed into the boards head-first. Rushed to hospital, he was diagnosed with a fractured nose and cheekbone, a concussion and possible brain damage. Emergency surgery relieved the pressure on his brain, but for a while, it looked as if he might not live through the night. In time, Howe made a full recovery.

With their injured star in hospital as their inspiration, the Red Wings won the Stanley Cup that season. The Detroit fans were euphoric, and the Olympia soon reverberated with chants of "Howe! Howe! Howe!" Gordie Howe was not forgotten. The early 1950s were Detroit's glory years (four Stanley Cups in six seasons), and although the Cup eluded him thereafter, Howe maintained his personal excellence through thick and thin. Still racking up points but suffering constant pain with arthritis, he retired in 1971. At the age of 43, Howe moved into a front-office "executive" position. He hated it, desperately wanting to be more than a ribbon cutter.

So in 1973, when the newly formed WHA invited him to join his young sons Mark and Marty on a line for the Houston Aeros, he jumped at the chance. Howe was an All-Star again and added 174 goals and 334 assists to his career totals. "His whole life is there in the rink, in the dressing room," claimed his wife Colleen in 1978. "He can't wait to get to practice just to see what some of the younger members of the team will do or say next. Then he can't wait to get home to tell me about it." Howe regarded the six seasons spent playing with his boys in the WHA the highlight of his 33 years in professional hockey.

Despite hints of disappointment at having his NHL career goal-scoring record broken by Wayne Gretzky, Howe has always maintained an amiable relationship with Gretzky, who has idolized Howe since he was a boy. "Stop this talk of early retirement," Howe advised him, "because the day will come when you won't want to stop." The last time their paths crossed in a meaningful way on the ice was in 1980, when Gretzky played his first NHL All-Star Game and Howe played his last. The loyalties of the 21,000 fans in Detroit's Joe Louis Arena were loud and clear. "I didn't know what to do with myself," Howe admitted later, for it seemed that the standing ovation for him would never end. "It's still hard to accept appreciation. I'd love to show that I accept this with a great amount of gratitude, but how do you do it?" A few months later, Howe hung up his skates for good.

Gordie Howe, above, completed his unparalleled career with the Hartford Whalers in 1979-80 at the age of 52. Facing page: Talented and relentlessly tough, "Mr. Hockey" mixes it up in front of the Toronto net as captain of the Detroit Red Wings in the late 1950s.

Bobby Hull

With his tremendous speed, muscular good looks and unprecedented goal-scoring ability, "The Golden Jet" electrified NHL audiences for 15 seasons. "You knew what he was going to do—you could read him like a book," maintained Gordie Howe, "but he was so strong, he'd do it anyway."

And yet all that power was tempered by good grace. "Always keep your composure," advised Bobby Hull, who won the Lady Byng Trophy in 1965. "You can't score from the penalty box; and to win, you have to score."

While Hull owns only one Stanley Cup ring, the goals and the wins certainly came for him. In 1965-66, he became the last NHL scoring champion to win with more goals than assists, and for seven seasons, he led the league in goals scored.

Hull entered the league in 1957 with a tremendous shot, but in the 1960s, he mastered the slap shot that Bernie Geoffrion had pioneered. Goaltender Cesare Maniago was slow to join the other NHL goalies and don a face mask full-time, and for years, he wore one only when he faced the Chicago Blackhawks and Hull's slap shot. He believed that "Hull could have killed somebody with the power of his shot" and had no desire to prove his theory.

An outspoken critic of violence in hockey, Hull even staged a one-man one-game strike during the 1977-78 season to publicize his cause. Yet he systematically terrorized opposition goalies, cranking noisy shots off the glass during warm-ups and publicly discussing his strategy of firing his first shots in a game at the goalie's head. Netminder Gump Worsley challenged Hull bare-faced for 15 seasons, maintaining that Hull only talked of firing the hard high one and, instead, rifled in a low shot, but most goalies were instinctively back on their heels.

When his teammate Stan Mikita started experimenting with a curved stick in the early 1960s, Hull joined him in tinkering with the new weapon. The "banana blade" was born, and Hull was thrilled with the results. "If you don't quite catch all of the puck as you let it go, it'll rise or drop suddenly, depending on the spin," he explained in 1966. "Drawing it toward you as you let it go sets up a different spin that produces a curve."

With 54 goals in the 1965-66 season, Hull broke the long-standing record of 50 goals in a season (he'd previously matched the 50-goal records of Maurice Richard and Bernie Geoffrion in 1961-62); the following season, he tallied 52 goals. Toronto netminder Johnny Bower complained, "He needs another shot like I need a hole in the head, which I may get."

In 1967, the NHL stepped in with a new rule limiting a stick's curve, and when Hull broke his own record in 1968-69 with 58 goals, the league further limited the curve. Yet it would be a gross overstatement to claim that the hooked blade was the key to Hull's success. Many experts believe that he would have scored more than 70 goals in 1968-69 without the big curve, suggesting that it impeded his accuracy.

Hull's career scoring record is impressive in every meaningful category. He won the Art Ross Trophy three times, and of the 10 first 50-goal seasons, 5 were his. Although he left the Chicago Blackhawks while still in his prime, Hull holds most of that franchise's career goal-scoring records.

Despite all his accomplishments on the ice, however, Hull's most lasting achievement may be the credibility he supplied the upstart WHA in its first season. Hull rocked the hockey world when he signed with the Winnipeg Jets in 1972. All the new franchises ponied up to give Hull a million-dollar signing bonus on top of the Jets' record-breaking salary offer, and Hull (who had initially made an outrageous demand just to get the WHA to leave him alone) felt compelled to accept the lucrative deal. "If I told you the big contract had nothing to do with my signing," he admitted after, "I'd be lying," but he cited a long-standing complaint about how Chicago had negotiated with him over the years. Almost immediately, every professional hockey player was able to command more money, for if a living legend such as Hull could jump to the new league, who couldn't?

Hull added 303 goals and 335 assists in just over six WHA seasons, most as left wing on a line with the elegant Swedes Anders Hedberg and Ulf Nilsson. He retired from hockey in the fall of 1978, but when the Jets joined the NHL the following year, he made a brief comeback. Hobbled by injuries and after a nine-game stint with the Hartford Whalers, he retired again before the 1979-80 season was out, but his name began to appear again in the NHL record book years later. When Bobby's son "The Golden Brett" received the Hart Trophy in 1991, the Hulls became the first father-son combination to win the award. Yet the younger Hull is unlikely to match one of his father's lasting accomplishments: In honor of one of hockey's most dynamic stars, Bobby Hull's number 9 jersey was eventually raised to the rafters in both Winnipeg and Chicago.

Facing page: Bobby Hull scored more goals against Soviet goaltender Vladislav Tretiak than any other Canadian player. "The Golden Jet" also led the NHL in goal scoring seven times as a member of the Chicago Blackhawks, right, and was the first player to break the 50-goal mark.

Brett Hull

"I'm a goal scorer," says Brett Hull. "That's not all I do, but that's what I do best." Hockey scouts were always convinced about Hull's sniping skills but not about whether he could play at the NHL level. As the son of Hall of Fame legend Bobby Hull, "The Golden Jet," Brett naturally attracted attention when he tallied 105 goals as a Junior B player to close out his teenage years. But at the same age, his father had been rifling in goals for the Chicago Blackhawks.

"Maybe I've got his genes, but I definitely don't have his personality," says Brett. "You're talking to the laziest man alive. I'm not into expending physical energy. I'm into expending mental energy. On the ice, my dad was like a thorough-bred. I'm more like a train. I chug."

The Calgary Flames decided to risk their sixth draft pick and made Hull the 117th player chosen in 1984. He also earned an invitation to the University of Minnesota at Duluth, where he potted 84 goals in 90 games over two seasons. A year with Moncton in the AHL followed, and on the strength of 50 goals and 42 assists, he got the long-awaited call-up to the Flames in the spring of 1987.

Doubts about his work ethic persisted, however, even through his official rookie year of 1987-88, when he tallied 26 goals and 50 points in 52 games. The Flames made a trade—debatable even then—dealing Hull to the St. Louis Blues at the March 1988 trading deadline. The move soon looked downright foolish.

Hull maintained his solid scoring pace with the Blues, contributing 7 playoff goals in 10 games and pacing his new club with 41 goals and 43 assists in the 1988-89 season. Magic ensued the following year, though. Newly acquired centerman Adam Oates, one of hockey's slickest passers, helped "The Golden Brett" erupt for 72 goals, a record for right-wingers. Hull shattered his own mark with 86 goals in the 1990-91 season and added 70 more the year after. Only Wayne Gretzky has ever found the net more often over a three-season span.

In addition to making the First All-Star Team three times running, Hull added the Lady Byng Trophy in 1990. "I'm not going to fight anyone," he once noted. "When I chase defensemen into the corner in the course of a game, I'm telling them I'm behind them and to move it. I don't want to hurt

anyone." In 1991, he received both the Hart Trophy and the Pearson Award. "My whole game is based on deception," he explained. "I'm there, and then I'm not. I don't want to be noticed. I barely raise my arms when I score. I don't want people mad at me for making them look stupid."

Still, his happy-go-lucky style grated on some. "I'm not a grinder," admitted Hull. "If we had 20 players like me, we wouldn't win five games all season." Lurking unobtrusively, Hull pounced on scoring opportunities. "There comes that moment when I have lost myself, and only the play finds me," he added mystically. "And I have nothing but confidence in my ability to bury the puck in the net at that moment."

Hull's production slackened over the next half-dozen seasons with the Blues, yet he still scored an average of more than 40 goals a year. In the middle of a lengthy feud with coach Mike Keenan, Hull boldly said, "You have one up on everyone if you can figure out what's going on in that guy's head." Keenan ultimately lost the public battle and was sacked.

Unafraid of controversy, Hull angered league officials by complaining about the interference that he and other finesse players faced nightly. "It's not the referees' fault," said Hull. "It's the people above them. They're ruining the game. It's embarrassing. I wouldn't pay money to watch that. The game's going to hell in a handbasket." Shortly thereafter, the NHL instituted tougher rules against obstruction.

"Brett Hull's goals are going to be missed," said St. Louis defenseman Al MacInnis when Hull signed a free-agent contract with the Dallas Stars for the 1998-99 season, "and no one guy is going to be able to replace him."

Hull hit a millennium milestone early in his tenure with the Stars. "It's a weird feeling," he said. "You hope to get one goal in this game, but to say I have 500 goals and 1,000 points is a thrill. I'll long remember this night." His dad called to congratulate him. "I told him that if I played when he did," Brett laughed, "I would have done this three years earlier."

As a member of the St. Louis Blues, Brett Hull, above, managed to skate—and shoot—himself out of his father's huge shadow, highlighted by an 86-goal 1990-91 season. Facing page: Hull joined the Dallas Stars in 1998-99, scoring several key goals in the battle for the Stanley Cup.

Jaromir Jagr

With a wild mane of curly hair spilling onto his shoulders from beneath his helmet, Jaromir Jagr still looks every bit the rebellious youth who roared onto the NHL scene in 1990. But he's undergone an unexpected metamorphosis. After Mario Lemieux retired in 1997 and Ron Francis joined the Carolina Hurricanes as a free agent in 1998, Jagr expressed his desire to captain the Pittsburgh Penguins. "I know the kind of person I am," he said, "and I knew I could do the job." His surprised teammates were unanimous in giving him the chance.

"I was a troublemaker," conceded Jagr. "When I wasn't happy, I would scream—I was uninterested in what I did on the ice or whatever the team did. I changed, because a lot of players look up to me now. I am trying to lead by example."

Pittsburgh coach Kevin Constantine, who had more than his share of run-ins with Jagr during his first season behind the Pittsburgh bench in 1997-98, has taken his young superstar's evolution in stride. "Jaromir's a smart guy," he said. "He saw a changing team that needed him to change and be a leader, and that's what he did."

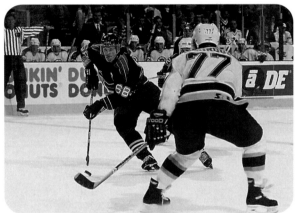

Jagr has come by his independent spirit honestly. His grandfather died in jail as a Czechoslovakian political prisoner in 1968. Born four years after Soviet Union tanks rolled in to strengthen a threatened Communist government, Jagr came of age during the next Czechoslovak uprising. Fortunately, the "Velvet Revolution" wasn't quashed, and Jagr became the first hockey player from his country to attend an NHL draft without having to defect. The Pittsburgh Penguins picked him early in the first round of the 1990 NHL entry draft. In memory of his grandfather, Jagr donned sweater number 68 and made an immediate impact.

Someone soon discovered that "Jaromir" was an anagram for "Mario Jr.," and indeed, Jagr seemed cut from the same cloth as team captain Lemieux. At six-foot-two and 230 pounds, he has Lemieux's reach, strength and "puck-on-a-string" stickhandling ability. His 27 goals and 30 assists in his rookie year helped the Penguins into first place in their division, and he added 13 playoff points toward Pittsburgh's first Stanley Cup victory in 1991. The following year, he was a dominant factor in defending the Cup, scoring 11 goals and 13 assists in the playoffs.

"There's so much innocence to him," said veteran Gordie Roberts in 1992. "He enjoys everything. He hasn't realized yet that hockey is a business."

Although "I play for fun" could have been Jagr's motto, his cockiness sometimes got him into trouble. Francis once verbally blasted Jagr for not setting a good example, but the veteran centerman was "blown away" by the 22-year-old Jagr's response: "Thank you. I needed that. Nobody ever gives me heck; the coaches never give me heck." He did receive a 10-game suspension for abusing an official on January 26, 1992, but otherwise, Jagr has rarely missed a game.

When Lemieux was out with a bad back, Jagr stepped more fully into the breach. During Lemieux's season off to convalesce from Hodgkin's disease, Jagr edged out Eric Lindros to take the 1994-95 scoring title. Lemieux returned the following year, drawing more of the opposition's attention, and Jagr erupted with his most productive season, scoring 62 goals and 87 assists.

"You always want to score a beautiful goal," says Jagr. "That's what you're trying to do. Score some goals like that, get more confidence for the other ones." Yet he sees himself as a "passer, not so much a goal scorer," and his scoring crown in the 1997-98 season came on the strength of his league-leading 67 assists. One of the most artistic and creative players of all time, Jagr also barges to the net, drawing hooks, slashes and power-play opportunities.

"Playing with him is a lot of fun," said Stu Barnes in 1998. "You never know what you're going to see next. But he's also a guy who really works hard off the ice, and that's something he doesn't get enough credit for."

Jagr often arrives at practice 45 minutes early to shoot pucks and stays late to skate uninhibited by a crowd of players. "I just go out and have fun," he says. "If you have fun, I think you play a lot better than if you take the game seriously."

"We used to all have our theories about how we're going to work against [Wayne] Gretzky," said veteran Toronto coach Pat Quinn. "Jagr is the same type of player. You stop one thing, and he finds something else to beat you with."

Midway through the 1998-99 season, en route to winning his third Art Ross Trophy as points leader, Jagr said, "Sometimes you feel you can do anything on the ice; sometimes you feel you can't do a thing. Right now, I feel better than I ever have, like I could play 50 minutes a night." Pittsburgh coach Constantine has tried many different players with Jagr, who gives all his new linemates the same instructions: "I don't want us chasing the puck down; that's how you get tired. Just keep it on my stick." It couldn't be in better hands.

Jaromir Jagr, right, won his third NHL scoring crown in 1998-99, with 44 goals, 83 assists and a 21-point bulge over his closest rival. Facing page: Perhaps the league's strongest one-on-one player, Jagr attempts a shifty move against veteran Boston defenseman Ray Bourque.

Jari Kurri

"There was a tremendous load off the back of the entire team," admitted Jari Kurri after the Edmonton Oilers won the Stanley Cup in 1990, "because we demonstrated that we weren't a one-man show." Kurri, who earned his fifth Stanley Cup ring with that win, probably felt more relief than anyone else on the Edmonton team. When Wayne Gretzky had been traded to the Los Angeles Kings in the summer of 1988, there were many who said that Kurri would be ordinary without him. The two had been the dominant offensive pairing of the 1980s, but Kurri proved his critics wrong. In his first NHL season without Gretzky as his center, Kurri made the Second All-Star Team with a 44-goal 58-assist campaign. During the 1990 Stanley Cup playoffs, he scored 10 goals and added 15 assists.

While Gretzky was at the peak of his offensive power in Edmonton, Kurri made more of a contribution than was sometimes acknowledged. Gretzky himself is always the first to credit his teammates for his success, and no one was closer to Gretzky than Kurri. In the end, the two played 13 seasons together. "We see the game the same way," said Gretzky. Coming from "The Great One," this is as generous a compliment as any ever given in hockey. The two seemed to operate on an intuitive level: Kurri found his way to open ice, and Gretzky found him with the puck.

Yet many of Kurri's goals came from his ability to make the most of the opportunities Gretzky provided him. His use of the "one-timer"—Europe's first major contribution to NHL hockey's evolution and the most difficult shot to execute—was only part of his secret. Kurri had the speed to create chances and the "soft" hands to finish them. He also made great passes; his 797 career assists are proof that he was a premier playmaker too.

Kurri was also more than an offensive force. "Jari Kurri is by far our most complete player," said Edmonton's chief scout Barry Fraser. Kurri was runner-up to Bobby Clarke in 1983 voting for the Frank Selke Trophy, but it's surprising that Kurri never won that award as the league's best defensive forward. Perhaps his offensive numbers threw the voters off. Assigned to Gretzky's line after a number of players had auditioned, Kurri knew from the start that two-way play would be critical to his success. He earned league-wide respect for his

clean defensive play (he was also a Lady Byng Trophy winner) but still had six 100-point seasons. Kurri had a career year in 1984-85, setting a new high for right-wingers, with 71 goals, and finishing with 135 points. He led the league with 68 tallies the following season.

Still, Kurri somehow managed to save his best hockey for the playoffs. He was the leading playoff goal scorer four times—the Oilers won the Cup on each occasion—and he shares a record with Philadelphia's Reggie Leach for 19 playoff goals in one season. Kurri's two overtime markers, seven hat tricks and 10 shorthanded scores helped him to a solid third place on both the all-time playoff goals and points lists.

A contract dispute in 1990-91 led to a year of play in Italy before a three-team trade sent Kurri to the Los Angeles Kings. Reunited with Gretzky, Kurri had two decent seasons before he helped the Kings to the 1993 Stanley Cup finals. However, the Kings failed to make the playoffs again, and Kurri was traded to the New York Rangers in 1996.

Kurri's defensive game had become his primary contribution, and he bounced to several teams before finishing his career in 1998 with the Colorado Avalanche. Having given advance notice of his retirement and notching his 600th career goal, one more highlight remained for Kurri. "Being chosen to come here one last time is wonderful," he said, after being invited to play at the 1998 All-Star Game by NHL commissioner Gary Bettman. Playing for the World Team (players born outside North America), Kurri scored only his second All-Star goal in eight appearances and was embarrassed when Gretzky slipped a pass by him to Mark Messier, who scored the game-winner for the North American side. "Wayne still fools even me," laughed Kurri. "I told him at the face-off, 'I back-check all those years for you, and that's how you treat me?' "

Once the requisite three years of retirement are up, Kurri is certain to be enshrined as Finland's first member of the Hockey Hall of Fame.

Jari Kurri, above, joined the Los Angeles Kings in 1991-92, having played a season in Italy after contract differences with Edmonton. Facing page: During his 10 seasons as an Oiler, Kurri won five All-Star selections and became only the third NHL player to score 70 goals in a season.

Guy Lafleur

When he got the puck on his stick, the Montreal Forum crowd came alive with cries of "Guy! Guy!" The fans edged forward in their seats, anticipating at least an exciting play if not a goal. And the focus of their attention, Guy Lafleur, rarely disappointed.

Heralded as a franchise player when he was drafted by the Montreal Canadiens in 1971 (cagey Canadiens general manager Sam Pollock had finessed the first-round draft pick from the California Golden Seals in a trade), Lafleur began his career with a heavy responsibility. Many saw him as a replacement for the legendary Jean Beliveau, who had retired the same year. Smart enough to decline Beliveau's sweater number 4, Lafleur had nonetheless created high expectations with his teenage scoring feats. When he finished an extraordinary junior career by tallying 130 goals and 79 assists in his last season with the junior league's Quebec Remparts, he rivaled even the sensational season enjoyed by his counterpart in Ontario's junior league, Marcel Dionne.

While Lafleur's rookie NHL campaign was excellent by normal standards (29 goals and 35 assists), he followed up with seasons of 55 and 56 points and was frequently portrayed by the media as a disappointment, especially since Dionne had fared much better on the vastly poorer Detroit team. In truth, Montreal boasted an incredible lineup in Lafleur's early years and intentionally broke in rookies slowly.

Lafleur finally had a breakthrough year in the 1974-75 season, with 53 goals and 66 assists, and many cited as a factor his decision to shed the headgear he had worn for his first three years in Montreal. Whether or not having the wind blow through his hair made Lafleur feel more creative and reckless, as some claimed, it certainly wouldn't have been quite the same for the fans if he'd had a helmet on. As he danced and whirled up the ice, "The Flower" was a beautiful sight, and Lafleur became a huge box-office draw as the first player to have six consecutive 50-goal seasons and six consecutive 100-point seasons.

Induction into the Hockey Hall of Fame represents the pinnacle of a successful hockey career. A player basks in the spotlight, while he and others reflect on his accomplishments and past glories. Not so for Lafleur. Late in the summer of

1988, while others were fondly looking back at his three scoring championships and five Stanley Cup victories with the Montreal Canadiens, Lafleur was anxiously looking ahead. He was only days away from finding out whether he could skate his way back into the NHL after three years of an unsatisfactory retirement.

Fellow Hall-of-Famers Ted Lindsay, Bernie "Boom-Boom" Geoffrion and Gordie Howe had all returned to league action after retiring, but only Howe had done so following his induction. Lafleur's attempt at a comeback caught most fans totally off guard. His name had been synonymous with the Canadiens' dynastic reign in the 1970s, and he had passed the 500-goal mark in 1983. What more could he hope to accomplish?

Yet Lafleur's retirement in 1985 had not been freely chosen. Although in 1978, Lafleur had described hockey as "like a dream to me," by 1984, it had become a nightmare under a new coach and general manager. Former teammate and then coach Jacques Lemaire imposed a tightly controlled defensive system that stifled Lafleur's natural gifts. (Lemaire later took his system to New Jersey and won the Stanley Cup in 1995.) Since Lafleur's game was offense, he saw a decreasing amount of ice time, poison to any scorer. Soon, some of the fans were starting to get on his back, for even when he got on the ice, Lafleur showed little of his famous flash and creativity. Claiming to be handcuffed by Lafleur's legendary stature and association with the Canadiens' tradition, team management ignored his appeals for a trade, so Lafleur quit in frustration. For three years, he missed the game terribly.

When the New York Rangers beckoned with the offer of a tryout in 1988, Lafleur proved that he could still play in the NHL. He had a decent season, with 18 goals and 27 assists, and played two more seasons after that with the Quebec Nordiques, in the city where he'd first received national attention. Age was finally catching up with him, however, and he was relatively inconspicuous on the score sheet, placing fifth and eighth on a team that finished out of the playoffs. But Lafleur had succeeded in proving to himself and to everyone else that he could have been a contributing player during his forced "sabbatical."

When Lafleur finally announced his forthcoming retirement in 1991, on *his* terms, he received an appreciative acknowledgment from every crowd in every city, but especially in Montreal. All past indignities and disputes were buried, and Lafleur later happily took an off-ice job as one of the Canadiens' exalted ambassadors.

Right: Guy Lafleur's blazing speed help to create the opportunities that earned him three consecutive Art Ross Trophies and five Stanley Cup rings in the 1970s. Facing page: Lafleur had three decent seasons wearing a helmet before doffing the protection and bursting into stardom with the Montreal Canadiens.

Ted Lindsay

Detroit hockey fans can thank Lady Luck for making Ted Lindsay a Red Wing. After Lindsay played well in his first game for Toronto's St. Mike's junior team, the Maple Leafs brass was alerted that the school had a rookie forward the Leafs should consider. At a subsequent game, the Toronto scouts put the best forward they saw on the ice on their "protected" list, making him their property. Unknown to them, however, this forward was *not* Lindsay—he had been knocked out of the lineup with a severe gash in his leg.

When the still-hobbled Lindsay resumed playing, he attracted little notice. By January, he was fully healed and showing the feisty vigor for which he would become legendary. In 1944, the day after a game against Detroit's junior affiliate, Lindsay was signed by the Red Wings organization.

"Terrible Ted" Lindsay was short of stature and temper. He eventually retired as the most penalized player of all time. "This is our profession. It's a game you get paid for," he said in a revealing comment as the Red Wings headed into the 1950 Stanley Cup playoffs. "But when it comes to the Leafs, we'd play them for nothing." Toronto had defeated Detroit in the finals the previous two seasons, but Lindsay's bitter feelings weren't entirely restricted to that club. He played a mean game, and the damage he inflicted often led to bloody retaliation, which was well documented by the 700 stitches he took in his face during his career. But the league's most-hated player earned nothing but appreciation in Detroit.

"He's the guy who holds us together," claimed Sid Abel, the center of the famous "Production Line" between Lindsay and Gordie Howe. "He keeps us at a high pitch. He won't allow anyone to let down when he's on the ice."

Lindsay commanded respect off the ice as well. "It was all in the tone of his voice," said Howe. "It was very authoritative."

And Lindsay wasn't hesitant about taking the initiative. He captained the Red Wings to a Stanley Cup victory in the spring of 1954. After the final game, the Stanley Cup was placed on a table at center ice, and the winning team stood around it drinking champagne. But Lindsay had a different idea. "It was an impulsive sort of thing," he later explained. "Everybody's emotions were running high, and I guess mine were a little higher." Lindsay hoisted the Cup over his head

and skated a lap around the ice near the boards to give the jubilant fans a better look. A tradition was born.

"As long as the fans don't boo you at home, you don't have to worry," he said in 1957. "If they boo you on the road, you must be doing something to help your own club. As for the other players, I'd like them all to be my friends—off the ice." The latter admission reflected a new approach, for in previous years, Lindsay admittedly "hated" his opposition *all* the time. But the injustices he saw inflicted, especially on less successful players, inspired him to form a Players' Association in 1956. When eight-time All-Star Lindsay began asking questions about the NHL pension fund, he couldn't get any straight answers. The "dictatorship" of NHL ownership allowed the players no recourse but to organize.

A lesser player would have been buried in the minor leagues or blacklisted entirely for even broaching the subject. Lindsay took advantage of his stature and the preseason All-Star Game to discuss his plan with players from other teams. Secret meetings were held until January 1957, when the first Players' Association press conference stunned league owners. Their rage was eventually vented on all the key figures.

Despite the distraction of his off-ice activity, Lindsay enjoyed his most productive NHL season in 1956-57, tallying 30 goals and 55 assists. But the following summer, he was dealt to the cellar-dwelling Chicago Blackhawks—as close to exile as existed in the NHL then—along with the outspoken young goalie Glenn Hall. Toronto's Conn Smythe sent *his* "troublemakers" to Chicago as well, and the threat of further retaliation against the Players' Association loomed. Detroit general manager Jack Adams successfully used an aggressive divide-and-conquer strategy to cow his players and destroy

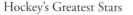

Lindsay's last-ditch effort at forming a protective players' union. Lindsay's organization effort was dead. "I'm not sore at Adams," Lindsay claimed. "I pity a man like that." But his trade to Chicago had struck Lindsay in the heart.

In the spring of 1960, Lindsay retired from hockey and returned to Detroit. He made a brief but successful one-season comeback in 1964-65, after Sid Abel had replaced Adams as Detroit's general manager. "Emotionally," said Lindsay, "I'd never left." His huge contribution to the franchise was fully acknowledged when his number 7 was officially retired, and he even served as Detroit's general manager and coach in the late 1970s. A lifelong fitness advocate, Lindsay—well into his seventies—remains a familiar figure at the Joe Louis Arena, where he continues to use the Red Wings' exercise facilities.

Ted Lindsay, above, looks for the rebound in front of the sprawling Maple Leafs goaltender Ed Chadwick. Facing page: "Terrible Ted," here dueling with Toronto defenseman Jimmy Thomson, put his natural combativeness aside in 1956 to form the first NHL Players' Association.

Frank Mahovlich

Few superstars have been as unappreciated for as long as was Frank Mahovlich, who spent nearly 11 years in a love-hate relationship with the Toronto Maple Leafs. While barely a teenager, he drew attention from several teams before the Leafs convinced him to join the St. Mike's junior team in Toronto.

Mahovlich burst onto the NHL scene in the 1957-58 season, edging out Bobby Hull in Calder Trophy voting for rookie of the year. The Leafs managed to get to the Stanley Cup finals the following two seasons, but the team's new savior couldn't quite take them to the promised land. That all looked to change when Mahovlich erupted with 38 goals in the first 35 games of the 1960-61 season. He eventually set the club record with 48 goals at season's end, but he was seen by some as a disappointment. A pattern had been set. "I don't really think I know myself completely," he said, in demonstrating his melancholic side, "or that I know when I'll fulfill my potential. Maybe it'll take three or four years, maybe never."

"No one else is so elegant, so electric, so furious, so fluid," wrote Peter Gzowski in 1961. "Other skaters stride, he swoops. They glide, he soars. They sprint, he explodes." But Toronto's coach and general manager Punch Imlach wanted his team to dominate through defense and rigid positional play. While Mahovlich scored dozens of beautiful goals in helping the Leafs win three consecutive Stanley Cups in 1962, 1963 and 1964, the autocratic Imlach encouraged Mahovlich—and the fans and media—to believe that there should have been dozens more goals.

"I actually liked the guy for about five years," said Mahovlich of his coach. "Then things weren't the same; he just wasn't the guy I once knew."

Mahovlich believed that Imlach made the team practice too hard. "It was like a horse running three days before the big race," he said, "and having nothing left." Mahovlich's long stride did make him appear to be loafing when he was actually skating quickly, but he withdrew further when Imlach tried to intimidate him to play harder.

"If Toronto fans would appreciate his great talent and give him the cheers he deserves instead of booing him," said Gordie Howe in the mid-1960s, "maybe the pressure wouldn't cook the guy."

The soft-spoken Mahovlich suffered two nervous breakdowns and was sent to hospital with a diagnosis of deep depression and tension. "I was just exhausted," he explained. "There was the pressure to perform from the fans, and here's some guy whipping you."

At the end of the 1964-65 campaign, Andy Bathgate, who was a creative winger like Mahovlich, said: "Imlach never spoke to Frank Mahovlich or me for most of the season, and when he did, it was to criticize. Frank usually got the worst. We are athletes, not machines, and Frank is the type that needs some encouragement, a pat on the shoulder every so often." That outspoken observation was Bathgate's last as a member of the Maple Leafs, but "The Big M" remained in Toronto for several more years.

Mahovlich sipped champagne from the Stanley Cup for a fourth time in 1967, before the Leafs made a blockbuster trade late in the following season that sent him to the Detroit Red Wings. The Maple Leaf Gardens switchboard was swamped with outraged callers, but for Mahovlich, "It was as if a piano had been lifted off my back." His production improved dramatically with the change of scenery, and he hit a career-high of 49 goals in 1968-69 on a line with Gordie Howe and Alex Delvecchio.

After two All-Star seasons, Mahovlich was deeply disappointed when he was traded to the Montreal Canadiens in January 1971. "The [Wings were] not doing well," he said, "and I felt that because they traded me, it was my fault." However, when the Habs sent someone to meet him at the airport—a courtesy he had never experienced before—he became optimistic that things were going to be different in Montreal.

"Hockey is fun again with this bunch," he admitted with a grin. "Even in practices, you can feel the Canadiens' love of sheer speed and what has become known as fire-wagon hockey." Mahovlich jelled immediately with his new team-

mates and found the net 14 times in the spring of 1971 to set a playoff goal-scoring record and help the Canadiens win the Stanley Cup. He followed up with his two highest regular-season point totals on the way to Montreal's Stanley Cup victory in 1973, before he was lured back to Toronto. This time, however, it was to play for the Toronto Toros of the World Hockey Association.

Mahovlich spent four years in the World Hockey Association, the last couple with the Birmingham Bulls, in Alabama, a stint that made for a rather ignominious end to a Hall of Fame career. But the rewards have come. In 1993, Canada's prime minister, Jean Chrétien, appointed Mahovlich to the Canadian Senate, an unelected position that he can hold until the age of 75.

Swift and freewheeling winger Frank Mahovlich, above, felt most at home as a member of the Montreal Canadiens, but he played much of his career for the Maple Leafs. Facing page: Mahovlich drives one of his 533 career goals past flinching Rangers goalie Ed Giacomin.

Dickie Moore

Dickie Moore was upset, wondering whether he was holding back his linemates by playing with a broken wrist. His center-man, Henri "The Pocket Rocket" Richard, looked as if he had a real shot at the 1957-58 Art Ross Trophy as scoring leader. On the other wing, the legendary Maurice "Rocket" Richard was still an offensive force and as fiery a personality as ever. When Moore offered to relinquish his spot on the line, Montreal coach Toe Blake called a meeting and asked the Richard brothers whether they wanted a change.

"We got here together," they quickly replied, "we end together." That vote of confidence, Moore believed, typified the attitude of the Montreal Canadiens in the 1950s. In the end, Moore did prevent Henri Richard from winning the scoring crown that year, but only because he took it home himself.

Three months with a specially de-signed cast helped Moore suit up for every match that season. Willing to do almost anything to play, he missed surprisingly few games over his career, despite myriad injuries. For all his formidable talent, Moore was fortunate even to have made it to the NHL. Two broken legs as a boy marked the beginning of a lifetime plagued with knee problems. Although hampered by numerous knee operations, separated shoulders and broken hands, wrists and col-larbones, not to mention more than the average number of stitches, bruises and sprains, Moore was never really stopped.

He followed up his Art Ross-winning campaign by setting a new record in defending his title the following year. His career-high 41 goals and 55 assists would not be beaten for seven seasons. Moore also made a huge contribution to six Stanley Cup victories for Montreal, including all five consecutive wins in the last half of the 1950s.

His team boasted eight future Hall of Fame members, and it took Moore some time to feel comfortable in that mi-lieu. "It was like a nightmare for me as a young player," he ad-mitted, "being around some of those great hockey players."

Moore had worked his way up through the Canadiens organization, helping both the Montreal Junior Canadiens and the Montreal Junior Royals win the Memorial Cup—Canadian junior hockey's championship—before joining the Montreal Royals of the Quebec senior league. Eager to test his skills in the big leagues but unwilling to sign for the NHL's

minimum salary, Moore didn't join the parent club until Christmas 1951. He then scored an impressive 18 goals in the 33 games remaining in his rookie season with the Habs, but injuries restricted him to only 31 NHL games—and three goals—over the next two seasons. Healthy through the 1953 playoffs, he contributed three goals to Montreal's Stanley Cup win. He then led all scorers in postseason action the following year, aided by a record-breaking 2-goal 4-assist game.

Although Moore jousted aggressively with the league's toughest players on a regular basis, part of his effectiveness came from the relatively few penalties he took. "The worst thing that [can] happen to a hockey player is that he starts to think," Moore once said. "A hockey player is not smart enough to think." Yet an obvious in-telligence added a dimension to his rugged approach to the game, and he resented the notion that he was uncontrolled. "I did anything I had to do to win and keep my job," he explained with self-awareness. "I had to play a certain style."

In 1962, Moore started an equipment-rental company, a venture that met with the disapproval of Canadiens brass, who thought it would distract him from hockey. "Who's going to look after me when I retire from the game?" he asked. When Montreal initiated conversations about trading him in 1963, Moore quit hockey to work at his business a little sooner than he had expected. "I couldn't think of playing for someone else," he claimed, although Toronto general manager Punch Imlach lured him back to the NHL for the 1964-65 season, after one year of retirement. Still only 33 years old, Moore was restricted by injuries to 38 games, and his 2 goals and 4 assists convinced him that it was time to hang up his skates again.

When league expansion in 1967 doubled the number of NHL players needed, the St. Louis Blues managed to per-suade Moore to come out of retirement one last time. Again limited by injuries, he played only 27 games but showed flashes of his former glory and helped his team to the Stanley Cup finals. While his team bowed out to the Montreal Canadiens in four straight games, Moore made his final exit with his head held high, distinguishing himself with 7 goals and 7 assists in 18 playoff games. In 1974, he was inducted into the Hockey Hall of Fame.

Despite a litany of injuries, Dickie Moore, above, battled his way through most of 12 seasons with the Montreal Canadiens, winning two scoring championships and leading all playoff scorers in both 1954 and 1959. Facing page: Moore finds the open net behind Toronto Maple Leafs goaltender Johnny Bower.

Maurice Richard

Rarely does a man gain mythic status while he is still alive, but early in his career, Maurice Richard transcended even the lofty role of folk hero. While the goals he battled for were achieved only by putting a puck in a net, "The Rocket" seemed to personify many of the aspirations and frustrations of French Canada as well. Nothing illustrated that relationship so well as the explosive night of March 18, 1955, in what became known as "The Richard Riot."

Two days earlier, Richard had been involved in a stick-swinging brawl. His explosive energy, best exemplified by his black eyes flashing with intensity as he bulled and weaved his way to the opposition's net, occasionally expressed itself in rage. Disarmed of his stick three times in a raucous melee, Richard committed the unpardonable sin of striking a linesman with his fist. NHL president Clarence Campbell responded by suspending the Montreal star for the final few games of the season as well as the playoffs.

At the time, Richard was leading the NHL scoring race and the Canadiens were vying with the Detroit Red Wings for first place, so Montreal fans felt that the rug had been pulled out from under them. Campbell was the target of numerous threats, but refusing to be intimidated, he took his regular seat at the next Montreal home game. On arrival, he was pelted with insults, eggs and debris. The Canadiens were soon losing to Detroit by a 4–1 margin, and the crowd grew angrier. Someone lit a tear-gas canister as the first period ended, and after consulting with the fire department, Campbell forfeited the match to Detroit.

The enraged fans streamed out of the Montreal Forum, joining several thousand others outside who were demonstrating against Richard's suspension. An estimated 5,000 people then went on a rampage, smashing windows and looting stores in downtown Montreal. The next day, while shopkeepers cleaned up the mess, Richard went on the radio and appealed, successfully, for calm.

Many have argued that "The Richard Riot" was the dawn of Quebec's Quiet Revolution, that it signaled an end to French-Canadian tolerance of English-Canadian subjugation. Regardless, it was a defining moment for Richard, the Montreal Canadiens and the NHL. The Canadiens lost to Detroit in seven games in the Stanley Cup final that year but

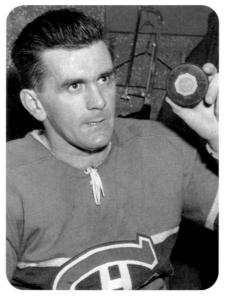

went on to win five consecutive Cups before "The Rocket" retired in 1960 and Montreal's remarkable streak ended.

Richard's record of 50 goals in 50 games, set during the 1944-45 season, stood until Mike Bossy equaled his achievement in 1981. Richard broke Nels Stewart's long-standing record of 325 regular-season goals and set a new high of 544 career goals before hanging up his skates. Yet he is best remembered for his playoff performances. Perhaps the ultimate clutch player, Richard scored six playoff overtime goals, still an NHL best. His 82 playoff tallies included 18 game-winners, four hat tricks, two four-goal games and a five-goal barrage against the Toronto Maple Leafs on March 23, 1944. In fact, he so dominated that game—a 5–1 Canadiens' victory—that he was chosen its first, second and third star.

Richard worked hard at developing new moves in practice, but he believed that there was only one thing which separated him from the rest: desire. "I had the same kind of determination from the time I was a boy of 7 or 8," he explained. "I wanted to win all the time, to score goals. That's all I had on my mind." Richard led the NHL in goals scored over five separate seasons but never won the Art Ross Trophy as scoring champion. He was runner-up five times, including that fateful 1954-55 season when teammate Bernie Geoffrion edged into the lead by one assist, while Richard sat out his suspension.

Although he claimed that he only shot to hit the net, Richard had tremendous accuracy on his forehand and backhand as well as a flair for the dramatic goal. In the seventh game of the 1952 semifinals against the Boston Bruins, he was knocked unconscious early on but returned to the ice late in the third period. Still woozy and with blood streaming down his face from a deep gash in his forehead, Richard began a rush behind his own net and maneuvered through

Above: The first NHL player to score 500 times, Maurice Richard buries one of his last goals behind Toronto's Johnny Bower. Facing page: Still showing a hint of "The Rocket's red glare" during a postgame dressing-room celebration, Richard displays one of his milestone-goal pucks.

the entire Bruins team before firing the tie-breaking goal past goalie Jim Henry.

Ever the target of Richard's enmity, Campbell paid tribute to him years ago. "Never have I met a man," he said, "with such singleness of purpose and so completely devoted to his profession."

Campbell's present-day counterpart, NHL commissioner Gary Bettman, echoed those comments in 1998 when he announced that the NHL would honor Richard by presenting a new trophy in his name. It will be awarded annually to the league's top goal scorer. "For generations of hockey players and fans, 'The Rocket' was *the* goal scorer," declared Bettman. "His determination and skill symbolized the best the game has to offer."

Pavel Bure

Exceptional detective work made Pavel Bure a Vancouver Canuck. By carefully perusing an entire season's score sheets, Vancouver's chief scout Mike Penny arrived at a surprising discovery: Bure had played 11 games over the 1987-88 season for the Central Red Army team in Moscow, although official NHL sources indicated that he'd only played five. NHL draft regulations stated that 18-year-olds could be drafted only in the first two rounds, unless they had played more than 10 games in a major league. When Vancouver chose Bure in the sixth round of the 1989 draft, 113th pick overall, an immediate controversy ensued, and the league declared him ineligible.

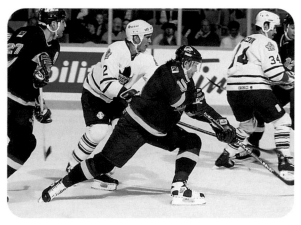

The Canucks presented their evidence, and after almost a year's consideration by NHL president John Ziegler, the initial decision was reversed. Bure was theirs.

Bure's talent was certainly no secret. He made a huge impact at the 1988 World Junior Championships with linemates Sergei Fedorov and Alexander Mogilny. Although Mogilny defected in 1989 and Fedorov a year later, Bure won the Soviet Union league's rookie-of-the-year award and postponed the lucrative future awaiting him in North America. He starred for both the Soviet junior and national teams for two more seasons before switching allegiances and signing a multiyear contract with Vancouver on October 31, 1991. Five days later, he played his first NHL game.

An immediate "impact" player, Bure grew stronger as the season progressed. "The Russian Rocket" led all rookies in scoring, with 34 goals and 26 assists, and the team went deeper into the playoffs than it had been in 10 years. Bure took the Calder Trophy as rookie of the year, but he didn't get a spot on the NHL All-Rookie Team—for a very good reason. Showing rare versatility, he played both left and right wing that season. Half of the voters chose him as the league's best right-winger; and half voted for him on the left side.

As a sophomore, Bure broke a franchise record with 60 goals. In the 1993-94 season, he led the league in goals with another 60 and added 50 assists, earning First All-Star Team honors at right wing. In the playoffs that year, Bure scored a spectacular double-overtime goal in game seven of the opening round and helped his team to the Stanley Cup finals. Although the Canucks lost the last game against the New York Rangers, Bure topped Vancouver playoff scorers, with 16 goals and 15 assists.

The NHL lockout of 1994-95 was a frustrating season for Bure, and he went down with a season-ending knee-ligament injury only 15 games into the following campaign. It really wasn't until 1997-98 that he played like his former self. He captained the Russian team at the 1998 Olympic Games, led his team in scoring and brought them a silver medal. The same year, he led the NHL in shots taken (329), and his 51 goals and 39 assists were good for third place in league scoring. Unfortunately for Vancouver, Bure dropped a bombshell when the season ended: Trade me—I will never play for the Canucks again.

"I have to admire Pavel for taking this stance, because he did make it clear for the last few years that he would like to be traded," said Canucks team captain Mark Messier, one of only a few people to side with Bure during a lengthy holdout. "He wasn't happy here, so instead of bringing that kind of energy into the locker room, he chose to sit out to force a trade."

On January 17, 1999, Vancouver general manager Brian Burke dealt Bure to the Florida Panthers. "Miami fans are in for a treat," said Wayne Gretzky. "He's an exceptional hockey player worth every penny he's paid." Bure finally explained the reason behind his trade request: disappointment in Vancouver management, especially at its failure to back him when rumors circulated that he had threatened to walk out on the team during the 1994 Stanley Cup finals. His new teammates, though, were much more interested in the future than the past.

"It's going to be nice to be embarrassed in practice instead of games," says Panthers defenseman Rhett Warrener.

"Everybody can do things at top speed," notes winger Ray Whitney. "His top speed is just faster. And the things he can do at top speed are different." Whitney had tied the Florida franchise record with 32 goals for the 1997-98 season, a mark Bure should eclipse easily.

"It's a dream come true," says Rob Niedermayer. "To get a chance to play with a guy like him—any centerman in the league would relish that."

Bure scored a beautiful goal in his first game, showing no ill effects from his long holdout, but after a thrilling couple of weeks with Florida, he strained his right knee and missed three weeks of action. The Panthers were patient, though, having signed Bure to a six-year contract. Bure was unhappy in Vancouver but still shone; it will be interesting to see what he'll do with a smile on his face. "I don't want to say I will score every game," he once said, "but I think it is possible."

Right: While his Florida Panthers teammates get into position on the power play, Pavel Bure patiently prepares to blast a shot from the point. Facing page: One of the league's fastest and most nimble players since breaking into the NHL with Vancouver in 1991-92, Bure dances toward the Toronto net.

Paul Kariya

"If I'm playing the game properly," said 50-goal-scorer Paul Kariya, "I should never get a penalty." He was about to embark upon his second consecutive Lady Byng-winning campaign in 1996. "I don't go out thinking I want to be the cleanest player in the league," he added, "but it makes sense if you're an offensive player and one of the leaders on the team. You can't be stuck in the penalty box." Kariya finished the 1996-97 season third in league scoring, accumulating only six minutes in the sin bin. Unfortunately, he soon felt forced to rethink his approach to the game.

"Obviously, I've got to protect myself a little better," he said two years later. "I don't think winning the Lady Byng is going to help me anymore. I'm not trying to be a tough guy, but if someone's going for my head, I'm going to get my elbow or my stick up to protect myself."

After sitting out two months in the autumn of 1997 due to contract negotiations with the Anaheim Mighty Ducks, Kariya had exploded for 17 goals and 14 assists in 22 games. The layoff seemed to have done him no harm. "Most others can't pass, defend or make an accurate shot at top speed," noted FOX analyst John Davidson, "but he can."

Kariya came to a crashing halt, however, on February 1, 1998. As he celebrated a goal, Chicago defenseman Gary Suter hit him with a vicious cross-check to the face, and Kariya went down in a heap. While Suter's foul earned him a four-game suspension, it cost Kariya his season, including a much-anticipated trip to Nagano with the Canadian Olympic Team.

Kariya had been looking forward to another chance at the Olympic gold medal he'd narrowly missed winning in 1994. "I still think of what could have been," he says, looking back at his failure to score in a final shootout against Sweden, leaving Canada with the silver medal. "I've gone over that penalty shot 200 times in my head, trying to change it." There was some consolation in helping Canada win the 1994 World Championship, but Kariya would have drawn the biggest crowds at the Nagano Olympics. He is of Japanese descent on his father's side, and it was hoped that he'd heal in time for the trip to Japan. Instead, Kariya spun out of control with post-concussion syndrome, which looked as if it might never end.

"There were some times—I won't lie to you—when I didn't think things were getting better, and I was thinking about other things I could do," says Kariya, explaining the months of severe headaches and dizziness and the lack of energy he endured. "But everything came back to hockey, and I am very glad that I was cleared by the doctors to do what I love."

He turned to workouts that included neck-strengthening exercises, he got a helmet with more padding and a secure chin strap, and he used a mouth guard for the first time—all to help him absorb the inevitable hits. "I have taken some good shots to the head," he said early in the 1998-99 season, "and I feel great. The biggest difficulty in getting back is just getting my legs underneath me. It's been almost seven months since I skated and played games."

The Mighty Ducks had acquired a couple of enforcers, but Kariya was also glad to see the league crack down on illegal hits. "When a guy is intentionally going after someone's head, he has got to be punished and punished severely, with longer suspensions and stiffer fines. We don't need that in the game of hockey."

"He's definitely changed after the postconcussion syndrome," claims linemate Teemu Selanne. "He's more aggressive on the ice, more outspoken with the media. I used to tease him that half my salary went for baby-sitting him." Kariya was partially responsible for getting his friend Selanne to the Ducks. A trip to the midseason All-Star Game in 1996 left Kariya with two profound impressions. "I was sitting next to Wayne Gretzky and Brett Hull," he recalls. "I pinched myself. Those are the guys I idolized growing up." But he was also struck by Selanne's skills and attitude and talked to Anaheim management, which acquired "The Finnish Flash" two weeks later. While the two are now sometimes separated to spread the offense around, they combined as linemates for 154 goals and 174 assists in their first 115 games together.

A dean's-list student at the University of Maine, Kariya is also a student of the game. Fortunately for the game of hockey, it looks as if he's figured out a way to stay healthy enough to star in the NHL for years to come.

Paul Kariya, above left, won the 1993 Hobey Baker Award as U.S. collegiate hockey's top player and was drafted by Anaheim the same year. Facing page: Team captain since 1996-97, Kariya brought an even higher intensity to the ice after injuries shortened his 1997 season to 22 games.

Zigmund Palffy

Zigmund Palffy picked the right moment to score his first NHL goal. Although he played five games in 1993-94, he was held off the score sheet. But when the next season finally got under way in January, after a protracted lockout, he scored both of the Islanders' goals in a come-from-behind victory over the Florida Panthers. Unfortunately, the Islanders maintained a winning record only until the tenth game of the season, before steadily falling out of contention for a playoff spot, a woeful status that they've maintained fairly consistently ever since. During that 1994-95 rookie campaign, Palffy added only eight more goals. The Islanders had good reason to believe that Palffy could score. In 1990-91, he'd notched 34 goals in a 50-game season to win rookie-of-the-year honors in Czechoslovakia, and he accumulated 13 points in just seven games at the 1991 World Junior Championships to help his country win a bronze medal. That was enough for the Islanders to make Palffy their second pick in the 1991 NHL entry draft.

Palffy renewed their faith with 41 goals and 33 assists the following year as Czechoslovakia's First All-Star Team right-winger, then tallied 38 goals and 41 assists to win the next season's scoring championship. Finally ready to emigrate, Palffy put in a respectable 1993-94 season with Salt Lake City in the International Hockey League, interrupted by his participation in the 1994 Olympic Games. Playing for Slovakia (after Czechoslovakia split to form two countries), he led all Olympians in scoring. It was only at the NHL level that Palffy had come up relatively empty. That, however, changed dramatically in his sophomore season with the Islanders.

Palffy wore jersey number 68 in honor of Czech star Jaromir Jagr, but 12 games into the 1995-96 season, he switched to number 16. It would be an overstatement to say that the change marked Palffy's emergence as his own man, but he went on an offensive tear.

His team-leading 43 goals and 44 assists included back-to-back hat-trick games and a seven-game goal-scoring streak. Islanders coach and general manager Mike Milbury acknowledged Palffy as a bona fide star just before the following season got under way. "He's my best player," he said, "and second place isn't close." Milbury selected Palffy to alternate with Derek King and Darius Kasparaitus as team captain for the year. "He's got a heavy responsibility now," Milbury added, "both as a player and an assistant captain."

Palffy took the announcement in stride. "I can do this thing," he said confidently. "No big deal."

Demonstrating that Milbury wasn't just spouting rhetoric, Palffy went on to beat second-place Islander Travis Green by 26 points in 1996-97, finishing eighth in NHL scoring, with 48 goals and 42 assists. Palffy earned his selection to the 1997 All-Star Game, but a mild shoulder separation prevented him from attending. Some consolation came in the end-of-season All-Star voting, when he finished in third place behind fellow European right-wingers Jagr and Teemu Selanne.

The Islanders as a team continued to flounder, but Palffy remained consistent, with a 45-goal 42-assist season in 1997-98, well ahead of any teammate. Although his team was barely better than average with a man advantage, Palffy led the league in power-play goals, with 17. He took his three-year record as the best Islander into contract negotiations that summer, but it took a half-season-long holdout before he signed a deal in January 1999.

"He's a special athlete that I would pay to watch," said Milbury, "and I have the privilege of seeing on a daily basis the things he can do. He's one of those people who happens to have a plethora of talent. Regardless of his conditioning, you can see [his talent] just jump out at you the minute he receives the puck, passes the puck or shoots the puck. We're very pleased to have him back."

Palffy scored 50 points in the remaining 47 games of the season, but the Islanders had begun an aggressive cost-cutting campaign. "It's not fun to have to shop around our best scorer and our best player," claimed Milbury, "but we're faced with unusual circumstances." In June 1999, Palffy was the key figure in a multi-player trade with the L.A. Kings. He's shown he has the tools to be one of the best. With the Kings, Palffy may finally get a chance to prove himself in the playoffs.

Above left: Zigmund Palffy, the Islanders' biggest scoring threat since 1995-96, has the full attention of Buffalo's Mike Peca (27). Facing page: Palffy shows the speed that was key to three consecutive 40-plus-goal seasons before a contract squabble cost him half of the 1998-99 season.

Teemu Selanne

Only three-quarters of the way through his 1992-93 rookie season, Teemu Selanne set a record that most pundits agree will never be touched. As a Winnipeg Jet, Selanne shattered Mike Bossy's 15-year-old rookie mark of 53 goals, becoming the first newcomer to lead the NHL in goals since Roy Conacher did so in 1938-39. Tying Buffalo's Alexander Mogilny with 76 goals, Selanne also set an NHL high for rookies, with 132 points.

But "The Finnish Flash" had almost become a Calgary Flame. The Jets had chosen Selanne in the first round of the 1988 NHL  entry draft based on his outstanding play in the Finnish junior leagues. Then only 18 years old, Selanne was determined to hone his skills on familiar ground and to fulfill a long-held dream to compete for his country. Four years later, he decided that the time had come to give the NHL a try. Since he'd failed to come to a contractual agreement with Winnipeg, Selanne had become a restricted free agent. The Calgary Flames made a lucrative long-term contract proposal in the summer of 1992, but Winnipeg invoked its right to match any offer. "I had a great time there," Selanne has said, "and what a hockey town Winnipeg is. It was unbelievable." The feeling was mutual.

While Selanne wasn't able to maintain the First All-Star Team pace of his premier season, he continued to post decent numbers. A severed Achilles tendon cut his second season off at the midpoint, but he spent the NHL lockout of 1994-95 playing back home in Finland. Although hobbled for months by tendinitis in both knees, Selanne tallied 48 points in 45 games once NHL competition began in January 1995. That proved to be his last complete season with the Jets. Stunned and angry, Selanne slowly digested the news that he'd been traded in February 1996.

"I was lucky that I left that way," he said in hindsight two years later, "because that was the Jets' last season anyway. I had a special relationship with Winnipeg fans, and it would

have been so much tougher to leave after the season ended and go through all those ceremonies." When the Jets were sold and became the Phoenix Coyotes, Selanne had already moved to sunnier climes.

The Anaheim Mighty Ducks provided Selanne with a gifted linemate in Paul Kariya, and the two complemented each other right from the start. Both speedsters, they each have a creative flair that forces defenders to focus on both wings simultaneously, a difficult if not impossible task. Selanne finished the season with a personal high of 68 assists, helping Kariya to his first 50-goal campaign while setting the franchise record with 51 goals of his own. Selanne and Kariya made the First All-Star Team in 1996-97, but Kariya missed most of the 1997-98 season due to contract negotiations and postconcussion syndrome.

"It's pretty frustrating right now," said Selanne, after taking over the team captaincy when Kariya was knocked out of the lineup by a cross-check from Chicago's Gary Suter. "We have to stick together and stay positive. It's the only way." Although he drew the undivided attention of the league's premier checkers, Selanne still managed to tie Peter Bondra for the league lead, with 52 goals, breaking his own team record. Responsible for more than 25 percent of Anaheim's goals, Selanne was also nominated for the Hart Trophy.

Yet he has remained one of the league's most down-to-earth players. In the midst of a contract which pays him far below current market rates, Selanne has rejected the notion that he should try to renegotiate terms, a common practice. "If the only problem I have is that I'm underpaid," he said in reference to his $3.4 million annual salary, "things have to be pretty good."

"Every player in the NHL and minor hockey around the world should follow this guy for a week," says ESPN analyst Darren Pang, "to see how well he handles people and demands. Besides, how can you not be enamored with one of the great pure goal scorers, who skates so quickly and effortlessly and then takes off the equipment and drives cars the same way?" Selanne owns dozens of cars that he likes to race. He once entered a competition under the pseudonym "Teddy Flash," out of fear that his hockey employer would frown on such a dangerous off-ice hobby.

Selanne added another vehicle to his collection at the 1998 All-Star Game but didn't pick up his reward for being the night's most valuable player until almost a year later. "I'm too lazy," he laughs, but anyone watching him on the ice would dispute that statement. Selanne gave much of the credit for his success that evening to Jari Kurri, who joined him on an all-Finnish line. "It's great to play with my countrymen," he says. "Jari has helped me a lot. He has been a great role model for the younger players." The same, undoubtedly, can be said for Selanne.

Teemu Selanne, right, won the inaugural Maurice "Rocket" Richard Trophy as the NHL's leading goal scorer in the 1998-99 season. Facing page: Seen pulling away from Toronto winger Igor Korolev, "The Finnish Flash" takes a modicum of penalties despite being frequently fouled.

Keith Tkachuk

"Goal scoring is nice," says Keith Tkachuk, "but everything is measured on winning. I don't need to prove I can score 50 goals. I've done that. I've got to prove I can lead this team and do the right things to get us there in the end. That's all I care about." As team captain of the Phoenix Coyotes, Tkachuk has borne criticism for his team's failure to win a playoff series and for twice holding out in contract disputes. Tagged with one of hockey's worst labels—selfish—he's redeemed himself the only way possible: doing whatever is necessary to help his team succeed. "Going to the net is not selfish," he says in

his own defense. "That's working hard and making a sacrifice for other people. A selfish player is a guy who sits out [on the fringes] and waits for a one-timer."

Tkachuk's role models are noted for their willingness to battle in the trenches. "Growing up, 'The Moose' was always one of my favorite players," he wrote about Mark Messier in a diary posted on the NHL's Website. "I liked him because of his speed, scoring and toughness, and I've tried to model my game after him. It's always a thrill to play against him. He's a winner."

At six-foot-two and 220 pounds, Tkachuk is even bigger than his first childhood hero, Cam Neely, who helped define the modern term "power forward" during an injury-plagued career with the Boston Bruins. Today, Tkachuk is generally regarded as the premier power forward in the NHL, but midway through the 1996-97 season, he was still fighting for respect.

"It's frustrating," he commented when he wasn't initially chosen to play in the All-Star Game. "Hopefully, I'll prove that I should have been named all along. I'm playing a lot feistier now. I'm really trying to get it going by bearing down harder and driving towards the net." Although Tkachuk would become a late addition to the Western Conference roster, the slight bothered him.

"He hasn't been himself since that [initial] decision,"

teammate Jeremy Roenick observed, but Tkachuk was a man on a mission. He finished the season as only the fourth player in NHL history to record at least 50 goals and 200 penalty minutes in a single season. Although he has tried to curb his time in the penalty box since then, especially by reducing retaliatory fouls, Tkachuk remains one of the game's most intimidating players. As much as his excellent scoring touch, his ability both to dish out and to absorb punishment has helped him win two end-of-year All-Star selections.

Tkachuk's 1996-97 campaign was also notable in that he became the first American-born player to lead the NHL in goals scored in a season. He's been one of the keys to the United States' rise in international hockey stature, although the 1998 Olympics were a major disappointment. An assistant captain when the United States won the inaugural World Cup tournament, Tkachuk was in the eye of a storm when his team flamed out early in Nagano. Quoted as saying that the 1998 Olympic Games were "a big waste of time," he claimed his comments were taken out of context, but he also had to deny repeatedly his involvement in an embarrassing room-trashing by unidentified American players.

Things had gone much better for a teenage Tkachuk at the 1992 Olympics. He used the experience of playing on a team that finished a respectable fourth place to springboard into the NHL for the remainder of the 1991-92 season. The Winnipeg Jets had selected Tkachuk right out of high school in the first round of the 1990 NHL entry draft, but he spent a year with Boston College—helping its team to the NCAA finals—before joining the American national team for a season that culminated with the Olympics. During 1992-93, Tkachuk really came into his own with Winnipeg, notching 28 goals and 23 assists and surpassing 200 minutes in penalties for the first time.

The Jets made 21-year-old Tkachuk team captain in the fall of 1993, and he put in two solid seasons before exercising his rights as a restricted free agent. After he agreed to terms with the Chicago Blackhawks, the Jets retained his services by matching the offer but stripped him of the "C" for 1995-96. Although upset, Tkachuk responded by joining the 50-goal club for the first time. When the team transferred to Phoenix, his captaincy was reinstated, and there's no evidence that he will relinquish his leadership role any time soon.

"I really think the most dominant player this season has been Keith Tkachuk," wrote ESPN analyst Barry Melrose midway through the 1998-99 season. "Most nights that I have watched him, he has been the best player in the world."

Keith Tkachuk, above, shows the fiery determination that has made him a team leader of the Phoenix Coyotes since their Winnipeg Jet days. Facing page: Going to the net is Tkachuk's forte, which he demonstrates here as he attempts to jam the puck past Toronto netminder Damien Rhodes while contending with a Leafs defender on his back.

The Defensemen

The defenseman's primary responsibility is to protect his goal from attack. He is allowed tremendous liberty in aggressively harassing opponents, especially in the slot—the critical area of ice in front of the net between the face-off circles—and generally, only the most blatant bludgeoning or tackling is penalized. For this reason, size and strength have traditionally been major factors in determining which players are assigned to the blue line. To achieve the status of the players in this position's upper echelon, though, it's important to contribute offensively as well.

Bobby Orr literally revolutionized defense, but finesse has always had its place, and the rushing defenseman harks back to the game's earliest days. King Clancy and Eddie Shore flamboyantly carried the puck up-ice in the 1920s and 1930s, and many pundits credit years of fine play by fleet-footed Red Kelly with inspiring the creation of the James Norris Memorial Trophy in 1953. Awarded annually to the NHL's defenseman showing "the greatest all-around ability," the Norris Trophy went to Kelly in its inaugural year but was then dominated by strong puck-handlers Doug Harvey and Pierre Pilote, who were both in or near the twilight of their Hall of Fame careers when Orr burst onto the NHL scene in 1966. What Orr did, however, was take a blue-liner's offensive prowess to a previously unimagined level.

Instead of following the norm and generally dishing the puck off after bringing it into the opponents' end, Orr routinely carried it right to the net, breaking the 30- and 40-goal marks by a defenseman for the first time and winning two scoring championships. But blocking shots and guarding the front of his own net after scampering back into position if his team failed to score were also intrinsic to Orr's game. "I'm glad I won the award now," said Harry Howell presciently after being presented with the 1967 Norris Trophy, "because I expect it's going to belong to Bobby Orr from now on." For the following eight consecutive years, Orr did indeed win the Norris, which has likewise gone almost unfailingly to a player cast in his image ever since. Rod Langway—a stay-at-home defensive stalwart for the Washington Capitals in the 1980s—stands as the only exception to date.

Brad Park and Denis Potvin typified the breed of rugged and offensively talented defenseman most highly sought after once Orr had shown what was possible. Having one of the team's principal scoring threats patrolling the blue line soon became an expectation rather than an anomaly. Three-time Norris winners Paul Coffey and Chris Chelios and five-time victor Ray Bourque have reinforced the standard for young blue-liners such as Scott Niedermayer and Nicklas Lidstrom. While hitting seems to be a dying art—particularly the open-ice body check—a more one-dimensional player such as Chris Pronger *can* still emerge as one of the league's better rear guards by superbly taking care of business in his own end. The position, after all, is still called defense.

Montreal defenseman Doug Harvey, above, breaks up a Toronto rush with a quick and effective poke-check. Facing page: Veteran Ray Bourque provides strong support for Boston Bruins goaltender Byron Dafoe.

Raymond Bourque

Raymond Bourque joined the Boston Bruins in 1979, grateful to be part of "old-time hockey" by playing with such veterans as Gerry Cheevers, Wayne Cashman and Jean Ratelle. In turn, Bourque has provided the same kind of experience to a new generation of Bruins, some of whom weren't even born when he was drafted. Just before his first NHL game, Bourque was handed sweater number 7, and he was naive enough not to fathom the implications of donning Phil Esposito's old number. Fortunately for Bourque, his success was immediate, and he didn't have to suffer the heckling most rookies wearing a legend's number would have faced. Bourque was awarded the Calder Trophy as rookie of the year and earned First All-Star Team status. Number 7 seemed to suit him just fine.

It wasn't really an issue for anyone until 1987, when the Bruins decided to honor Esposito by "retiring" his number, although the club said that Bourque could continue to wear what had become "his" number. Bourque had great respect for all that Esposito had done for the Bruins organization, however, so a secret plan was hatched. On "Phil Esposito Night," in front of a sellout crowd in the intimate Boston Garden, Bourque stripped off his number 7 jersey and handed it to Esposito. The retired star was shocked and visibly moved by the gesture. Underneath, Bourque wore his new number, 77, a sweater that undoubtedly will one day join the other team legends up in the rafters.

While Bourque was virtually an annual fixture at the NHL All-Star Game throughout the 1980s, he had an even greater opportunity to show off his abilities when the league instituted a skills competition as part of the festivities in 1990. He has won the accuracy-shooting contest most years, and his success in the breakaway competition led Team Canada management to select him as one of five participants in a pressure-filled shootout against Dominik Hasek and the Czech Republic at the 1998 Olympic Games. Bourque (and the rest of his teammates) failed to score.

But it was with Hasek as a teammate that Bourque had his most glorious personal moment to date. Hasek entered the net for the third period of the 1996 All-Star Game, held in Boston, on behalf of the Eastern Conference. For the first time in a generation, the goaltenders outshone most of the scorers that

night, but Teemu Selanne of the Western side finally got a puck past Hasek to tie the game 4–4. With only 37 seconds remaining, Bourque snared the puck and rifled the winning goal past Felix Potvin. The hometown crowd erupted with joy, much more for the goal scorer than for the victory. The ovation lasted for several minutes and was renewed when Bourque was named the game's most valuable player. Seeing the respected veteran bask in the limelight, the other players seemed almost as pleased as Bourque himself.

Bourque's official All-Star selection at the end of his rookie year was the first of an incredible 17 consecutive nominations. Only Gordie Howe has been named more often—and that was over a 26-season NHL career. His five Norris Trophies rank behind only Doug Harvey and Bobby Orr. Like them, Bourque has been the dominant defenseman of his era, starting with an All-Star presence on the blue line as a teenager and lasting until the present. He now takes his place as one of the league's elder statesmen. "I love playing the game," he replied when retirement was mentioned. "That's why I'm doing well. I'm still looking at it like a little kid."

Bourque broke the 1,000-assist marker late in the 1996-97 season and is challenging Paul Coffey—the only defenseman ever to tally more career points than he has—for the all-time scoring crown among blue-liners.

Unfortunately for Bourque, the Bruins club has not always surrounded him with a sufficiently strong complement of players. He's been to the Stanley Cup finals twice and both times led all defensemen in playoff scoring. But after the Bruins finally defeated the Montreal Canadiens, their nemesis of the 1970s, they fell easily to the Edmonton Oilers of the 1980s on each occasion. "A Stanley Cup," said Bourque, "would be unbelievable," but he seems fated to join a small number of illustrious players who will never see their names engraved on the Cup. Bourque remains undaunted: "Every day, you've got to prove yourself, and that's how I've played this game my whole career."

Boston's all-time leading scorer, Ray Bourque, above and facing page, is a master at the point, taking a great number of chances and shots from the blue line. When Bourque scored 10 goals in the 1998-99 season, he hit double digits for the twentieth consecutive time in his NHL career.

Chris Chelios

After emigrating from Greece to the United States in 1951, Gus Chelios developed a passion for hockey and his hometown Chicago Blackhawks, which he passed on to his children. "It's that pit-bull upbringing," his son Chris once joked. "They grow 'em tough in those small European countries, and I've got this temper that gets me into trouble now and then." But Chris Chelios has also managed to channel some of that ferocity into stardom in the NHL.

Chosen fortieth overall by the Montreal Canadiens in the 1981 NHL entry draft, Chelios then spent two seasons at the University of Wisconsin and a year with the American national team. After Chelios played at the 1984 Olympic Games, Montreal was ready for him. He played the remainder of the 1983-84 campaign and six more seasons with the Habs, highlighted by a Stanley Cup championship in 1986. "Those were great years," he recalled. "I listened and learned a lot. Playing for the Canadiens is like getting a Harvard law degree. Montreal players know what it's like to win." Chelios developed under the watchful gaze of Hall of Fame blue-liners Larry Robinson and Jacques Laperriere and was awarded the Norris Trophy as the NHL's finest defenseman for his 1988-89 season, an honor that he received again in 1993 and 1996.

Chelios grew as a player, but his penalty minutes also increased. "I was a real pain in my first 8 to 10 years in the league," he has confessed. "I liked going out there and being the guy people hate to play against. I thought I was more effective being mean and getting at their top players." Yet all too often, Chelios took a bad penalty. After the Canadiens made a quick exit in the 1990 playoffs, Chelios was traded to the Blackhawks for the flashy little centerman Denis Savard.

Savard had been a crowd favorite in the Windy City, and the trade for Chelios was an unpopular move with the Blackhawk fans. "When you've got a player of his size and speed," John Davidson remarked about Chelios in 1991, "he's going to hurt you when he hits you. People hate a player when he hurts others." But those feelings inevitably change when the hitter is on your side, and Chelios quickly endeared himself to the Chicago fans. He played a nasty game, accumulating career-high penalty time in his first three seasons as a Blackhawk, with 192, 245 and 282 minutes, respectively.

"I'm going to have to find a line between being mean and taking penalties," Chelios remarked after serving a suspension in 1994, and he has been somewhat successful. "I'm trying to control myself more now," he said recently. "I don't want to be known as the type of player who is constantly in trouble. I want to show I can play aggressively and be mean but not jeopardize the team's success." That team success with Chicago was fleeting at best, although Chelios's play remained stellar. He was uneasy about being chosen team captain after the 1994-95 season, but his teammates were convinced that he was the right man for the job.

"The greatest thing I've learned from Chris is, you can't take a night off, can't take a shift off," said defenseman Eric Weinrich. "You just have to play 100 percent every night, which is what he does—and usually in twice as many minutes as most people."

Another Chicago defenseman, Keith Carney, echoed those sentiments: "There is no better player to watch and to practice with and to learn from than Chris. He's our leader."

Even Denis Savard, who eventually made it back to the Blackhawks via Tampa Bay, said: "You can't replace a guy like Chris. He adds too much to the team, not only in talent but in leadership."

Although Chelios made headlines during the 1994 NHL lockout with his death threat against NHL commissioner Gary Bettman (he quickly apologized), he prefers to stay out of the spotlight. "He's always been like that," said Frank Kiszka, the hockey moderator at Mount Carmel High School, where Chelios played for two years. "He was hardworking and down-to-earth in high school, and he's still like that today. He's still very much 'South Side.' "

Chelios was criticized for not testing the free-agent waters in 1997, but his willingness to sign a contract extension that committed him to Chicago until age 38—for less than a market-value salary—struck many as a breath of fresh air. "Money doesn't motivate me," claimed Chelios, although his extension was to pay him $11.5 million. "I play hockey because I love it, and I was fortunate enough to go back home and have my whole family together again. I don't think there are too many guys in the NHL who get in that situation. To me, it's a great honor to play in the NHL and especially for the Blackhawks."

But trade rumors persisted throughout the 1998-99 season. Chelios tried to squelch the speculation, but when he asked the Blackhawks for an extra year's contract extension and his request was denied, he waived his no-trade agreement and joined the Detroit Red Wings in time for their 1999 Stanley Cup run. Unfortunately, Detroit did not make it past the second round of the playoffs, but playing for a contender again could extend Chelios's career even more.

Chris Chelios, right, won two of his three Norris Trophies in Chicago and seemed determined to retire as a Blackhawk until he agreed to a trade-deadline swap with the Red Wings late in the 1998-99 season. Facing page: A late addition but a key player on the U.S. roster, Chelios helped his country win the inaugural World Cup in 1996.

King Clancy

At first, Frank Clancy's nickname "King" was an inside joke. His father, an Ottawa sports celebrity with a reputation for toughness, had earned the royal designation "King of the Heelers" back in the 1890s for his ability to "heel" the ball out of a football scrum. Although Frank was only an 18-year-old 127-pound sprite when he first approached the Ottawa Senators in 1921, the junior "King" earned a spot on the defending Stanley Cup champion Ottawa roster because of his spirit and fleetness. Signed as a substitution player, Clancy

saw little ice time for a couple of years except in practice.

"They wanted me on their team, and the only opening was on defense," said Clancy. "I had to take it or leave it, and I took it." He didn't get his first real chance until the 1923 Stanley Cup finals against the Edmonton Eskimos, champions of the Western Canada Hockey League. In the final game of a two-game total-goals playoff, injuries knocked out two defensemen, and Clancy substituted admirably. Then he spelled Hall of Fame center Frank Nighbor and both wingers

in turn. In those days, no substitution was allowed for a penalized goalie, so when Ottawa goaltender Clint Benedict took a penalty, Clancy went between the pipes. He didn't allow a goal and even raced up the ice with Benedict's big goalie stick for a shot on net. Ottawa won the Cup, and Clancy was hailed as the team's hero.

Defenseman Eddie Gerard retired, and Clancy became a regular in the 1923-24 season. In 1927, he helped Ottawa win another Stanley Cup, and in the 1929-30 season, he led all NHL defensemen in scoring, with a career-high 17 goals and 23 assists, before being traded to the Toronto Maple Leafs for the then ex- orbitant sum of $35,000 and two players. Toronto's owner Conn Smythe was looking for someone to fill the building he planned to construct for the start of the 1931-32 season, and Clancy didn't disappoint him. He led the Leafs to their first Stanley Cup victory in the spring of 1932 in the new Maple Leaf Gardens before capacity crowds.

Clancy was as determined and effective as any defenseman in the league, earning All-Star Team honors in his first four sea- sons with Toronto, but he combined his hockey prowess with clownlike theatrics. He once pro- voked Boston's notorious Eddie Shore into drop- ping his gloves, then shook Shore's hand enthusi- astically while grinning and said: "Good evening, Eddie. How are you tonight?" Everyone, including Shore, was left laughing. Although Clancy en- gaged in plenty of fights over the years and dished out his hits indiscriminately, he didn't make many lasting enemies.

The Leafs decided to honor Clancy on St.

Toronto owner Conn Smythe bought King Clancy, above and facing page, from the Ottawa Senators in 1930 to help fill the new rink he was planning to build—Maple Leaf Gardens. A rough-and-tumble defenseman with a delight- ful sense of humor, Clancy played for 16 NHL seasons.

Patrick's Day, 1934. A number of floats were paraded onto the ice, pulled by stars of both the hometown Maple Leafs and the visiting New York Rangers, and the ceremony culmi- nated in the presentation of the guest of honor dressed as Old King Cole. When the lights were momentarily extinguished, Clancy doffed a big white beard, regal robes and a crown to reveal himself garbed in a brilliant emerald-green uniform. Clancy was presented with gifts while a band played *When Irish Eyes Are Smiling*. He remained decked out in green when the game began, but the celebration was clearly over for the Rangers. They gave Clancy such a rough time that he donned the Leafs' blue-and-white uniform for the second and third periods.

After playing only six games for Toronto in the 1936-37 season, Clancy hung up his skates—briefly. He coached the Montreal Maroons for half a season be- fore receiving an unexpected call from NHL president Frank Calder. "I suppose Mr. Calder figured out I knew a lot about the rule book," Clancy said in announcing that he was becoming an NHL referee, "after having spent so much time sitting and thinking in the penalty box."

Clancy retained his sense of humor despite now representing the voice of au- thority. "If that comes down," he once said to Babe Pratt, who'd just thrown his glove into the air in disgust at Clancy's penalty call, "you've got a game misconduct." But he was tolerant. "If at all possible, I avoided giving miscon- duct penalties," he said. "If a youngster blew his top, I quietly told him to keep cool or he would hurt his team. If an older player became abusive, I found that it helped to give him a second chance. So I would look tough and say, 'Just repeat what you said.' Usually, [the player] took the warning and skated away. Calling me names never hurt me. I never wanted to be a showboater, and I didn't mind them having a little fun."

Clancy coached the Leafs in the mid-1950s and again in 1972, but he served the Leafs best as an unofficial goodwill ambassador until his death in 1986. In a fitting tribute, the NHL established the King Clancy Memorial Trophy in 1988, which is awarded annually to the player who best exemplifies leadership both on and off the ice while making a significant humanitarian contribution to his community.

Dit Clapper

Dit Clapper unintentionally coined his own nickname as a child. Called "Vic" by his parents, the toddler could only say "Dit," and soon, that's how he was known to everyone. Playing all his games for the Boston Bruins, Clapper became hockey's first 20-year man, setting the NHL longevity record. Coincidentally, Clapper's last season was Gordie Howe's first.

After Howe had established himself in the league, he summoned the courage to admit to one ambition—to play for 20 years, "just like Clapper." While he eventually lasted even longer than Boston's wonder, Howe was unable to challenge Clapper's other distinction in the history books. A right-winger for his first 11 years in the league, Clapper hit even greater heights on the blue line. He remains the only NHL player to be awarded All-Star status both as a forward and as a defenseman.

Clapper joined Boston in 1927 at the age of 19. In his first two campaigns, he scored only 4 and 9 goals, respectively, but the Bruins won the Stanley Cup in 1929. The following season was different: Clapper erupted with 41 goals and 20 assists in what was only a 44-game season, good for third in the NHL scoring race. His performance was well deserving of an All-Star berth, but the NHL didn't begin honoring its elite in that manner until the 1930-31 season. Although his production slowed somewhat, Clapper was the NHL's Second All-Star Team's right-winger for the next two seasons.

Named team captain during the 1932-33 season, Clapper had already cultivated a reputation for high achievement while keeping his emotions in check. At six-foot-two and 200 pounds, he had a size advantage over most NHL players and the strength to match. No pacifist, Clapper nonetheless didn't play the Boston-style roughhouse as defined by bruising defensemen Lionel Hitchman and Eddie Shore. He was even known to break up fights on occasion, although once he reached his boiling point, he was capable of inflicting heavy damage with his fists. One such punch almost got him into severe trouble.

Avenging a butt-end administered to a Boston rookie in the 1936 playoffs, Clapper was punching the offending Montreal Maroons player when the referee yanked him back by the hair. That was the referee's first mistake, for Clapper took great pride in his meticulously combed jet-black hair

with the razor-sharp part. The young official then further enraged Clapper by denigrating his mother. Stunned by the comment, Clapper asked the referee to repeat himself. When he did, Clapper decked him.

The referee was Clarence Campbell, who 10 years later would become president of the NHL. Knowing Clapper's character and recognizing the role he himself had played, Campbell made a public apology and explained the circumstances to league president Frank Calder. Instead of receiving a lengthy suspension, Clapper was fined $100.

After 11 seasons at right wing, Clapper moved back to defense. At the end of the season, Clapper joined Shore as 1938-39's First All-Star Team defensemen. The two rear guards were an important part of Boston's Stanley Cup victory that spring. Clapper made the First All-Star Team the next two years as well.

Boston's 1940-41 team emerged as one of the strongest in NHL history. Clapper was runner-up in Hart Trophy voting to teammate Bill Cowley, and the Bruins swept Detroit in the Stanley Cup finals. Clapper won a Second All-Star Team spot in 1943-44. Before the 1945-46 campaign got under way, Boston's general manager Art Ross gave him another big job. In addition to retaining him as captain, Ross relinquished his coaching responsibilities and appointed Clapper player/coach.

Clapper filled the role for a little more than two years before hanging up his skates and moving into coaching full-time. After almost three seasons behind the bench, though, Clapper had had enough. "Being a coach is a lousy job," he said in a surprise resignation speech on April 1, 1949. "I couldn't abuse these players. They're my friends." The president of the Boston Garden said that Clapper's announcement "hit me like a wet towel." Goaltender Frank Brimsek grew even more determined to be traded when he heard of the popular coach's retirement. Under Clapper's direction, the team had never finished lower than third place. The season after Clapper left, Boston finished out of the playoffs.

Clapper had been inducted into the Hockey Hall of Fame the day after he retired from active play, and his number 5 jersey was raised to the rafters of the Boston Garden almost as quickly.

Dit Clapper, above, made a successful transition in 1938-39 when he immediately established himself as one of the league's best defensemen and made the First All-Star Team. Facing page: Clapper (left), with fellow "Dynamite Trio" linemates "Cooney" Weiland and "Dutch" Gainor, spent 11 of his 20 seasons with Boston at right wing.

Paul Coffey

Paul Coffey's name is peppered throughout the record book for defensemen, and he accomplished this with a style rarely seen on a hockey rink. When Coffey emerged as an offensive star in the early 1980s, whirling and swirling up and down the ice at full speed, he drew inevitable comparisons to the just-retired Bobby Orr. But he has borne that burden of heavy expectation successfully, flattered rather than pressured by such talk. His 48 goals in the 1985-86 season topped Orr's record of 46, set in 1974-75, and Coffey passed Denis Potvin in 1991-92 to become the leading career scorer among defensemen, a position he still holds.

Frank Mahovlich made a huge impression on Coffey's father, and as a boy, Paul was coaxed to emulate "The Big M" and make every stride as long and strong as possible. "I would never have become a hockey player," he once admitted, "but for my father." Coffey's fluid and graceful style has led many to remark that he can glide faster than most players can skate. He crams his feet into boots several sizes too small and has his blades sharpened without the rocker curve that most players find necessary in order to pivot easily. And, like a speed skater, he uses as long a blade as possible to increase his glide. As a child, he was a fan of center Dave Keon—another Toronto Maple Leaf renowned for his skating ability—but he moved back to defense from center as Orr redefined the position in the NHL.

Coffey made occasional forays toward the opposition net, but playing for Glen Sather on the Edmonton Oilers added a further dimension to his game. Sather noted his rookie's speed and coaxed Coffey to jump up into the play more often. "I'd never done that before," said Coffey, "even in junior." The results were dramatic. As the fourth man in the rush, Coffey was a key to the Oilers' offense—not only did he skate fast, he was also capable of making a sterling setup or finishing a play with his accurate shot.

After a decent rookie year, with 9 goals and 23 assists, Coffey almost tripled his offensive production with an 89-point sophomore season in 1981-82 and made either the First or Second All-Star Team for the next five seasons. His point totals continued to climb as he helped Edmonton win the franchise's first two Stanley Cups, in 1983-84 and 1984-85. His stellar play, which included 12 goals and 25 assists in the

1985 playoffs, led many to believe that he should have won the Conn Smythe Trophy that year, but Wayne Gretzky, who had amassed 10 more points, won the award. Coffey peaked offensively with a record-breaking 48-goal 90-assist campaign in 1985-86 and won his second consecutive Norris Trophy as the NHL's dominant defenseman, but the Oilers were eliminated in the second round of the playoffs. The team rebounded to win the Cup again the next year, but in the midst of the celebrations, Coffey dropped a bombshell: His days as an Edmonton Oiler were over.

Coffey felt denigrated by Edmonton owner Peter Pocklington when he sought to renegotiate his contract, as Gretzky and Messier had already done, and was adamant that he wouldn't play for "Peter Puck" again. "A lot of things were said that hurt me personally," he revealed. He was traded to the Pittsburgh Penguins in the summer of 1987. Coffey missed the fleet of top-notch scorers he'd played with in Edmonton, but Mario Lemieux, who liked to play high in the defensive zone, was the perfect receiver for the long-bomb passes for which Coffey was famous. In 1991, Lemieux got the Stanley Cup ring he coveted, and Coffey earned his fourth, but once again, the All-Star defenseman had found himself in the shadow of a bigger celebrity. While the Penguins were en route to their second consecutive Cup, Coffey was traded to the Los Angeles Kings.

"Hockey's a funny game," Coffey has observed. "You have to prove yourself every shift, every game." Despite all that he has done, Coffey hasn't always received his due.

In his 1988 autobiography, *Robinson for the Defence*, Larry Robinson went on record with his high regard for Coffey: "Coffey has the uncanny ability to make a defensive play in his own end and start the puck back the other way before the other team can react." Robinson decried the lack of respect the transition player receives in hockey (such a player is "revered" in basketball) and opined that Coffey is "probably the best player in hockey today when it comes to the transition game."

Coffey has frequently been accused of being a defensive liability, but despite his detractors, he won his third Norris Trophy in 1995 as a Red Wing. "When we've got the puck," Coffey has wryly noted, "they can't score." When the

Colorado Avalanche successfully targeted him in the 1996 Stanley Cup finals, however, ruthlessly pounding him every time he touched the puck, he was out of Detroit. Unhappy with his trade to the Hartford Whalers, Coffey was dealt to Philadelphia midway through the 1996-97 campaign, but in 1998-99, he was sent to the Chicago Blackhawks, then to the Carolina Hurricanes. Despite the trades and even though the points are coming farther apart, Coffey still manages to retain his positive attitude: "It's not up to anybody else. You have to take pride in yourself."

Facing page: Paul Coffey joined Edmonton in 1980-81 and went on to break Bobby Orr's single-season goal-scoring record for a defenseman while winning three Stanley Cup rings with the Oilers in seven years. One of the best skaters ever to play in the NHL, Coffey, right, won his third Norris Trophy while playing for the Detroit Red Wings in the 1994-95 season.

Doug Harvey

Few kings have fallen further from grace than Doug Harvey, who died in 1989 at the age of 65 in a Montreal hospital after living for several impoverished years on the fringes of society. At his peak, Harvey had ruled the NHL blue line for more than a dozen years, winning the Norris Trophy as the league's best defenseman seven out of eight seasons between 1955 and 1962. One could argue that his death from cirrhosis was the predictable result of his dedication to fun and the bottle. Although he had quit drinking three years before his death, the damage to his liver was irreversible.

Harvey was one of the smartest players ever to lace on skates, but he wasn't always appreciated. His deliberate and efficient manner initially struck many as lackadaisical, especially in Montreal, where the "fire wagon" brand of hockey dominated. He broke into the NHL with the Canadiens in 1947, but it took several successful seasons before he received the respect he deserved.

Instead of racing up and down the ice, Harvey moved methodically, breaking up opposition rushes with an economical poke-check or coolly intercepting a pass when it looked as if he were out of position. He defied convention. He'd keep the puck on his stick while almost motionless, then just before the opposition stripped him of it, he'd flick a beautiful pass. Nor was Harvey averse to carrying the puck in front of his own net.

Such hockey heresy gave management fits until they realized that his apparently reckless and lazy maneuvers were actually planned and typically executed almost perfectly. His "slowness" inevitably lured a forechecker in deep and soon right out of the play. In the meantime, his teammates were gathering a head of steam in anticipation of his pass.

When Harvey did make a mistake, he generally made amends immediately. While he preferred to pass the puck rather than shoot it, his occasional forays deep into the enemy end were usually made to atone single-handedly for causing a goal to be scored against his team.

Although he was on a team of superstars in Montreal, Harvey had the ability to dictate play. Often referred to as the team's "quarterback," Harvey could slow a game's pace by corralling the puck and shepherding his team up the ice, or he could ignite the action by snapping long lead passes to a fleet of sharpshooters. The combination was so deadly on the power play, with Montreal exploding for two or three goals in a two-minute span, that the league was forced to change the rules in 1956 and allow a penalized player back on the ice as soon as his team was scored upon.

Harvey was such an integral part of Montreal's dynasty in the 1950s that in 1957, when he teamed up with Detroit's Ted Lindsay in a failed attempt to form a Players' Association, the Canadiens refused to "exile" their star defenseman to the lowly Chicago Blackhawks, as some clubs had done to other association supporters. Harvey was a leader both on the ice and in the locker room, where his sense of humor and lighthearted approach made him the life of every party. While this endeared him to his teammates, Montreal management eventually decided that he was more trouble than he was worth and traded him in 1961.

In 1961-62, Harvey joined the New York Rangers as player/coach, and even with his additional responsibilities, he won his seventh Norris Trophy and got the sad-sack Rangers into the playoffs. Missing being "one of the boys," however, Harvey relinquished his coaching duties the following season, preferring to have a beer with his teammates after a game rather than socialize with team management.

Harvey continued to play, but while his mental skills were still sharp, his age and lifestyle were starting to catch up with him. Early in the 1963-64 season with the Rangers, he was demoted to the minors, where he bounced around for five years with a number of teams. The Detroit Red Wings tried him out for a couple of games in 1966, but it was the NHL expansion in 1967 that allowed him to return to the NHL fold. He joined the St. Louis Blues for the 1967-68 playoffs, chipping in four assists, and he played for them the following season, at the age of 44. He then scouted professionally for a while, but before long, he had worked himself out of hockey altogether, gathering notice for a few days only when news of his fatal illness and subsequent death was broadcast.

Doug Harvey, facing page, was both an offensive catalyst and a defensive stalwart for the Montreal Canadiens. Here, he muscles himself into position against the Toronto Maple Leafs. Above: Harvey finished his playing career with the St. Louis Blues in 1968-69.

Tim Horton

Tim Horton's name lives on through the chain of coffee and doughnut shops he founded, but regrettably, few patrons remember the outstanding hockey player who launched the business. Horton was recognized as an NHL All-Star six times and was runner-up in Norris Trophy voting twice, the second time when he was 39 years old. But his tragic death at the age of 44 means that there is no longer the face of a hockey player to go with the universally recognized name.

Generally acknowledged as the strongest man in the game when he was playing, Horton skated through most of 24 NHL seasons. "There were defensemen you had to fear because they were vicious and would slam you into the boards from behind," declared Bobby Hull, perhaps the only player in the league who possessed more muscles than Horton. "But you respected Horton because he didn't need that type of intimidation. He used his tremendous strength and talent to keep you in check."

Horton was a punishing hitter, but his lack of malice was

legendary. "If he'd only get angry," King Clancy once lamented, "no one would top him in this league." But Horton believed that he had taken too many penalties early in his career because of his "hot temper."

Although Horton mellowed over time, the lack of a mean streak never affected his intensity. He just approached the game in his own way. Rather than punching back at an opponent who dropped the gloves with him, he'd envelop his foe in a crushing bear hug. Derek Sanderson once bit Horton during a fight. Years later, Horton's widow Lori asked him how he could have done such a thing. "Well," Sanderson replied, "I felt one rib go, and I felt another rib go, so I just had to get out of there!"

Horton possessed a devastating slap shot and was one of the NHL's best rushing defensemen for almost two decades. He accumulated 518 points over his lengthy career, a huge total in his day. Even though he used a methodical approach and reportedly measured a couple of inches less than his official five-foot-ten, Horton was a menacing sight as he crossed the opposition blue line with his almost fully erect skating style and the momentum of a freight train.

In 1955, defenseman Bill Gadsby, who played 20 NHL seasons, caught Horton on a rare occasion when his head was down with "the hardest check in my life." Horton suffered a broken leg and jaw, the worst of a litany of injuries suffered over the years. Horton's daughters begged him to let his crew-cut grow longer in the 1970s, not so much to keep up with the day's fashion but to hide the numerous scars which made his head resemble that of Frankenstein's monster. Yet injuries and age

Tim Horton was well into his forties when his old friend Punch Imlach talked him into playing for the Buffalo Sabres. Above: Horton moves the puck while being pursued by Montreal's Mahovlich. Facing page: Horton gets ready to make a hurried pass under pressure from Earl Ingarfield of the Oakland Seals.

seemed to be little more than minor inconveniences to Horton.

"What I get paid for is the practices," Horton often said. "I'd play the games for nothing." His "retirement" was an almost routine event at contract-renewal time, but when the Leafs fired Punch Imlach, who liked to prolong and resurrect older players' careers, the 39-year-old Horton declared, "If this team doesn't want Imlach, I guess it doesn't want me."

Toronto owner Harold Ballard bit the bait and asked Horton later in the summer of 1969 whether he'd consider playing again for more money. "If somebody said they'd double my salary," Horton joked, "I might consider it." But Ballard took him up on his jest, and Horton went from $45,000 to $90,000 a season. The Leafs' show of faith in their veteran, however, didn't stop them from dealing Horton to the New York Rangers late in the 1969-70 season in exchange for wingers Guy Trottier and Denis Dupere and goaltender Jacques Plante, who was one year Horton's senior.

Horton retired after his second year with the Rangers, but his old teammate Red Kelly convinced him to play a year for him in Pittsburgh. Although Horton's business partner wanted him to focus on the doughnut business, which had grown from a single store to a national franchise, Imlach had something else in mind. He talked Horton into joining his new club, the Buffalo Sabres, in the summer of 1972. "Maybe it's just a bad habit I've acquired," Horton joked. "I like to play hockey. I have a long time ahead of me to sit behind a desk."

In negotiating what proved to be Horton's final contract, Imlach, to his lasting regret, gave in to Horton's request for the car of his choice as part of his compensation. A lifelong automobile enthusiast, Horton chose a Ford Pantera—a sports car capable of dangerously high speeds. The car did what no one had managed to do—it stopped Tim Horton from playing hockey. He was killed instantly in a single-vehicle accident in 1974 while returning home to Buffalo from a game where, fittingly, he had been named third star in Maple Leaf Gardens.

Although Horton was only in his second season in Buffalo when he died, he had already made such an impression that the team officially retired the number 2 jersey he had worn for the Sabres. At his funeral, his pallbearers were all friends from his years with the Toronto Maple Leafs.

Red Kelly

Red Kelly is the last defenseman to win the Lady Byng Trophy. In the early 1950s, he made the award almost a personal possession by winning it three out of four years and coming second in the other. "Kelly is as good a player as I've seen in my long connection with hockey, which dates back to 1906," said Montreal manager Frank Selke Sr. in 1952. "More than that, he exemplifies everything that is desirable in a young man, and the Detroit club is fortunate to have a man of his integrity and character in its lineup."

Kelly didn't lack toughness—he won a welterweight boxing championship during his junior days at St. Mike's in Toronto. Looking back at his hockey career, Kelly recalled: "I had some good fights with some tough players. But I also knew that fighting hurts the hands and takes you off the ice."

Always fleet of foot and creative with the puck, Kelly apprenticed under the rugged "Black Jack" Stewart for three seasons, honing his defensive skills. He was a league All-Star for eight consecutive seasons and the first winner of the Norris Trophy in 1953-54. Yet the red-haired defender remained an offensive threat; he led NHL defensemen in goals eight times. His role in Detroit's four Stanley Cup wins is often forgotten, but Kelly was a critical component of a powerhouse club. He played up to 55 minutes a game, leading many to believe that he would quickly burn out, but he was indefatigable and lasted 20 years in the NHL.

Early in 1960, Kelly was prodded into revealing that the Red Wings had coaxed him into playing on a broken ankle during the previous season. General manager Jack Adams immediately traded him to the New York Rangers. Kelly refused to report, announcing his retirement, and despite threats from Adams and NHL president Clarence Campbell, he began a life outside the game, an eventuality that he had been preparing for every summer. He went to work for his off-season employer, but an exploratory call from King Clancy and the Toronto Maple Leafs 10 days later proved fruitful, and a new deal was swung.

"I think you could be the last piece of the puzzle," said Toronto's coach and general manager Punch Imlach, believing that Kelly could help break Montreal's stranglehold on the Stanley Cup. Imlach knew that Kelly could play center.

"One year, Sid Abel got hurt in the playoffs," said Kelly, "and they moved me to center between Howe and Lindsay. I believe I also lost a First All-Star selection one year because of helping out on the forward line. The voters didn't know where to put me." Kelly did the job Imlach had envisioned, but the unexpected bonus was the effect he had on Frank Mahovlich. With Kelly as his centerman in 1960-61, Mahovlich finally realized his potential, netting 48 goals. Kelly had his first 20-goal season and 50 helpers, with a paltry 12 minutes in penalties, to earn his fourth and final Lady Byng Trophy.

While Kelly helped the Leafs win the Stanley Cup four out of the next six years, he also served as a Member of Parliament for his Toronto riding, commuting to Ottawa for four seasons. "The House generally closed in time for me to get to games," he recalled, "although I had a few close scrapes, arriving at the arena just before the opening whistle." He was elected twice but finally gave up his second job to focus on the game. "I thought that the greatest stick-handlers were in hockey," he said, after retiring from elected office, "but I found out they were in Parliament."

Although he helped the Leafs win the Stanley Cup in his last season, the 40-year-old Kelly said, "I didn't have the extra overshift I used to have." He retired from active play as the recordholder for the most playoff games, at 164, and took a coaching position with the Los Angeles Kings in 1967-68 for their inaugural season. The Kings were expected to be the weakest expansion team, but Kelly guided them to second place in their division. After two years with the Kings, he joined the Pittsburgh Penguins for several seasons before returning to Toronto to coach.

Kelly guided the Leafs for four complete seasons, longer than any other coach managed to do during the tumultuous years when owner Harold Ballard ruled the roost. Kelly is fondly remembered in Toronto for his introduction of "Pyramid Power," a positive-thinking campaign meant to nullify Kate Smith's singing of *God Bless America*, the Philadelphia Flyers' good-luck charm. Kelly had pyramids under the bench and in the dressing room and provided smaller ones for his players to sleep with. The novelty eventually wore off—Toronto lost to the Flyers in the quarter-finals for three successive years—and Kelly retired from the game after the 1976-77 season. He successfully entered the business world and ran an aircraft-maintenance company, while reserving time to watch several of his children compete as speed skaters in the Olympic Games.

Red Kelly, right, was an eight-time All-Star defenseman with the Detroit Red Wings and the inaugural Norris Trophy winner in 1953-54. Facing page: Kelly, who joined the Toronto Maple Leafs during the 1959-60 season and was made a centerman, is tripped up by a sprawling Jacques Plante. Kelly matched the four Stanley Cup triumphs he'd celebrated in Detroit with four more in Toronto.

Bobby Orr

Doug Orr was one of the speediest hockey players ever seen in Parry Sound, Ontario, and he had a young son with tremendous potential. He thought that his boy Bobby should play forward, as he himself had done in his youth. After all, Bobby was fast on his skates, could stickhandle like the devil and had a hard shot and a deft scoring touch.

Fortunately for hockey, Bucko McDonald—a standout NHL defenseman in the 1930s and 1940s—was head coach of all the Parry Sound boys' teams when Bobby Orr was 11 and 12 years old. McDonald felt that Bobby should play defense, maintaining that he was a natural at the position. "Bucko taught me almost everything I know," Orr later declared graciously.

"It wasn't hard," McDonald confessed, "because even at that age, you could see that Bobby was special." The little defenseman soon came to the attention of the Boston Bruins, who did everything they could to ensure that Orr became, and remained, their exclusive property.

In deference to Orr's youth, Boston made exceptional arrangements to allow him to play for the Oshawa Generals of Ontario's junior league in 1962. The 14-year-old Orr continued to live at home, 150 miles from Oshawa, and was driven to every game. He didn't practice with the team once, yet at season's end, he was selected to the Second All-Star Team in a league that included 20-year-old men.

Orr boarded in Oshawa the following season and dominated junior hockey for three more years, while weary Boston fans tried to be patient. When Orr finally made his Boston debut in 1966, the club slipped from fifth to sixth place for its eighth consecutive season out of the playoffs, but the hockey prodigy lived up to his advance billing—and more.

Orr's 13 goals and 41 points in his first NHL campaign may seem humble when compared with the

standards he later set, but only Chicago's Pierre Pilote tallied more as a defenseman that season. Orr won the Calder Trophy as the NHL's outstanding rookie and a Second All-Star Team selection. (He made the First All-Star Team in every other season in which he played more than 20 games.)

While most teams had included at least one rushing defenseman since Eddie Shore's day, Orr took the concept to another level. His radical approach to the game invited argument, including the one McDonald had won years earlier. "We played him at center for six of seven games in his rookie year," said Boston coach Harry Sinden (now president and general manager). "He was only tremendous. On defense, he was phenomenal."

Bobby Orr, above, is launched by St. Louis Blues defenseman Noel Picard after scoring the 1970 Stanley Cup-winning overtime goal. In 1969-70, Orr became the first NHL defenseman to score 30 goals in a season, adding a league-record 87 assists to win the scoring championship. Facing page: Not even fleet Toronto center Dave Keon could catch Orr when he wound up for a dazzling end-to-end rush.

Veteran Toronto sportswriter Jim Proudfoot called him "a Doug Harvey with additional speed and power." Orr went on to set offensive records that would have thrilled history's greatest forwards, twice winning the Art Ross Trophy as the NHL's leading scorer and finishing as runner-up to teammate Phil Esposito three times. In 1970-71, Orr set the high mark for assists and total points by a defenseman, with 37 goals and 102 assists, a record that still stands. In fact, to date, only centers Wayne Gretzky and Mario Lemieux have counted more assists in a season.

His speed was so great that Orr could lead or join an offensive foray and still get back to his position when play wheeled the other way. He was a tough and stalwart defenseman and won the Norris Trophy for eight consecutive years as the league's best blue-liner. He blocked shots and cleared the front of his net, and while he was never a mean player, Orr dropped his gloves when the situation called for it and won most of his fights. But his lasting legacy is the way he spearheaded the attack. "One of his great gifts," noted the analytical Eddie Shore, "is the ability to gauge precisely the speed of the man he is passing to."

Orr's 1970 goal to win Boston's first Stanley Cup in 29 years is remembered best—his hands raised in celebration even as he is being catapulted through the air by St. Louis defenseman Noel Picard—but his game was frequently dramatic. Derek Sanderson, who fed him the puck that day, commented: "We had the one player who could finish a play like that."

"Winning the Cup twice was great," Orr told *The Hockey News* in 1981, "but I wonder why we didn't win it more often." Due in part to his betrayal at the hands of his now disgraced agent Alan Eagleson, Orr forsook Boston to sign a free-agent contract with the Chicago Blackhawks. But his greatest disappointment was his forced early retirement. Plagued by knee injuries throughout his career (he even sat out all of 1977-78 to recover), Orr was finished at the age of 30. Twenty years have passed since he last laced up his skates for an NHL game, but time has only sharpened the memories of his greatness. He actually played fewer than 10 seasons, but he left an indelible mark on the game. "Losing Bobby," said Gordie Howe, "was the biggest blow the NHL has ever suffered."

Brad Park

When he negotiated his son's first NHL contract, Brad Park's father got a verbal agreement from New York Rangers general manager Emile Francis that Brad would be paired with defenseman Harry Howell, a 16-year NHL veteran. "I knew that I could learn a lot by watching Harry," said Park, "but he really went out of his way to work with me. I learned so many little things just in the four weeks I spent in my first Rangers training camp. Most of them were mental aspects of the game—how to foresee or deal with different situations."

Howell, traded after Park's rookie campaign, likewise has good memories of his young protégé. "I didn't have to teach him much," smiled Howell, who only recently learned of the "tutoring" arrangement. Park played in his first NHL game in the fall of 1968, and by his second season, he was a league All-Star, a status he upheld for 7 of the next 10 years.

Park played a rugged, hard-hitting game and became the team's "policeman." He fought a lot—not the best strategy when you're the team's most talented defenseman—yet his point totals continued to rise along with his penalty minutes. The Rangers made it to the Stanley Cup finals in 1972 for the first time in 22 years before losing to the Boston Bruins in a six-game battle. "Bobby Orr was the difference," said Park, who finished runner-up to Orr in Norris Trophy voting that season for the third time in a row.

After Park led his team in assists (57) and points (82) in 1973-74, he lost out to Orr again. "For a while, I guess I was trying to compete with him," admitted Park that year. The self-assured, sometimes cocky Park allowed that he might be slightly better defensively than his rival but that Orr's speed allowed him to make mistakes and still get back into position. "But let's face it," Park added, "there's only one Bobby Orr. From now on, I'm just going to be Brad Park."

Park was named team captain for the 1974-75 season, but the Rangers lost in the preliminary round of the playoffs. Early the following year, Rangers management deemed a shake-up necessary, and with the Bruins struggling in Boston with Orr on the injured list, the scenario was set for one of the biggest trades in hockey history: Park, Jean Ratelle and Joe Zanussi were sent to archrival Boston in return for Phil Esposito and Carol Vadnais. On record as hating both the Boston Bruins and their fans, Park couldn't have been less

pleased. For a time, he even had an FBI escort while entering and leaving the Boston Garden. There was a silver lining, though: He would be playing with Bobby Orr.

Once Orr returned to the lineup, Boston coach Don Cherry decided that his two blue-line stars would spell each other so that one would be on the ice at all times, but they would also work the power play together. The combination was overwhelming. Park described their efficiency in converting the manpower advantage into goals as "about 50 percent"; unfortunately, the combination lasted for only 10 games before Orr's knees gave out again. By the 1976-77 season, Orr was a Chicago Blackhawk, and change was in the works for Park as well.

"Don Cherry asked me to sit back and concentrate on the defensive side of the game," said Park, "unless I was on the power play or we were behind late in the game. Many wondered if I had lost a step." Cherry later speculated that his instructions cost Park a Norris Trophy—he came second behind Denis Potvin twice—but noted that he probably helped prolong a Hall of Fame career at the same time. Although Park underwent nine operations on his left knee, he didn't miss a season or the Stanley Cup playoffs for 17 years. He went to the finals twice with the Bruins, but a championship was just not in the cards.

A free agent in 1983, Park joined the Red Wings and finished his playing career in Detroit, where he finally got his name on some NHL hardware: He was awarded the Bill Masterton Trophy in 1984 in recognition of his perseverance and dedication to hockey. His subsequent coaching career in Detroit was short. "I took over a last-place team," said Park, "and I kept them there." He was fired after 45 games.

"I'm still a huge fan of this game," said Park recently, despite helping to launch a legal suit against NHL owners for salary collusion in the 1970s. Always a student of the sport, Park is now working on a program to develop the skills of minor-league players.

A six-time runner-up for the Norris Trophy, Brad Park, above, anchored the Boston blue line for most of eight seasons. Facing page: Park protects New York Rangers goaltender Gilles Villemure and moves for the bouncing puck before Toronto's Dave Keon can snag it.

TOP 15 DEFENSEMEN

Pierre Pilote

"My first pair of skates was my mother's," said Pierre Pilote, "and I didn't play organized hockey until I was 17." From such humble beginnings arose one of the NHL's premier defensemen. Pilote won the Norris Trophy three years in a row and sandwiched those victories with three second-place finishes. A successful rushing defenseman in the NHL's "Original Six" era, Pilote was honored as an NHL All-Star for eight consecutive years, five in a row on the First Team. That Pilote's name is not as celebrated as some who accomplished less may owe as much to the nasty side of his game as it does to his team's relative lack of success. For back then, if you weren't a Chicago Blackhawks' fan, you probably *hated* Pilote.

"When penalties came, I always made sure I got my money's worth," confessed Pilote. "The guy paid for it, whether it was from boarding or charging, and I saw that as a sign that I was in the game." A definite part of his strategy was intimidation, a technique he first honed as a teenager. After moving to Fort Erie, Ontario, from Kenogami, Quebec, he started to play industrial-league hockey. "You'd call it a butcher league now," claimed Pilote. He once joked that the first English words he learned were "Do you want to fight?" but he hit with his hips and shoulders as well as his fists. With an eagerness to learn and a willingness to do what he had to, Pilote made an impression on a number of Junior B teams and entered the Blackhawks system.

After graduating to Junior A hockey and playing two years for the St. Catharines Tee Pees, Pilote moved up to the Buffalo Bisons of the American Hockey League. Still an extremely raw talent, he apprenticed for over three years under player/coach Frank Eddolls, a former defenseman for the Montreal Canadiens and New York Rangers. "Frank taught me that the game was simple and uncomplicated, if you played it right," said Pilote. "The short pass rather than the long rink-wide kind was the key to movement, the key to the attack." Everything came together for him during the 1955-56 season. Pilote got his first call-up to the Blackhawks, and by the next year, he was there to stay.

Although only five-foot-nine and 180 pounds, Pilote played with determination and an obvious mean streak. He pulled no punches when clearing the front of his net and

engaged in numerous fights. Yet he had a light touch in moving the puck, either by passing or by skating it up-ice, and he steadily refined every facet of his emerging skills.

By the 1959-60 season, he was the NHL's leading scorer among defensemen, with 7 goals and 38 assists, and was named to the Second All-Star Team. His own club was also improving. The following season, Pilote led the league with 165 penalty minutes and made a major contribution to Chicago's greatest success in the past 60 years—and counting. In the spring of 1961, he tied Gordie Howe for the most playoff points, with 3 goals and 12 helpers, including assists on three game-winners in the finals, and the Blackhawks defeated the Detroit Red Wings for their first Stanley Cup victory in 23 years. Pilote looked back on that season as his career high-light, for another championship was not to be.

Named captain for the 1961-62 campaign, Pilote brought his team back to the Stanley Cup finals that season before losing to the Toronto Maple Leafs. Despite Pilote's lofty personal accomplishments, either the Leafs or the Canadiens—who defeated the Blackhawks in the seven-game 1965 finals—won the Cup over the course of the rest of his career.

A pioneer in the use of visualization, Pilote spent hours analyzing his own play and that of his teammates and opponents and imagining possible situations on the ice. "Tommy Ivan [Chicago's general manager] once told me I could see things other players couldn't," said Pilote, but his quick reactions and uncanny anticipation came both from his mental practice and from continuous hard work. He also set high personal goals for himself. Pilote won his first Norris Trophy in 1962-63, and the next season, he recorded 46 assists, tying an NHL best. In 1964-65, he broke Babe Pratt's record of 57 points by a defenseman, set in the 1943-44 season, with

14 goals and 45 assists. Pilote's new mark was topped by Bobby Orr four years later.

Pilote was still team captain when Chicago traded him to the Toronto Maple Leafs in the summer of 1968. His subsequent season's total of 46 penalty minutes with Toronto was a career low, a sign that some of the edge was gone from his game. When Leafs coach and general manager Punch Imlach, the older players' best friend, was fired at the end of the 1968-69 season, Pilote decided that it was time to retire.

"I don't think I did too badly," he once acknowledged. "I wish I had done better, but I guess that's what drives you."

Pilote's pursuit of excellence was rewarded by the game one last time. He was elected to the Hockey Hall of Fame in 1975.

Facing page: A late bloomer due to the lack of opportunity as a youth, Pierre Pilote went on to win three consecutive Norris Trophies and to captain the Chicago Blackhawks from 1961 until 1968. Above: Pilote keeps Toronto's Frank Mahovlich away from the puck while Chicago goaltender Glenn Hall deals with a rebound.

Denis Potvin

A precocious child, bigger and stronger than others his age, Denis Potvin had a temperament that would make him one of the most intimidating defensemen in NHL history. "I didn't want to become known as a bully," he recalled, "yet I had a fanatical obsession with being the best." His brother Jean, five years his senior, was an excellent hockey player and provided a worthy role model, but before long, the hockey world had set a higher mark for the younger Potvin. At the age of 13, he joined his brother's junior team, the Ottawa 67s, and made an immediate impression on all who saw him. "Potvin Touted as Next Bobby Orr" was the headline of the day and the next decade.

Potvin first experienced the pleasures of hitting in football and discovered that he could have that feeling on the ice too. "I found a similar thrill going into the corners, feeling the crunch of body against body, stick against stick," he said. "In a purely impersonal sense, I enjoyed hurting people with my body, as long as they weren't seriously injured." That, he believed, was the difference between him and his brother Jean, who had a more-than-respectable 11-season NHL career of his own. "Jean never had a mean streak when he was on the ice," Potvin noted, "and I think that aspect of his play hurt him; he was never a hitter."

Leo Boivin, one of the most devastating body checkers in NHL history, coached Potvin for his last year of junior eligibility and helped him fine-tune his hip-checking technique—a dying art. But Potvin was frustrated. He felt that he should already be in the NHL, but NHL rules then strictly prohibited players under the age of 20. Nevertheless, with 123 points in 1972-73, Potvin beat Bobby Orr's record and set a new mark for junior defensemen that lasted for 16 seasons. "Orr does things I don't do, and I do things he doesn't do," he said confidently. "You can't compare us."

The New York Islanders, having finished their inaugural NHL season deeply mired in the NHL basement, had an eye on Potvin as a potential cornerstone for their young franchise. But so did a number of World Hockey Association clubs. Upping the ante somewhat, the Islanders traded for Jean Potvin and surprised no one when they selected Denis Potvin as their first pick in the 1973 entry draft. They soon signed him to a contract.

"Now that I'm here," said Potvin in his rookie NHL season, "I ask myself, What am I going to do next? Well, I want to be the best. I set my goals high. It keeps you working; it keeps you alive." He won rookie-of-the-year honors, and although he was regarded as distant by some, Potvin was becoming a team leader, a position that was formalized when he was named team captain in the fall of 1979.

"We know we can beat the Rangers," Potvin said when entering the 1975 playoffs against the Islanders' crosstown rivals. "We're younger, stronger, better. For some reason, though, we have too much respect for them. We treat them like gods." His team then proceeded to sweep the Rangers out of the playoffs. Potvin's first selection as First All-Star Team defenseman coincided with Orr's last.

While he alienated many people with his arrogance, Potvin later admitted that the confidence he displayed was a "security blanket," masking a deep-seated fear of failure. He hit the 30-goal mark late in his third season—a magic number for a defenseman that only Orr had reached—and he almost collapsed with relief. "I skated to the bench," recalled Potvin, "fell to the wooden plank and bawled as quietly as I could before 14,865 friends." He won the Norris Trophy for the first of three times, ending Orr's eight-year monopoly. Due to injury, Orr played only 10 games that season.

When the two played together in the 1976 Canada Cup tournament that fall, Potvin led the international meet in points and in the plus/minus category, but Orr received the award as most valuable player. "Is Bobby Orr only going to have to play to be known as the best defenseman?" he fumed in a candid diary he kept for a Canadian magazine. His outspokenness did not earn him many new fans, but he gradually received more of the respect he craved.

"Potvin could hurt you in so many ways," said Islanders coach Al Arbour, "with a defensive play or a pass or a goal from the point. He also had a mean streak, so he could hurt with his stick or just physically, with his body." While Potvin won two more Norris Trophies during the 1970s, he felt hobbled by Arbour, who had been a "defensive defenseman" for 16 NHL seasons. Potvin's offensive numbers did decline, but his all-round game was a key to the Islanders' four consecutive Stanley Cup wins in the 1980s.

When he noticed he'd lost some of his competitive drive, Potvin decided to retire in 1988. After 15 seasons in the game, he held the records for the most goals, assists and points by an NHL defenseman. In 1991, Potvin entered the Hockey Hall of Fame, and on February 5, 1992, his number 5 sweater was officially retired, making him the first New York Islander to be so honored.

Denis Potvin, right, captained the New York Islanders for eight seasons and was a seven-time All-Star. Facing page: The Islanders acquired Jean Potvin (left) from the Philadelphia Flyers just prior to drafting Denis Potvin (right) in 1973, and both brothers were on the blue line in 1980 when the team won its first of four consecutive Stanley Cups.

Larry Robinson

Larry Robinson's selection at the 1971 NHL entry draft was not a big story at the time. Montreal made Guy Lafleur its first prize, although general manager Sam Pollock had a pocketful of extra picks as usual, typically hornswoggled from NHL expansion teams. Robinson was the Habs' fourth choice. But "Big Bird" Robinson, gangly and tough, and "The Flower" Lafleur, smooth and graceful, would soon represent the careful balance of yet another Montreal team dynasty. Before that day came, however, each would have to serve an apprenticeship.

Lafleur joined "Les Canadiens" immediately and struggled in the limelight for a time, but Robinson was sent to the Nova Scotia Voyageurs for seasoning. Montreal was as interested in Robinson's size as in his puck-handling skills, even though he had posted 52 points in each of his last two years in Ontario's junior league. Arriving at his first professional training camp at 193 pounds, Robinson, who was six-foot-four, was told that he had work to do. With effort, he played most of his career between 215 and 220 pounds. Although Robinson remained wiry, his added heft and more aggressive approach were key developments over two seasons with the Voyageurs.

Robinson was called up to Montreal midway through the 1972-73 campaign. Although the Canadiens tried to break him in gently, the rookie defenseman was able to sip champagne from the Stanley Cup for the first time that spring.

Concentrating on the defensive side of his game, Robinson cleared the front of his net with authority. He accumulated his highest penalty totals in his first two complete NHL seasons, partly through the mistakes that any young defenseman makes but also through establishing a presence. It took several more years before he really settled in to the kind of game he enjoyed most: hard-hitting but clean. After Robinson took apart the Philadelphia Flyers' notorious pugilist Dave "The Hammer" Schultz in the 1976 Stanley Cup finals, his reputation was forged, and he rarely had to brandish his fists again.

The Canadiens won the Cup that year, the first of four consecutive championships, and Robinson significantly contributed to the team's success. Joining Serge Savard and Guy Lapointe, he was part of Montreal's trio of All-Star defense-

men known as "The Big Three." He emerged as an offensive threat as well as being one of "the trees in front of the net" that Boston coach Don Cherry cited as key to Montreal's domination of the Bruins in the Stanley Cup playoffs. While his main asset was his passing, Robinson often surprised opposing teams by using his size and long reach to carry the puck right to the goalmouth.

He won the first of two Norris Trophies as the NHL's premier defender and the first of five consecutive All-Star Team selections with a career-high 19 goals and 66 assists over the 1976-77 season. He followed that up with a particularly fine effort in the spring of 1978. Robinson notched 4 goals and 17 assists, tying regular-season scoring-champion Guy Lafleur for most playoff points, and won the Conn Smythe Trophy. In 1986, he won his sixth Stanley Cup ring with another All-Star season under his belt. Then, after 17 years in Montreal, it was time for a change.

"That's why we all wear numbers," Robinson humbly noted after being traded to the Los Angeles Kings in 1989, "so that when we're gone, they [can] put another player in the jersey." He concluded his Hall of Fame career after three seasons with the Kings, with 20 consecutive playoff appearances on the record books.

Robinson took off one season before being lured back into the NHL in 1993-94 as an assistant to former teammate Jacques Lemaire, coach of the New Jersey Devils. In only his second season with the Devils, Robinson had his name inscribed on the Stanley Cup again, when New Jersey swept the Detroit Red Wings in the 1995 finals. He was rewarded with a head coaching job with the Los Angeles Kings the next year, a post he held for four seasons before agreeing to rejoin the Devils as an assistant in 1999-2000.

"I try to stay as positive as I can," he said during his tumultuous final season in Los Angeles, "but I'm my own worst enemy, my biggest critic. I was like that when I played. That's what helped me become a great player."

Larry Robinson, facing page, holds the Montreal Canadiens' career playoff records for most games played (203) and most assists (109). Robinson finished off his on-ice career with the Los Angeles Kings, above, a team that he later coached for four seasons.

Serge Savard

Broadcaster Danny Gallivan, who loved a colorful phrase, dubbed one of hockey's most deceptive maneuvers the "Savardian Spinnerama." While other legendary defensemen, such as Doug Harvey and Bobby Orr, occasionally used the move, Serge Savard made it his own with regular success. "Savard would skate up the right-wing boards out of our zone," recalled teammate Larry Robinson, "usually right at an oncoming winger. Just as both reached the vicinity of the blue line, Serge would spin around 360 degrees and skate away from the checker. He'd perfected the move in both directions, clockwise and counterclockwise. Teams that sent in one or two forecheckers were reluctant to get too close to Serge, because he'd burn them."

It took years of practice before Savard made such an audacious gambit in game situations, but his poise on the blue line was evident early in his career. After a two-game call-up in 1966-67, he joined the Canadiens on a full-time basis the following season. He contributed two playoff goals, despite seeing only irregular postseason duty in Montreal's Stanley Cup victory. Then, in his second NHL season, he was awarded the Conn Smythe Trophy when the Canadiens successfully defended the Stanley Cup. Appropriate to his subsequent Hall of Fame career, Savard received the award as most valuable player not for some uncharacteristic heroics but for his solid two-way play. That was to be the individual hallmark for an astonishingly undecorated standout defenseman.

For the first time in 22 seasons, the Canadiens did not qualify to vie for the Stanley Cup the following year. Unfortunately, Savard missed the playoff action in 1971 as well. A broken leg cost him his place on the Stanley Cup-winning team of 1970-71 (Montreal won without him). He broke his leg again the following year, and it looked as if he might be too brittle for NHL action. But he came back, played the last 23 games of the season and playoffs and missed very little action for the rest of the decade.

Savard had resumed his dependable play so impressively that he was chosen as a member of Team Canada in the famous Summit Series in September 1972. He didn't play in the entire eight-game showdown between Canada's NHL professionals and the Soviet Union's national team, but he never dressed for a losing game either—the only Canadian player

with that distinction. Fearful of losing the series at the very end, the Canadian coaches had Savard on defense for the final minute of the eighth game, so Savard has the added distinction of being on the ice when Paul Henderson broke a tie with only 32 seconds remaining.

Montreal won the Stanley Cup the following spring, with rookie defenseman Larry Robinson in the lineup. Savard, Robinson and Guy Lapointe, who had joined the Canadiens in 1970, became known as "The Big Three" and were as powerful a blue-line triumvirate as hockey has ever seen. The Canadiens won four consecutive Cups, but wresting the crown from Philadelphia's "Broad Street Bullies" in 1976 was particularly sweet for Savard. "This is not only a victory for the Canadiens," claimed Savard, "it is a victory for hockey. I hope this era of intimidation and violence that is hurting our national sport is coming to an end. Young people have seen that a team can play electrifying, fascinating hockey while still behaving like gentlemen."

Savard received his only All-Star nomination for his 1978-79 season, the year he was also awarded the Bill Masterton Trophy—for perseverance, sportsmanship and dedication. The NHL wasn't alone in finally acknowledging Savard's distinguished career. Montreal made him team captain, an honor he held for two seasons until announcing his retirement. His old teammate John Ferguson had other ideas for him, though. Then general manager of the Winnipeg Jets, Ferguson picked up Savard for a $2,500 waiver fee and convinced him to play two more seasons for him. For the first time in franchise history, the Jets made the playoffs both years before Savard retired for good.

Long known as "The Senator" by his teammates, because of the three-piece suits he often wore for business meetings, Savard made an easy transition when he became Montreal's managing director in 1983. He held that post for 12 years and his name was engraved on the Stanley Cup two more times.

A member of seven of Montreal's Stanley Cup-winning teams, Serge Savard, above and facing page, won the Conn Smythe Trophy for his solid play in the Canadiens' 1968 triumph. Savard was a rock-steady defender, but he also carried the puck with confidence and style.

Eddie Shore

They called him the "Edmonton Express" and "Mr. Hockey"—until that title was usurped by a more modern legend named Gordie Howe—but "Old Blood and Guts" remains this defenseman's most apt epithet. Over the course of his career, Eddie Shore took 978 stitches in more than 80 lacerations to his body. His nose was broken 14 times and his jaw 5, and he lost every tooth in his head through bloody contact with his opponents' sticks, elbows and knuckles. His back was fractured, his hip broken and his collarbone cracked. His eyes were frequently blackened, and he suffered cuts to the eyeballs. And every wound dramatically embellished Shore's reputation as the toughest player in hockey.

Several wild seasons as a minor-league professional earned Shore an invitation to the Boston Bruins' training camp in 1926. Veteran tough-guy Billy Coutu took an immediate dislike to the newcomer and, in a bull-like rush down the ice, slammed into the significantly smaller Shore at full speed. Coutu hit the ice semiconscious, while Shore remained standing, his left ear split from top to bottom and blood gushing onto his face.

When the Bruins' doctor warned Shore that his ear would have to be amputated, Shore sought a second opinion and found someone willing to stitch up the wound instead. As vain as he was gutsy, Shore held a mirror to watch the stitching. "I was just a farm boy who didn't want his looks messed up," he later explained. "I made him change the last stitch; he'd have left a scar." Shore kept his ear, and Boston had a player to be reckoned with.

He played his first NHL game on November 16, 1926, and according to newspaper accounts, he "caught the fancy of the fans." Shore scored his first goal in his third game—he finished the season with 12, second among NHL defensemen—and his penalty totals of 130 minutes were second in the league. He followed up his rookie campaign with a total of 165 penalty minutes (an NHL record that lasted for seven years) and 11 goals, tops for defensemen that 1927-28 season.

Shore had become a dynamic skater, with a low crouch and a long, flowing stride. He was as hard-hitting as ever, but his stickhandling made him a constant offensive threat as well. At the end of the 1930-31 season, Shore was named to the NHL's First All-Star Team, as he was six times after that.

For the 1933-34 season, however, he was selected only to the Second All-Star Team, probably the result of his 16-game suspension for hitting Ace Bailey from behind at full speed on December 12, 1933. Shore himself suffered a head injury when Toronto's Red Horner dropped him with an uppercut even as Bailey writhed on the ice—Shore wore a helmet for the rest of his playing life. But the incident brought Bailey's hockey career to an end and also left an indelible black mark on Shore's Hall of Fame career.

Scrambling to avoid a Bailey lawsuit against Shore and the Boston Bruins, the NHL staged the Ace Bailey Benefit All-Star Game on February 14, 1934. Bailey shook hands with Shore at center ice in a magnanimous gesture that did much to restore the game's image. Although Shore was unrepentant, his penalty-minute totals did drop significantly thereafter.

Shore won four Hart Trophies in the 1930s as the league's most valuable player, a greater number than any defenseman ever—even Bobby Orr won only three. But after leading his team to a Stanley Cup victory in the spring of 1939, he made the bold decision to buy and manage the Springfield Indians of the International Hockey League. Shore and Boston's general manager, Art Ross, were at loggerheads over the purchase, until Shore's NHL contract was traded to the New York Americans. Shore agreed to play all their games and as many games for Springfield as he could.

Shore helped pull the Americans into the playoffs, while packing his own rink whenever he played for Springfield, but that 1939-40 season was his last in the NHL. He played one more season for Springfield before moving into management full-time, where he quickly became notorious for his miserly penny-pinching (thinking he was being shortchanged in a one-for-one player trade with Hershey, he insisted that a new net be part of the deal) and for his bizarre training methods. He "cured" goaltender Don Simmons of falling to the ice by tying his arms to the crossbar; he also introduced tap dancing in the dressing room and ballet steps on the ice to "improve balance, the foundation of an athlete's ability."

Shore kept several extra players on hand—an ever-changing group that became known as Shore's Black Aces—so that he could bench or suspend anyone at will. Those not playing sold popcorn or did odd jobs around the rink. Former player Kent Douglas claimed that "studying with Shore was like getting your doctorate in hockey science," yet for each flattering comment "Old Blood and Guts" received, there were several stories highlighting his eccentricities and meanness. When he died in 1985, Shore made sports headlines one last time, with colorful obituaries.

Eddie Shore, right, won the Hart Trophy as the league's most valuable player four times. Facing page: All-Star Shore stands at center ice in Maple Leaf Gardens as fallen Leaf Ace Bailey presents him with a commemorative windbreaker at Bailey's benefit game in 1934. NHL president Frank Calder is at left, while Toronto Maple Leafs owner/manager Conn Smythe is to the right.

Bryan Berard

"Bryan Berard is probably going to make me look silly," said New York Islanders general manager Mike Milbury, "because he has such a bright future." In dealing for Felix Potvin, a much-needed number-one goalie, the Islanders sent Berard to the Toronto Maple Leafs in January 1999. One of the league's most promising defensemen, Berard had been developing too slowly for Milbury, a former defenseman who had played 11 seasons with the Boston Bruins. In fact, Milbury frequently grew irate over Berard's defensive lapses. "There were certain flaws that we tried to address and correct," he said. "Some we

had success with, and others we didn't. He did come a long way defensively, maybe at the expense of his offense. Maybe they'll find the right blend in Toronto."

The Leafs' unhurried management style may now provide Berard with all the patience that Milbury and the Islanders lacked. "They tried to run a defensive system, where I didn't fit in," Berard explained when comparing the two teams. "Toronto runs more of an offensive system, and I'm looking forward to it. I think I'll fit in better."

"He is not nearly as bad defensively as his supposed reputation," observed Leafs coach Pat Quinn after Berard's first game in Toronto. "He has quick feet. He seems to handle the one-on-ones. One thing I like is that he shows an ability to jump up and recognize the time to go. Now whether he knows the time to shut it down or not is another question, but he jumped up and recognized an opportunity early in the game and got a breakaway."

One glance at the Islanders' worst plus/minus record in 1997-98 shows that Berard did indeed commit a number of mistakes, but he also came third in team scoring. And although he scored only 4 goals for the Islanders in the 1998-99 season, three of them were game-winners. "He's got an immense amount of talent," said Quinn, also a former defenseman, "especially in his stickhandling and skating. He's a young man, and I'm sure he's got a lot to learn about play-

ing defense, but you just don't find those skills every day."

Berard grew up in Rhode Island, where he earned a scholarship to the distinguished Mount St. Charles Academy. After helping his high school team win three state hockey championships, he tested his skills in the more competitive Ontario Hockey League. Berard joined Detroit's Junior Red Wings in the otherwise Canadian league and contributed to the team's 1994-95 OHL championship win. His 75 points in 58 games resulted in his being named Canadian Major Junior Rookie of the Year and earned him a place on the First All-Star Team. That spring, the Ottawa Senators selected Berard as the number-one pick of the 1995 NHL entry draft. The draft introduced the first hiccup to Berard's career.

The 1995 draftees were the first to be affected by the NHL's rookie-salary cap. Berard's agent tried to negotiate an incentive-laden contract that would effectively earn his client more money, but he failed to come to terms with the Senators. As discussions broke down, Berard followed through on a threat. "It wasn't that I didn't want to stay in Ottawa," he recalled. "At that time, the organization was in a little bit of trouble, and we couldn't work anything out by camp time. So we decided to go back and play another year of junior and see what happened. People think it had to do with not wanting to go to a Canadian team, but I played junior in the OHL. It just wasn't the best thing for my career at that time, that's all."

Berard had another all-star season in the OHL, tallying 31 goals and 58 assists. Midway through that campaign, however, Ottawa dealt his rights to the New York Islanders as part of a three-way trade with Toronto. Berard signed his first NHL contract that summer and played every game of the 1996-97 season for the Islanders. He won the Calder Trophy as the league's best rookie, and his 8 goals and 40 assists also placed him among the top-10-scoring NHL defensemen.

When things didn't go as well in his second season, Berard seemed unconcerned, which aggravated Milbury further. "I do have a cocky side," admitted Berard. "To be the player I want to be—the best player on the ice at all times—you have to have a cocky attitude. But off the ice, the guys know that I'll do whatever it takes to help the team." That's the player the Maple Leafs were counting on when they made the trade. Time will tell whether they have him.

Speedy Bryan Berard, facing page, joined the Toronto Maple Leafs midway through the 1998-99 campaign. Above left: Buffalo goalie Dominik Hasek sends New York Islander Berard flying with a sprawling check as both race for a loose puck at the blue line.

Nicklas Lidstrom

Detroit Red Wing Nicklas Lidstrom is one of the NHL's best defensemen, yet he seriously entertains thoughts of forsaking his North American hockey career. Married and the father of two preschool boys, Lidstrom talks about returning to Sweden to give his children a more rooted upbringing and to continue to educate them in their native tongue. "My family comes first," said Lidstrom. "I've always said that."

Lidstrom is entering his prime years and would be missed. "I'd be shocked," said his defense partner Larry Murphy when asked about the possibility of Lidstrom's leaving the NHL, "espe-

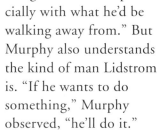

cially with what he'd be walking away from." But Murphy also understands the kind of man Lidstrom is. "If he wants to do something," Murphy observed, "he'll do it."

By the fall of 1998, Lidstrom had spent almost a year wrestling with the decision. "I have to make up my mind," he stated firmly. "I know I can live with either decision."

Lidstrom himself has experienced the challenge of learning a new language. "You aren't used to yelling in English on the ice," he recalled, describing his NHL rookie year, "so at first, you are just reacting. You are thinking in Swedish and slowly translating into English. I had to simplify my game. I had to play safe, minimize mistakes and get rid of the puck a lot quicker."

Not that anyone noticed. Lidstrom finished second in 1992 rookie-of-the-year voting behind Pavel Bure, displaying a maturity rarely seen in first-year defensemen. That season, the Red Wings had played him alongside veteran Brad McCrimmon, and this model has been used successfully throughout Lidstrom's years in Detroit. Paul Coffey was his partner for most of the next three years, and late in the 1996-97 campaign, Wings coach Scotty Bowman hit upon an almost magical combination when he paired Lidstrom with Murphy, a former Maple Leaf thought to be at the end of the line by Toronto management. Lidstrom and Murphy were key to the unraveling of Eric Lindros in the 1997 Stanley

Cup finals, and Lidstrom led all defensemen in playoff points in 1998, when Detroit repeated as Cup champions.

Lidstrom's scoring prowess was no real surprise, since he led the NHL's defensemen through the regular season as well. Yet for all Lidstrom's success, individual recognition has been slow in coming. He placed second in Norris Trophy voting for top defenseman in 1997-98, behind Rob Blake of the Los Angeles Kings, but he did garner his first All-Star Team honors.

"It's nice to see a steady player like that get recognized for his game," said two-time Norris Trophy winner Brian Leetch. "Here's a guy that does everything right—makes the pass, makes the shot, plays the one-on-one. In every team meeting, ever since he came into the league, we'd say, 'Stay close to him, watch him coming in late, you have to finish on him.' He's [Detroit's] strength."

Lidstrom has never finished an NHL season with a negative number in the plus/minus category. Those figures, though, count only even-strength goals. He's made his biggest offensive contributions on the power play, which accounts for 130 of his 240 points over four consecutive seasons, ending with 1998-99. His greatest gift is his consistency in posting both solid offensive numbers and a minimum of penalty minutes. He gets the job done without being overtly physical. "I always try to be in the right position," he explained, "because I'm not going to go out and put the big hit on someone. That's just not my game."

"He makes the right move just about all the time," said Bowman. "He plays in control, and his stick is almost always in the right position." The praise is welcomed, but not all the attention that Lidstrom has started to garner has been helpful.

"All of a sudden, people started talking about him," said Detroit's associate coach Dave Lewis midway through the 1998-99 season. "They're paying much more attention to him than [to] any of our other players. I think they try to chase him down more, put more pressure on him, be more physical with him."

While making the necessary adjustments to this increased targeting on the ice, Lidstrom announced that he would wait until the summer after the 1998-99 season ended before deciding whether to re-sign with the Red Wings or not.

"When I first came over, I thought I might stay two or three years," he said with typical humility. "I just wanted to see if I could play at this level." He's certainly accomplished that, and Detroit fans who hope to see the Red Wings reclaim the Stanley Cup want to see Lidstrom in the lineup for many years to come.

Detroit Red Wing Nicklas Lidstrom, above, has quietly established himself as one of the NHL's premier defensemen. He was a Norris Trophy finalist in 1998 and 1999. Facing page: Lidstrom calmly moves the puck out of his own end with an eye on the traffic ahead, while goaltender Chris Osgood watches attentively.

Scott Niedermayer

As a teenager, Scott Niedermayer had one of the brightest futures in hockey. Only 17 when the New Jersey Devils picked him third overall in the 1991 NHL entry draft, Niedermayer had already been a junior All-Star as well as the Canadian Major Junior Scholastic Player of the Year. But although he led all Devils defensemen in scoring through his first NHL training camp, he couldn't quite crack the lineup. After four games, he was sent back to his junior team in Kamloops, British Columbia. There, Niedermayer led his team to a Memorial Cup—Canada's national junior championship—

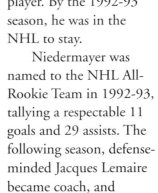

and in addition to receiving a slew of other awards, he was voted the tournament's most valuable player. By the 1992-93 season, he was in the NHL to stay.

Niedermayer was named to the NHL All-Rookie Team in 1992-93, tallying a respectable 11 goals and 29 assists. The following season, defense-minded Jacques Lemaire became coach, and Niedermayer proved that he could take care of business in his own end, placing third on the team with a plus-34 rating. He frequently chafed under orders to curb "creative" instincts construed as undisciplined, but Niedermayer played a large role in the Devils' greatest achievement. His 4 goals and 7 assists in the playoffs helped his team win the Stanley Cup after the lockout-shortened 1994-95 season. His end-to-end rush in the second game of the finals was particularly brilliant. One-on-one against Detroit's Paul Coffey, he shot wide but deposited the rebound off the back boards to tie the score. The Devils eventually swept the Red Wings in four straight games.

Niedermayer was able to savor the Stanley Cup win for only a few weeks before contract negotiations captured his attention. "We look to him to do big things for us," general manager Lou Lamoriello said in the summer of 1995. "He is a pure Devil. He wants to be a Devil. We want him to be a Devil. Scotty is a bright, young player. He is a very talented individual. But those talents have to be used in the framework of the team for us to be successful." A three-year deal

was finally agreed upon just before training camp began.

One of hockey's fastest and most mobile skaters, Niedermayer looked and felt stifled under Lemaire's system, but he did manage to make important contributions. Three of his five goals in 1996-97 were game-winners. He has been used as a winger in a pinch, even in critical playoff games, and he frequently plays the forward position when the Devils have two men in the penalty box. But he's a devastating point man on the power play and is most at home as a blueliner. His 14 goals and 43 assists in 1997-98 earned him a berth on the Second All-Star Team, and he was fifth in Norris Trophy voting.

Lemaire resigned after the Devils lost the first round of the 1998 playoffs, and the more offense-minded Robbie Ftorek was hired to replace him. The change boded well for Niedermayer, whose contract expired that summer. A restricted free agent for the second time, he was mindful of keeping his demands below the pay levels earned by team stars Martin Brodeur and Scott Stevens. The Devils, however, are one of the stingiest NHL clubs, and Niedermayer's offer was rejected. Niedermayer demanded a trade and made arrangements to play with the Utah Grizzlies of the International Hockey League.

However, three weeks into the NHL season, Niedermayer blinked. After only a week with the Grizzlies, he signed a two-year $6.5 million deal with the Devils and rescinded his trade request. His teammates were anxious for his return. "He just brings so much flow to the game with his great skating," said defenseman Kevin Dean. "He's obviously going to help our power play a ton. Even five-on-five, offensively we suffered. I think Scott's a great penalty killer and a great defensive player as well." Niedermayer didn't score any points in his first game back, but he sparked his club to a 3–1 victory.

"Niedermayer was pretty much everywhere," noted Ftorek with approval. "He was flying all over the place."

"If I saw open ice and an opportunity," said Niedermayer, "I jumped in." Under Lemaire, that would have been forbidden, but the entire team was ready to experiment. "I got a few different passes I haven't seen in a while from our forwards," he added. "There are going to be a few different things to get used to." Niedermayer enjoys his new freedom. "I'd watch him, for sure," he said of the New York Rangers' freewheeling defenseman Brian Leetch. "I'd see what he was doing and think, 'That looks like fun.' It was frustrating for me at times, and I didn't think I'd get to that point." Although the Devils were handed another first-round knockout in the 1999 playoffs, a new era has begun for New Jersey and Niedermayer.

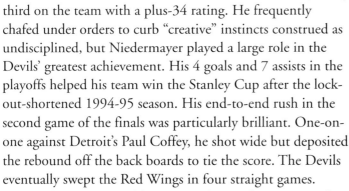

One of the most mobile defensemen in the NHL since joining the New Jersey Devils for the 1992-93 season, Scott Niedermayer, above, serves occasional spot duty at forward. Facing page: Niedermayer unleashes a slap shot in a game against the Toronto Maple Leafs. His younger brother, Rob, is a center for the Florida Panthers.

Sandis Ozolinsh

That the San Jose Sharks selected Sandis Ozolinsh as the thirtieth pick in the 1991 NHL entry draft is a tribute to the scouts who saw his potential. Ozolinsh, a native of Riga, Latvia, had dreamed of following in the footsteps of Helmet Balderis—"The Riga Express" of the Soviet Union's powerhouse national hockey team—but he accumulated just 3 assists and no goals for his hometown club during his draft year.

Over the course of 30 games, he scored only 6 goals and no assists in 1991-92, but he did help the Commonwealth of Independent States (formerly the U.S.S.R.) win the gold medal at the 1992 World

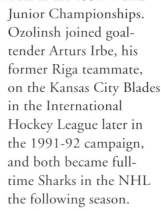

Junior Championships. Ozolinsh joined goaltender Arturs Irbe, his former Riga teammate, on the Kansas City Blades in the International Hockey League later in the 1991-92 campaign, and both became full-time Sharks in the NHL the following season.

As a 1992-93 NHL rookie, Ozolinsh tallied 7 goals and 16 assists in only 37 games before hitting his stride the following season, when he notched 26 goals and 38 assists and earned a trip to the mid-season All-Star Game. There, he scored 2 goals and added an assist. More significantly, the Sharks made their first-ever trip to the NHL postseason. Ozolinsh added 10 playoff assists as San Jose upset the conference-leading Detroit Red Wings in the first round before falling to the Toronto Maple Leafs in seven games.

Ozolinsh tied for third place in team scoring in 1994-95, which convinced him to hold out for a big raise. During contract negotiations, Ozolinsh, now a restricted free agent, upped the ante by returning to the IHL, joining the San Francisco Spiders for two games before reaching an agreement with the Sharks. "I'm glad this situation has come to a conclusion," said San Jose's general manager Dean Lombardi. "Sandis is an important part of our club and has shown the ability to be a great player in this league. Now we can begin the season with our complete team." After only seven games, however, Ozolinsh was

traded to the Colorado Avalanche for winger Owen Nolan.

When Patrick Roy was traded to Colorado six weeks later, all the ingredients were in place for a successful Stanley Cup run. Ozolinsh had the satisfaction of chalking up a career-high 4 assists in one game against the Sharks on March 28, 1996, but it was in the playoffs that he really shone. He scored a dramatic second-overtime goal to eliminate the Chicago Blackhawks in the Western Conference semifinals, sneaking in from the blue line for a point-blank shot that hit the post before he buried the rebound. By the time he lifted the Cup in triumph, Ozolinsh was leading all defensemen in playoff points.

The following year was a banner one for Ozolinsh. He started in the 1997 All-Star Game that was played in the San Jose Arena and counted 3 assists. With a personal record of 23 goals (first among defensemen) and 45 assists over the regular season, including a league-high 42 points on the power play, Ozolinsh was a finalist for the Norris Trophy and was voted to the First All-Star Team. Once again, he led all blue-liners in postseason points, even though the Avalanche fell to the Red Wings in the semifinals.

The 1997-98 season was a weak one for Colorado, which bowed out in the first playoff round. Again holding out for higher pay, Ozolinsh didn't return to the ice until midway through the following season. "I'm happy to be back," he said, after finally signing a contract in January 1999. "I was so excited, I couldn't sleep a minute last night." His return sparked a 12-game winning streak that turned the season around for the Avalanche.

"Everybody was so pumped up when he got back," said team captain Joe Sakic. "The way he plays, the game really opens up the ice for the forwards. You know he is going to play 20 to 25 minutes a game, and in that time, you are always going to have that fourth guy coming late in the play or even leading the rush. And he has been our [power-play] quarterback for a number of years."

Ozolinsh refused to take credit for the team's turn-around. "Not anymore," he said. "Now it's getting more serious. The first three, four games, yeah. Not when it's 12 games. It's getting kind of old. After each game, everybody wants to rub my head." Ozolinsh tallied 32 points in the remaining 39 games, and the Avalanche not only won their division but succeeded in battling their way to the 1999 Western Conference finals before falling to the Dallas Stars in seven games. Like it or not, Ozolinsh is a vital key to his team's success.

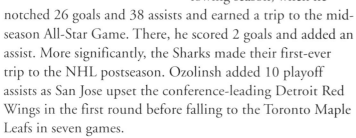

*Sandis Ozolinsh, above, is especially strong on offense, frequently join-
ing the rush and heading for the opposition net, and he's a key member
of the Colorado Avalanche power play. Facing page: Ozolinsh keeps
Toronto's Mathieu Schneider at bay by shielding the puck with his
lanky six-foot-three frame.*

Chris Pronger

Fear that Chris Pronger might be dying gripped the other players on the ice, but Pronger himself was oblivious. "I didn't know what was going on," he later recalled. Pronger had taken a Dmitri Mironov slap shot on the chest, just to the left of his heart, while killing a penalty against the Detroit Red Wings in the 1998 playoffs. "The puck was rolling when he shot it," Pronger told Dave Luecking of *The St. Louis Post-Dispatch*. "I leaned back to get my head out of the way, and the puck hit me. It hurt a little bit, but not a lot. I went down and kind of corralled the puck and got the whistle. Then I gasped for a breath. I went down on my knees and blacked out."

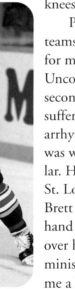

Players from both teams frantically waved for medical assistance. Unconscious for 20 to 30 seconds, Pronger was suffering from cardiac arrhythmia—his heartbeat was weak, slow and irregular. He woke up to find St. Louis Blues teammate Brett Hull squeezing his hand and players leaning over him, poised to administer CPR. "Geez, give me a little room, guys," he complained. "You're crowding me." Although Pronger lay on the ice for 15 minutes before being moved to a stretcher and rushed by ambulance to a Detroit hospital, his heart quickly recovered. After one night under close observation, he flew home to St. Louis for a battery of tests.

"Chris is in great spirits," said St. Louis Blues trainer Ray Barile. "He's a competitor, a warrior, but we have to make sure his health is taken care of. If Chris Pronger the person is okay, then we ask if he can play hockey." Pronger was given a full medical clearance and didn't miss a game.

Pronger's astonishing recovery has parallels to his career. Voted Canada's Junior Defenseman of the Year in 1992-93 with the Peterborough Petes, Pronger was chosen second overall in the 1993 NHL entry draft by the Hartford Whalers. Although the 19-year-old made the NHL All-Rookie Team the following season, the Whalers quickly grew disenchanted with him. His attitude and work habits left much to be desired. One could cite his age and sudden

wealth, but the high expectations placed on his shoulders by a perennially sad-sack team must be added to the equation. "Sometimes they're putting too much pressure on you," Pronger explained, "and you're putting too much pressure on yourself. They don't know they're doing it; you don't know you're doing it. And it isn't working out." The Whalers jumped at an offer to swap him for 50-goal-scorer Brendan Shanahan. After two seasons as a Whaler, Pronger joined the St. Louis Blues in the summer of 1995.

He had a rough beginning in St. Louis. "I could trade you for Alexei Yashin!" Blues coach and general manager Mike Keenan would scream at Pronger. "Do you want to play in Ottawa?" Pronger eventually got into shape and learned to use his size (six-foot-five, 220 pounds) and strength.

Keenan's earlier comparison of Pronger to Hall-of-Famer Larry Robinson no longer sounded quite so inflated. "It's a great comparison," said Joel Quenneville, who replaced Keenan as coach midway through Pronger's second season with the Blues. "I think Chris is turning out to be one of the top guys, and if he can continue to play and mature the way he has, the resemblance is pretty amazing."

Robinson, then coach of the L.A. Kings, was also impressed. "He's a tower of strength out there, and he's got a little bit of bite to him," he said. "He gives his shots out there, controls the play and plays with a lot of poise for a young man."

Pronger was embarrassed by such talk: "It's neat to be mentioned with him, but I don't think I deserve to be in the Larry Robinson category just yet. I've got to get another 15 years in me."

Quenneville selected him as team captain just before the 1997-98 season. The youngest player ever to serve in that role in St. Louis Blues history, 23-year-old Pronger had earned his teammates' respect. "Chris needed to be a little bit more consistent in his game and get a little fire under him," said veteran St. Louis defenseman Al MacInnis, "and he certainly has done that the past couple of years."

Pronger led his team over the 1996-97 season in the plus/minus category and repeated the feat the following year with a league-leading plus-47, winning the NHL's Bud Ice Plus/Minus Award. More significantly, he also garnered his first Norris Trophy nomination, an award likely to be in his future.

Chris Pronger, facing page, is a blue-line workhorse for the St. Louis Blues. In the 1999 playoffs, he averaged over 36 minutes of ice time per game. Pronger broke into the NHL with the Hartford Whalers, above left, and made the 1993-94 NHL All-Rookie Team.

The Goaltenders

"What pitching is in a short series in baseball," noted Detroit general manager Jack Adams, "goaltending is in the Stanley Cup playoffs." That such respect for the position comes from the man who traded Hall of Fame netminders Turk Broda, Alex Connell, Harry Lumley, Glenn Hall and, twice, Terry Sawchuk affirms what every fan of the game already knows: Tending goal is the most vulnerable position in hockey.

"How would you like it," Jacques Plante once asked rhetorically, "if every time you made a small mistake in your job, a red light went on over your desk and 15,000 people stood up and yelled at you?" While stories of other hockey players suffering nervous breakdowns are uncommon, they are legion about goaltenders.

"Goalies are insane," Glenn Hall once warned teenager Grant Fuhr, but the enthusiastic young student remained undeterred.

Perhaps Fuhr had heard Gump Worsley's take on the position: "Not all goaltenders are nuts; only about 90 percent of them."

What is surprising is how many of hockey's premier goalies first went between the pipes simply because they had no choice. At age 14, the four-foot-eleven Worsley was given an ultimatum. "You're going to have to forget about playing forward," his coach said, "and put on those goalie pads."

Said center Phil Esposito of his brother Tony, "He was younger, so he had to be the goalie."

While hockey has evolved over the years, nowhere have the changes been more dramatic than in goaltending. Until 1917, a goalie was penalized for dropping to his knees. Various restrictions on a goalie's ability to hold and freeze the puck were implemented in the first half of this century, and even the blocker and catcher—now seen as rudimentary tools of the trade—didn't become standard issue until the 1940s. In 1959, Jacques Plante literally changed the face of goaltending when he ushered in the era of the mask. Continual refinements have succeeded in making the position safer, but the tremendous increase in the size of the goaler's equipment raises the question about whether a form of cheating is now allowed.

Because of such profound transformations, it is more difficult to draw comparisons between goalies of different eras than it is to compare, for instance, different generations of skaters. But what these goaltending legends do share are the skills and fortitude to adjust to the demands of goaltending as we now understand it.

Wisdom has it that a goalie's skills peak at about age 30. If so, then the younger netminders highlighted here still have some of their best hockey ahead of them. Goaltending has never been as strong as it is today—perhaps the by-product of better equipment and coaching. But since television highlight reels concentrate on the pucks that go in more than the pucks the goalies turn away, the NHL is once more tinkering with the rules to increase scoring. Like their counterparts before them, though, these young goalies will continue to develop better ways to keep the puck out of the net.

Montreal's Bill Durnan, above (left), shares a warm handshake with fellow goalie Turk Broda of the Toronto Maple Leafs. Facing page: New Jersey Devil Martin Brodeur makes a beautiful split save.

Johnny Bower

It's difficult to picture Johnny Bower as a young man, much less a boy. His wizened face, unmasked until his final season, was almost as creased and laugh-lined when he entered the league at the age of 29 as it was when he retired at 45. Of course, Bower added hundreds more scars over the span of his career, but he accepted them as an occupational hazard. "I just made up my mind I was going to lose teeth and have my face cut to pieces," he said in explaining his decision to become a goalie. "It was easy."

Bower's real age was a subject of some debate, since he had lied about it in order to join the army and fight in World War II. Amazingly, the four-year war veteran was still eligible to play junior hockey when he returned to civilian life. Bower spent a season back home in Saskatchewan, then joined the Cleveland Barons in the American Hockey League in 1945.

He had an eight-year apprenticeship in Cleveland before the New York Rangers gave him his first shot at the big time in the 1953-54 season. Goaltender Chuck Rayner, who had just retired, gave the rookie goalie tips on his stick work, particularly the poke-check. It would become Bower's signature move.

Acquitting himself admirably that season with New York, Bower played every minute of every game. He had five shutouts on a team that finished out of the playoffs, posting a 2.60 goals-against average. But the Rangers disappointed him the following year when they brought in goalie Gump Worsley and gave Bower a ticket back to the minors.

Convinced that he had NHL skills, Bower nevertheless spent the 1954-55 season in Vancouver in the Western Hockey League. A five-game call-up to the Rangers that year went well, but Bower was soon back to the AHL. He played only a couple of 1956-57 NHL games yet continued to work hard, racking up numerous AHL awards. Back in net for Cleveland in the 1957-58 season, Bower played brilliantly against the Springfield Indians in the playoffs. Fortuitously, the Indians were managed by Punch Imlach, soon to be installed as manager and coach of the Toronto Maple Leafs. That was just the break Bower needed.

Almost 34 years old when he was drafted by the Leafs in 1958, Bower was somewhat pessimistic about his chances,

but Imlach convinced him to give the NHL another try. In his first season with the Leafs, Bower shared duties with Ed Chadwick before establishing himself as Toronto's number-one, and only, goaltender for the next three years. With a willingness that further ingratiated him with Imlach, Bower spent hours perfecting his poke-check. Jabbing his stick with his arm outstretched—often after making a spectacular dive both to cover more distance and to exercise the element of surprise—Bower could knock the puck off his opponent's stick so that his teammates could clear it out of harm's way.

He won the Vezina Trophy and First All-Star Team honors in 1960-61 and was poised for greatness.

As genial a player as any who has ever skated in the NHL, Bower was also extremely competitive. "I always played best under pressure," he said. "Maybe it was the money and prestige that went with the big games." Bower was the underpinning of Toronto's three consecutive Stanley Cup victories in the early 1960s. The icing on the cake was the shutout he registered in game seven of the 1964 Stanley Cup finals, for opposite him in the Detroit Red Wings goal was the legendary Terry Sawchuk. Neither knew that they were about to become teammates, as Sawchuk would be traded to Toronto for the 1964-65 season.

Sawchuk and Bower made a potent team. They shared the Vezina Trophy in 1965, and their success prompted the NHL to institute a new rule requiring each club to dress two goalies for every game. "I wasn't all that glad to see the two-goalie system come in," maintained Bower. "I wanted to play in all the games I possibly could." But the two veterans tag-teamed to a surprising victory for Toronto in the 1967 Stanley Cup finals.

While his reflexes remained sharp, Bower's vision had deteriorated enough to prompt him to consider retirement, and when his friend Imlach was fired after the 1968-69 campaign, the 44-year-old goalie had all the confirmation he needed. Although he was persuaded to suit up for one more game in the 1969-70 season, Bower turned his attention to other pursuits. At the summer goalie school he runs, students—prompted by parents and grandparents—still ask him to teach them how to poke-check.

*Johnny Bower, above, makes full use of his goaler's paddle to stop the
puck and steer it into the corner. He was a fully seasoned minor-league
veteran when he joined the Toronto Maple Leafs in the fall of 1958.
Facing page: Bower kicks out another shot in the efficient manner that
helped Toronto to four Stanley Cup victories in the 1960s.*

Frank Brimsek

"Usually when the Bruins entered, there would be a lot of cheering," recalled goaltender Frank Brimsek, looking back at a game against the Montreal Canadiens on December 1, 1938. "But when I hit the ice, things were so quiet that I could hear the people breathing. They were just waiting for me to blow one."

Earlier in the season, Brimsek had made a quiet rookie debut in the Boston net as a temporary substitute for the legendary "Tiny" Thompson. After missing only two games due to an eye infection, Thompson returned, but Brimsek had made a huge impression on Boston's management. A month later, Boston sold Thompson, their aging All-Star, to Detroit.

The announcement of Thompson's departure and Brimsek's ascension sent shock waves through Boston. Several players, including the levelheaded Dit Clapper, threatened to quit, convinced that they'd never win without Thompson. Not only was Brimsek American-born—a rarity amongst the almost exclusively Canadian fraternity of hockey players—but his parents were Slovenian emigrants. How could he ever succeed?

The young goalie lost his test against Montreal 2–0, and the fans were on him throughout. But Brimsek went on to shut out his opponents in the next three games, posted another victory, then three more consecutive shutouts. "Kid Zero"—soon to become "Mr. Zero" for the remainder of his career—received standing ovations from the Bruins faithful for the rest of the season. After posting a minuscule 1.56 goals-against average over 43 games, Brimsek received the Vezina and Calder trophies and became the first NHL rookie to be named to the First All-Star Team. He lowered his average to 1.50 in the playoffs to help Boston win the Stanley Cup for the first time in 10 years.

Brimsek anchored the league's best team in the regular season the following two years, and Boston won its second Cup in 1941. "He's as quick as a cat," said New York Rangers manager Lester Patrick. "And trying to get him to make the first move is like pushing over [the] Washington Monument."

Detroit goalie Johnny Mowers added, "He's got the best left hand in the business, and nobody plays the angles as well as he does."

Constantly looking for an "edge on the offense," Brimsek also played a sharp mental game. "I tried to make the opposition player do what I wanted him to," he explained. "I always felt that the glove side was the strongest side for a goaltender. And I would make the shooter believe this too. In that way, I would make most shooters fire the puck to my stick side, which is what I wanted them to do in the first place."

A soft-spoken man of few words, Brimsek let his actions speak for him. In 1943, when almost half of the NHL enlisted in military service, he joined the U.S. Coast Guard. While Brimsek spent some time tending goal for the Coast Guard Clippers, he then endured 18 months of active duty in the South Pacific with a Coast Guard supply ship. The experience changed him profoundly. "I came back too soon after being in the service," admitted Brimsek. "My nerves were jumpy. I should have taken a rest before coming back, but I needed the money."

Although he returned to the NHL midway through the 1945-46 season and helped his team advance to the Stanley Cup finals, Brimsek's playing days were numbered. "When I got out of the war, I knew I wasn't going to play long. I didn't have that same feeling for the game," he said. "I had a hard time even going back to training camp." Yet Rocket Richard, who became a league star during Brimsek's military leave, called Brimsek "the toughest goalie I ever faced."

Brimsek made the Second All-Star Team three years in a row. Meanwhile, he was preparing for his retirement. "I had spoken to [general manager] Art Ross in 1947 and told him that I would like to leave Boston in '49 to go to Chicago," said Brimsek. "My brother was starting a business there, and I thought I might help him open a few doors. Ross agreed, but when it came time, he didn't like the idea anymore. 'If that's the way you feel,' I told him, 'I'll quit altogether!'"

Brimsek soon got his trade to Chicago, and even with the last-place Blackhawks, he added five more career shutouts in his final NHL season in 1950. In 1966, he became the first American elected to the Hockey Hall of Fame.

In a mad scramble around the Boston net, above, Frank Brimsek successfully denies a goal to the Toronto Maple Leafs. Facing page: "Mr. Zero" displays his prowess at stopping pucks on the stick side, where he intentionally lured shooters to aim.

Turk Broda

"He's the best playoff player in all hockey," claimed Toronto Maple Leafs owner and manager Conn Smythe, and when Turk Broda died in 1972, his record of 13 playoff shutouts still stood.

"The bonus money for winning wasn't much," laughed the lighthearted Broda, "but I always needed it." On average, he allowed fewer than two goals a game in postseason action over 14 NHL campaigns and was on five Stanley Cup winners.

Walter Broda earned his nickname as a child, when his class was told the story of an old English king called "Turkey Egg" by his subjects because of his freckles. Since Broda had more freckles than any of his schoolmates, the moniker became his as well. Soon, it was just "Turk," and the tag stuck.

Originally deemed too short to play any position other than goal—he was five-foot-nine—Broda eventually turned professional with Detroit's International Hockey League farm club in 1935. "He hasn't a nerve in his body," declared Red Wings general manager Jack Adams. "He could play in a tornado and never blink an eye." But in 1936, Smythe acquired the promising netminder for $8,000.

Broda played well in his first five seasons with the Leafs, but his team always came up a little short in the end, losing in the Stanley Cup finals three years in a row. He seemed destined for also-ran status again when he trailed Detroit's rookie goalie Johnny Mowers by one goal in competition for the 1941 Vezina Trophy. Toronto finished out its regular season and traveled to Boston to await the Bruins, who still had a game to play against Detroit. Cool as a cucumber, Broda took a seat in the Boston Garden to see whether the Bruins could help his cause. Boston scored twice, and Broda had his first Vezina.

Toronto lost to the Bruins that year, but in 1942, Broda backstopped his team in the most remarkable comeback in Stanley Cup history. Down three games to none, he allowed only seven goals in the next four games to help the Leafs to their first championship in 10 years.

By 1945, the next time Toronto won the Stanley Cup, Broda had been in the army for almost two years. A public controversy had erupted over the preferential treatment that professional athletes were receiving when Broda went to enlist. The Royal Canadian Mounted Police stopped his

train en route to Montreal, arrested Broda and returned him to Toronto—all so that he would play hockey for the Toronto Army Daggers rather than the Montreal military team which had offered him a $2,400 bonus. The frustrated Broda would later complain that he had been drafted to stop pucks rather than bullets.

Broda returned to NHL duty late in the 1945-46 season and soon regained his form. "We were outplayed and out-chanced in scoring opportunities, I would think, by about three to two," said Toronto rookie Howie Meeker. "Turk Broda was the guy who won that series." The Leafs won their first of three consecutive Stanley Cups, and Broda's already low playoff average continued to drop every year.

Broda's colorful character also made him a crowd favorite. Before accepting his teammates' congratulations after a victory, he would rush around the ice scooping up the cigars his fans had showered down. His chubby face and portly build made him an unlikely-looking NHL star, and when the Leafs faltered, 35-year-old Broda was an easy target.

"If it isn't Turk's fault, we'll find out whose it is," said Smythe after the Leafs stumbled halfway through the 1949-50 season. "I'm taking Broda out of the nets, and he's not going back until he shows some common sense." To back up his threat that Broda wouldn't play until he shed seven of his 197 pounds, Smythe called up his reserve goalie and then traded for up-and-coming netminder Al Rollins. "Two seasons ago, [Turk] weighed 185. Last season, he went up to 190—and now this," complained Smythe. "A goalie has to have fast reflexes, and you can't move fast when you're overweight."

Broda, who hadn't missed a single game with the Leafs apart from his military service, won the celebrated "Battle of the Bulge" by fasting and sweating his way down to his prescribed weight. He earned a shutout in his first game back.

Although Broda played in 31 games, Rollins played more and was awarded the Vezina Trophy for the 1950-51 season. But it was Broda who sparkled in 8 of the Leafs' 11 playoff games. His minuscule 1.13 goals-against average helped Toronto to another Stanley Cup victory. That series, however, was Broda's swan song. He appeared in only three games the next year before retiring.

Turk Broda, above, was at his acrobatic best in the playoffs—he retired with five Stanley Cup rings and a 1.98 goals-against average in post-season action. Although Broda apprenticed in the Detroit farm system he made his NHL debut with Toronto in 1936-37. Facing page: Broda squares himself against an attack from Detroit center Sid Abel.

Ken Dryden

In 1972, Ken Dryden took time out from sight-seeing with Team Canada to visit the hockey department of the Institute of Physical Culture and Sport in Moscow. The Soviets' scientific approach led one official to insist that Dryden was too tall to be a goaltender. "There are disadvantages," the six-foot-four Dryden conceded, "but there are advantages too: my reach. I can cover a lot of goal." His host was unconvinced, but NHL shooters knew better. While he played fewer than eight NHL seasons, Dryden was goalie for six Stanley Cup-winning teams, and he never lost more than 10 games in any one campaign.

Many cite the troika of defensemen in front of him—Serge Savard, Larry Robinson and Guy Lapointe—as key to Dryden's five Vezina Trophies. In those days, the award went to the goalkeepers on the *team* allowing the fewest goals. But Dryden also made the league's First All-Star Team in each of those five seasons. "The team always felt that [Dryden] could win them a big game if he had to," said coaching legend Scotty Bowman, whose career with the Habs began in Dryden's rookie year (1971-72) and ended with his netminder's retirement in 1979. "He was the most consistent goaltender I have ever coached and a fierce competitor."

Dryden followed his brother Dave's lead. Their first meeting on NHL ice on March 2, 1971—with veteran Dave in net for the Buffalo Sabres and call-up Ken guarding Montreal's cage—replicated hundreds of backyard games. But the two brothers had taken radically different routes to the NHL. Dryden spurned Canadian junior hockey to play four years at Cornell University while working toward a law degree, an unlikely path to the NHL in the 1960s. Although the Montreal Canadiens were interested in his services, Dryden accepted an offer with the Canadian national team that would allow him to continue his education.

When the national-team program folded a year later, Dryden entered the Montreal farm system. It wasn't long before he was brought up to the parent club, and he played in the last six games of the 1970-71 season. He won every match and posted a 1.65 goals-against average, but the hockey world was stunned when Montreal started him against the defending Stanley Cup champion Boston Bruins in the first playoff game that spring.

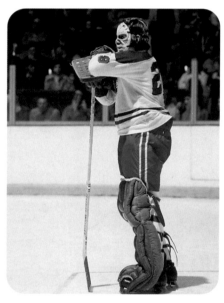

The Bruins had poured a league-record 399 goals into enemy nets. It looked as if Dryden were being fed to the wolves, but he backstopped the Canadiens to a seven-game upset and eventually won the Conn Smythe Trophy for his part in vanquishing Minnesota and Chicago en route to a Stanley Cup victory. Dryden proved that it was more than beginner's luck when he won the 1972 Calder Trophy the next season, his rookie year. He earned his second Stanley Cup ring in 1973, yet it looked then as though Dryden was already through with hockey. Dissatisfied with his contract, Dryden shocked fans and pundits alike when he quit the game in 1973 to return to school, article and get on with his legal career.

When Montreal faltered badly without Dryden in the 1973-74 season, the club offered to quadruple his salary, raising it to the going rate for the NHL's best talent. The following season, Dryden once again traded his legal pads for goalie pads.

His "leave of absence" had just been part of hard bargaining, and he quickly picked up where he had left off. Dryden helped his team to the semifinals before backstopping the Canadiens to four consecutive Stanley Cups as the league's premier netminder.

Dryden's iconic pose—gloves stacked on the butt end of his stick, chin resting on his blocker—was original and unforgettable. While the image epitomized the thinker he was, it was also a ritual that helped him stretch out a long spine which spent too much time in a crouch. Unfortunately, Dryden's back finally got the better of him, and in 1979, he announced his retirement, this time for good.

His book *The Game*, arguably hockey's greatest tome, launched him into a successful writing and broadcasting career, but Dryden remained open to new challenges. In 1997, he moved into an executive position with the Toronto Maple Leafs, where it is hoped that his thoughtful approach will lead to the Stanley Cup.

Ken Dryden's patient pose, above, was a novelty when he was the surprise starter for the Montreal Canadiens in the 1971 playoffs, but the silhouette soon epitomized the cerebral and athletic goaltender. Facing page: A five-time Vezina Trophy winner, Dryden kicks the puck wide.

Bill Durnan

Bill Durnan tended goal with a unique pair of gloves—fingered catching mitts that allowed him to hold his goalie's stick in either hand—for he had the remarkable ability to adjust his stance to face an attacker with a glove always in the optimum position, covering the wider part of the net. He credited Steve Faulkner, his boyhood coach, with his ambidextrous ability. "He worked me by the hour," explained Durnan, "until I had the technique down pat, and we won five city championships in six years. At first, it felt as though I was transferring a telephone pole from one hand to the other, but after a while, I'd hardly realize I was doing it." Not only ambidextrous, Durnan also had lightning reflexes, particularly in his hands, a combination that confounded shooters throughout his career.

Although he became a Montreal Canadiens legend, Durnan was originally signed by the Toronto Maple Leafs in 1936. He won the Memorial Cup, junior hockey's championship, while playing in the Leafs' farm system, and at 20 years of age, he was ready to go to his first NHL training camp. Unfortunately, just before camp opened, Durnan injured his knee in a playful tussle with a friend. When the Leafs heard about his injury, they immediately dropped him from their protected list.

Durnan felt that he had been treated shabbily and vowed never to play in the NHL, even drifting from hockey for a time after his knee healed. Before long, though, he was active in the mercantile leagues, playing goal in the winter and pitching baseball in the summer, always with a guaranteed company job to augment his income. He starred for several teams, including the Kirkland Lake Blue Devils, which won hockey's Allan Cup in 1940—a prestigious trophy at the time.

At 29 years of age, Durnan was tending net for the Montreal Royals in the Quebec senior league and earning considerable attention with his stellar play. By day, he worked in the accounting department of a firm run by a director of the Montreal Canadiens club. Durnan was content, but in 1943, he started to feel considerable pressure to play for the Canadiens. "Somehow, I managed to hold out until the day of the opening game," he explained years after he finally gave in. "I signed for the huge sum of $4,200 and found myself on a hockey team just beginning to jell." Durnan won the Vezina

Trophy and a First All-Star Team selection, as he would in five of the next six seasons, establishing himself as one of hockey's greatest goalies ever. Despite his success, however, he remained a reluctant NHL star.

Durnan and the rest of the Canadiens slumped badly in the 1947-48 season, and the Montreal fans voiced their displeasure. "They booed me and made me feel six inches high," Durnan lamented. "I don't know whether you've ever heard 13,000 people all calling you the same bad name at the same time, but it sure makes a loud noise." Although he had the support of the team—he was named captain in early 1948—Durnan threatened to quit while he still had his health and his nerves. He was persuaded to stay and rebounded with two more excellent seasons. For all that, he viewed hockey as a string of one-year careers. "I figure I may be fired next week, or I may decide to quit the week after," he explained. "In that way, I gear myself for shock. If it doesn't come, so much the better. I carry on the best I can."

Durnan looked back at the 1949-50 campaign as "the beginning of the end." Most of the fun had gone out of the game for him, and he decided to quit at season's end. "I'll admit," he conceded in 1972, "if they were paying the kind of money goaltenders get today, they'd have had to shoot me to get me out of the game. But at the end of any given season, I never had more than $2,000 in the bank. I wasn't educated and had two little girls to raise. All this worried me a great deal, and I was also hurting."

Yet Durnan's threat of retirement had become an almost annual statement, and if he was prepared for "shock," most others were not. His retirement was the stuff of legend. Heavily favored Montreal faced fourth-place New York in the first round of the 1950 playoffs, but the Rangers jumped into a surprising 3–0 lead in games. Durnan, not playing particu-

larly well, lost what remained of his confidence and decided that Gerry McNeil, a promising young goalie pegged as his eventual replacement, might as well start the next game. He told coach Dick Irvin of his intention to retire, and despite Irvin's and even McNeil's protestations, Durnan was adamant. In an emotional locker-room meeting, he explained his deci- sion to his teammates.

While admitting that the emotional turmoil he felt was agonizing, "the nerves and all the accompanying crap," Durnan attested, "were built up." Yet the story went out that Durnan couldn't handle the pressure and had suffered a nervous breakdown. McNeil started game four, which the Canadiens won, before going down in defeat to the Rangers in the fifth game. Durnan never played another hockey game.

Bill Durnan, above, captained the Montreal Canadiens for the remain- der of the 1947-48 season after Toe Blake retired. His long forays out of the crease to discuss the game with the referee led the NHL to ban goaltenders from holding the title. Facing page: Durnan displays his unusual ambidextrous goalie gloves.

Grant Fuhr

Grant Fuhr got off to an inauspicious start with the St. Louis Blues by showing up for training camp in 1995 almost 25 pounds overweight. Rumored to have refused to complete the team's routine physical examination, the goalie was immediately sent packing by coach and general manager "Iron Mike" Keenan. A week later—and 14 pounds lighter—Fuhr returned. By the beginning of the season, he was down to his regular 200-pound weight and back in Keenan's good graces. Fuhr was in net for the first match of that campaign and went on to set an NHL record for goaltenders by starting 79 games—76 in succession.

The move to St. Louis proved to be a tonic for Fuhr. Following 10 spectacular and glory-filled seasons with the Edmonton Oilers, Fuhr had been traded to the Toronto Maple Leafs in 1991 after publicly acknowledging a drug-abuse problem. He had a decent season with the Leafs, but Felix Potvin also arrived that year. Fuhr took the young goalie under his wing and coached him well enough that Potvin unseated him as Toronto's "go-to" goaltender.

Early in 1993, the Leafs sent Fuhr to the Buffalo Sabres. Unfortunately for Fuhr, Dominik Hasek was just emerging as a star. While the two shared the William M. Jennings Trophy with the league's lowest average in the 1993-94 season, Fuhr, as second-stringer, had played only three games midway through the following season when the Sabres dealt him to the Los Angeles Kings. He played so poorly there that his average, never his strong suit, ballooned for the first time to more than four goals a game. In the summer of 1995, he arrived in St. Louis as a free agent.

After his initial blowup with Keenan, Fuhr found the fountain of youth in physical fitness with St. Louis. Once again, he was at his acrobatic best—with perhaps the league's sharpest reflexes—and posted his lowest seasonal average. "I've often learned things the hard way," said Fuhr, but for the longest time, everything had seemed to come easily to him. His 78–21–1 junior record had prompted Edmonton to use its first-round (eighth overall) draft pick in 1981 to choose him. Midway through his rookie NHL season, at the age of 19, Fuhr became the youngest goalie to play in an NHL All-Star Game. At season's end, he was runner-up to Billy Smith in Vezina Trophy voting and was selected for

the Second All-Star Team. "He was born to be a goaltender," Mark Messier once said. "I'm sure he feels more comfortable in his hockey equipment than he does in his pajamas."

In Edmonton, a power struggle between goalies Fuhr and Andy Moog soon emerged. Within a couple of years, a pattern had been set. Both netminders shared regular-season duties, but Fuhr got almost all the calls in the playoffs. "Fuhr is one of the most unflappable athletes I have ever met," said ESPN broadcaster Darren Pang, a former NHL goaltender. "There is no pulse in the most pressurized situations, and that has always been his greatest asset."

Fuhr was at his best in backing the Oilers to four Stanley Cup victories in five years. While Edmonton's run-and-gun style meant that they gave up almost as many scoring opportunities as they created, Fuhr shone under the heavy workload. Although he preferred the sanctuary of his crease and didn't play the puck as much as many goalers, he nevertheless set an NHL record in 1983-84 for most points in a season, with 14 assists.

Fuhr starred in net for Canada's winning team in the 1987 Canada Cup tournament and used his experience that autumn as a springboard for his best NHL season. When Moog departed in frustration, Fuhr led the league in minutes played en route to his selection to the First All-Star Team and his only Vezina Trophy. He succumbed to his first serious injury two years later, and Bill Ranford stepped into the breach. Healed but on the bench, Fuhr watched his team win the Stanley Cup again in 1990.

Not until he joined St. Louis in 1995 did Fuhr once again get the workload he craved. He has started to pick up more frequent injuries, though, and recovery seems to take longer. "One more year after this one, and that's it," he said late in the 1998-99 season. Time will tell whether Fuhr remains true to his word and retires or surprises everyone by stretching his career. It would not be the first time he did the unpredictable.

Grant Fuhr, above, resurrected his career with the St. Louis Blues in 1995 and remains one of the NHL's best netminders. Facing page: Fuhr's stellar play with the Edmonton Oilers allowed his team to develop the run-and-gun style that came to define hockey in the 1980s.

Glenn Hall

Records are made to be broken, but goaltender Glenn Hall's record for consecutive games will never be bettered. From the first game of the 1955-56 season until 12 games into the 1962-63 season, Hall never missed a minute of NHL action. Finally, on November 7, 1962, Hall pulled himself out of a game against the Boston Bruins. His back had bothered him the previous game, but he'd felt good in the pregame warm-up, and the team doctor had given him the green light. When the Bruins scored on their first shot of the game, however, Hall went to the bench, conferred briefly with coach Rudy Pilous, then headed for the dressing room.

As Hall explained later, "I was able to take a comfortable stance, but I couldn't move with the play when it crossed in front of the net. A goalie who can't do that might as well be up in the stands." Denis DeJordy had been rushed in from the farm team in Buffalo when Hall first complained of a sore back, and he replaced Hall that night and played the next game in Montreal three days later. Hall's streak ended at 502 games—552 if you include the playoffs. It remains one of the most remarkable accomplishments in hockey history.

Not only was Hall an iron man, he also played net in a record 13 All-Star Games, his first in 1955. In that game, he played for the defending Stanley Cup champion Detroit Red Wings (he had played just eight NHL games before that preseason game but showed such promise during his minor-league apprenticeship that the Red Wings traded away the great Terry Sawchuk). Hall finished the season by winning the Calder Trophy as rookie of the year, leading the league in shutouts, a feat he would repeat five more times.

Hall always spoke his mind, even if it meant criticizing the game, its fans or team management, a trait that probably led Detroit general manager Jack Adams to trade him in 1957 to the sad-sack Chicago Blackhawks along with Players' Association organizer Ted Lindsay. Hall, however, never missed a beat. Four years later, he backstopped the Blackhawks to their first Stanley Cup triumph in 23 years.

Hall knew what worked for him and had the courage to stick with it despite the criticism he faced. He pioneered the "butterfly" style of goaltending, having discovered that by crouching and keeping his legs spread below the knees, he could cover more of the net and still keep his body upright, ready to spring back to his feet. This style dominates the game today. Protected by better equipment, goalies now spend most of their time fending off attackers while down in the butterfly position. In Hall's day, a goalie who went down too often risked taking a shot in the face. "Back then, the goalkeepers always thought survival," Hall said years later. "The styles have changed so much since the mask came in. We tried to get our feet over in front of the puck and the head out of the way. It was survival, number one." Hall himself did not wear a mask until the final 2½ seasons of his career.

Ironically, "Mr. Goalie," as he was called, appeared to hate hockey. He was sick to his stomach before every game and often between periods. "Five minutes before a game or between periods, I didn't hear what a coach was saying because I was in total preparation," recalled Hall. "All I would be thinking about was what I had to do. During a game, when someone got ready to shoot, I'd already looked at the shot in my mind. I tried to prepare myself for every option."

Hall's vomit bucket became part of his legend, along with a paint bucket and the barn back home in Stony Plain, Alberta. The latter story derived from a flip answer Hall once gave to the press when explaining why he wasn't at training camp yet. "I'm painting the barn," he claimed, but it was actually part of his contract-negotiating ritual. Hall didn't think he needed training camp or even much practice during the season. Concentrating solely on games, he maintained, was the key to his consecutive-game streak, and his record supports that view.

In 1967, Blackhawks management deemed Hall expendable and left the 36-year-old unprotected in the league's first expansion draft. The St. Louis Blues quickly made him their first selection. Although Hall described his

new teammates as "kids and castoffs," his play was so spectacular while his team was being swept out of the 1968 Stanley Cup finals by the Montreal Canadiens that he was awarded the Conn Smythe Trophy as best playoff performer. He won the Vezina Trophy for lowest goals-against average for a third time when he shared goaltending duties with the even older Jacques Plante in 1968-69, earning a First All-Star Team selection the same season.

Hall finally retired in 1971 at the age of 40. He had moved into third place among the all-time shutout leaders with 84, a position he has held ever since. In 1975, Hall was inducted into the Hockey Hall of Fame; in 1988, his number 1 jersey was retired by Chicago, a late but fitting tribute to one of the franchise's greatest goalies.

Above: Montreal's Claude Larose tries to lift the puck over veteran Glenn Hall of the St. Louis Blues. Facing page: Shown down in the butterfly position that he developed, "Mr. Goalie" played an incredible 552 consecutive games, including playoffs, spanning years in Detroit and Chicago.

Dominik Hasek

"I would say, without question," said Wayne Gretzky in 1998, "that Dominik Hasek has proven to be the best player in the world the last two years—not only for what he did for the Buffalo Sabres and for the NHL but for what he did for his country in the Olympic Games." Although only half of the team in front of him had NHL experience, Hasek took the Czech Republic into the medal round of the 1998 Winter Olympics in Nagano. He helped eliminate an NHL star-studded American squad before facing the Canadian favorites.

"We're going to fire a lot of rubber and go to the net," said Canadian captain Eric Lindros before the game, but Hasek was almost perfect. He nursed a 1–0 lead with dozens of brilliant saves before Canada's Trevor Linden found a chink in Hasek's armor with a minute left on the clock. Both Hasek and Canadian netminder Patrick Roy were flawless in an overtime period, but under Olympic rules, there was a shootout to decide the winner. It was the "most intense pressure of my life," said Hasek, but he blanked all five Canadians, while the Czechs managed to slip one by Roy.

Facing Russia in the final game, Hasek posted a shutout in a tense 1–0 victory. He went home with a gold medal around his neck and an Olympic goals-against average of less than one. "Hasek to the castle!" ("Hasek for President!" is a rough translation) was the cry that rang out in Prague's central square, as hundreds of thousands milled about in celebration. A Czech astronomer even named a comet after him.

The Chicago Blackhawks had drafted Hasek with the 199th pick in the 1983 NHL entry draft, but despite lucrative Blackhawk contract offers, Hasek had no interest in coming to North America then. He was the Czechoslovakian goaltender of the year from 1986-90 before joining Chicago's minor-league affiliate in Indianapolis in the 1990-91 season. He appeared in five games with the Blackhawks before splitting the following season between Chicago and Indianapolis. He compiled a 10–4–1 record with the Blackhawks, but teammate Eddie Belfour was clearly number one. Although Hasek was named to the 1992 NHL All-Rookie Team, Chicago coach Mike Keenan almost ran him out of the NHL because of his unconventional style. A trade to the Buffalo Sabres in August 1992 convinced Hasek not to head for home, and within a year, "The Dominator" had established himself as the league's premier goaltender.

Hasek won the Vezina Trophy in his second season as a Sabre and three times after that. His 1.95 goals-against average in 1993-94 marked the first time a goalie had dropped below 2.00 in 20 years. The prestigious Hart Trophy, which had not been awarded to a goaltender since Jacques Plante won it in 1962, went to Hasek in both 1997 and 1998, along with the NHL Players' Association's Pearson Award. But a run-in with popular Buffalo coach Ted Nolan and a punch-up in 1997 with a reporter who had suggested that he might be faking a playoff injury got the fans on his back. "It's very important that I feel people like me here [in Buffalo]," he said. "It's why I play so well, because the players, coaches, the people in the stadium, believe in me." Hasek struggled through the first part of the 1997-98 season before notching an incredible six shutouts in December and winning back his supporters.

"He's got an advantage on a lot of shooters because of the reputation he's built up," observed Mats Sundin of the Toronto Maple Leafs. "Guys see him in the net and think they have to try something special to score a goal."

Hasek is unconvinced. "I really don't feel I have any edge on the players," he has commented. "I always believe only in my hard work and my skills. I look at the stick. I look at the players, and I just try to stop the puck, try to win the game—stop the puck with my head, whatever it takes. Ever since I can remember, I always made straight for the goal—in soccer, in hockey, in everything. Coaches never told me anything, except keep my stick on the ice."

Buffalo coach Lindy Ruff doesn't have much to say either, although he's a huge admirer. Hasek "has pretty well redefined how goaltending is being played," he said. "He's done some things nobody's seen before—dropping his stick and using his other hand, making saves with his head, rolling over and laying his arm on the ice, rolling over and kicking his legs up. He never says 'never' on any play."

Hasek is looking for a Stanley Cup ring now. "It bothers me to see all the other goalies who have won the Stanley Cup, and I haven't," he said. "The pressure is on our team and me also, but I don't mind. It makes me play better."

Dominik Hasek, above, shows how little net he offers to opposition shooters, but his quick reflexes are what has made him "The Dominator" of the 1990s. Facing page: Unorthodox in almost every way, Hasek gets a toe on the puck as his Buffalo Sabres teammate Alexei Zhitnik looks on.

Bernie Parent

"The mask gives you protection, saves you a few hundred stitches," noted Bernie Parent, "but the best thing it does is hide your face from the crowd." Fame rather than shame was Parent's desire for concealing his features—the slogan "Only the Lord Saves More Than Bernie Parent" appeared frequently on signs in the Philadelphia Spectrum and on bumper stickers all over town.

Signed by the Boston Bruins organization when he was a teenager, Parent got his first big break in Junior A hockey playing for coach Hap Emms in Niagara Falls. "Until I turned 18, I didn't know what a goaltender was supposed to do," he has said. "I just did things by instinct."

Emms taught him how to play the angles, and Parent made an auspicious NHL debut in 1965 when both of Boston's starting goalies were injured. "Parent has given this club the lift it needs," said Bruins coach Milt Schmidt. "He has all the moves, he stays up, and he stays remarkably cool."

Although Parent completed a decent rookie year, his play slipped in his second season. "If an athlete ever tells you booing doesn't bother him," said Parent, "he's either in a trance or just plain ignorant." Parent was sent to the minors, and the Philadelphia Flyers made him their first pick in the expansion draft the following summer. He shared duties with Doug Favell for 3½ seasons before being sent to the Toronto Maple Leafs midway through the 1970-71 season.

Upset by the trade, Parent entered Maple Leaf Gardens and sadly wandered the halls, looking at the framed pictures of Toronto's storied past. As he did, however, his feelings started to change, and by the time Jacques Plante shook his hand in the dressing room, Parent realized that the trade was fortuitous. "Plante was like a god to me," he later recalled. "Now I was on the same team with him."

His nervousness about how the 43-year-old veteran would treat a young newcomer was soon eased. "We'll be playing together," said Plante warmly, "so just ask if there is anything I can help you with." Plante worked with his young protégé on clearing the puck and playing the angles better. Parent discovered that his idol literally had a book on every shooter in the league and wrote notes on every arena regarding the play of the boards and even the lighting. Realizing that he had been a raw talent when he arrived in Toronto, Parent left as a polished goaltender, having made Plante's scientific goaltending system his own.

A lucrative offer from the Miami Screaming Eagles of the fledgling World Hockey Association enticed Parent to jump to the new league in 1972. When Miami folded its team before playing a single game, Parent's contract was picked up by the Philadelphia Blazers, an even newer WHA entry. He was ecstatic about returning to Philadelphia, and the heavy barrage of shots he faced in 65 games for the Blazers was just what he needed after Plante's tutoring. But one season in the WHA was enough. The club struggled to meet its financial obligations and ceased operations, while Parent managed to force Toronto to trade his NHL rights to the Philadelphia Flyers for the 1973-74 season.

"My first game back with the Flyers was a forgettable one," Parent laughingly recalled. "The papers were saying that I was back and could help the team win. My first game was an exhibition against the New York Rangers, and after 12 minutes, I had let in seven goals." But he notched four shutouts in his first 10 games of the regular season, and the Flyers went on to win their division. Parent shared the Vezina Trophy with Chicago's Tony Esposito, and his stingy 2.02 goals-against average in the ensuing playoffs helped the Flyers march to the Stanley Cup finals and defeat the favored Boston Bruins. Parent's stellar performance—punctuated with a 1–0 shutout in the clinching game—earned him the Conn Smythe Trophy.

"We know the exhilarating feeling only a player on a Stanley Cup winner can appreciate," he exclaimed after repeating his most-valuable-player performance when the Flyers won their second consecutive Cup. "It won't be easy for any team to take the Cup away." But Montreal swept them in the

finals the next season, and Parent never got that close again.

"Once a game starts, I forget about the shots and getting hurt," he said, but off the ice, he became increasingly worried about injuries, which prompted him to sign a lifetime deal with the Flyers in 1975. His concerns proved well founded when he was struck down midway through the 1978-79 season. A stick glanced up in a goalmouth scramble, poked through an eye hole in his mask and jabbed him in the eye. A sympathetic reaction in the other eye left the goaltender in complete darkness for two weeks.

Fortunately, Parent's sight returned, but his playing career was over. His jersey was officially retired, and he turned his attention to sharing his wisdom with new generations of Philadelphia goalies.

A remarkably poised Bernie Parent, above, was the backbone of the Philadelphia Flyers' Stanley Cup victories in 1974 and 1975—and won the Conn Smythe Trophy both years. Facing page: Parent grabs the puck in front of St. Louis Blue Ted Irvine and his own teammate Don Saleski.

Jacques Plante

If Jacques Plante had not stood up to Montreal Canadiens coach Toe Blake on the night of November 2, 1959, the number of career-ending injuries suffered by the sport's goaltenders would have been far higher by now. When sniper Andy Bathgate of the New York Rangers ripped open Plante's nose with a backhand, sending him into the trainer's room, Plante informed Blake that the only way he would go back in the nets that night was with his mask on, the one he had worn in practice for years.

Blake had repeatedly denied Plante's requests to wear the mask in games, but with no backup goalie dressed and his team enjoying a 4–1 lead, he relented. Plante was allowed to wear the face protection until his nose healed. The Canadiens promptly won their next 11 games with a masked man in net. Still, Blake made Plante stick to their agreement, and a healed and bare-faced Plante started the next game. The team lost, and Blake let Plante decide whether the mask had helped or hindered his play. Plante's mask went on for good, and the face of goaltending was forever changed.

Clint Benedict, in 1930, had been the first NHL goalie to wear a mask. When the padded leather contraption failed to save him from a nose-breaking forehead-slashing shot from Howie Morenz, Benedict retired, taking his invention with him. Plante, an innovator by nature, was recuperating from a fractured cheekbone when he mentioned in a televised interview that if anyone had a mask a goalie might wear, he'd try it. A listening fan sent one in, and Plante wore it in practice for several years before switching to an improved fiberglass model. Blake claimed that he was opposed to the mask because it would impair Plante's performance in a game, but there is no doubt that at the time, using a mask was seen as a sign of cowardice.

It took someone like Plante, an independent thinker with All-Star skills, to disprove that notion, and 10 years later, he was able to argue that the mask had saved his life. The 41-year-old Plante was playing excellent goal for the St. Louis Blues in the 1970 Stanley Cup finals when Phil Esposito tipped Fred Stanfield's shot from the point. The rising puck caught Plante just above the left eye, putting him out of the series with a concussion but no cut or fracture. Without the mask, said Plante, "I would have been dead. No question."

Plante was as eccentric as he was brilliant in the nets. He found knitting relaxing and made the tuques he liked to wear in net (he claimed they spared him a chill). Denied this comfort by Blake, who didn't like the look of it, Plante knit undershirts instead. An asthmatic, he often complained about breathing problems in certain locations and occasionally stayed in a different hotel from that of his teammates. Considered questionable practice at the time, it further distanced him from those who saw camaraderie as integral to success.

Plante *was* a private man off the ice and egotistical to boot, but on the ice, he was the ultimate team player. He constantly called out helpful advice to his teammates and was the first goalie to signal impending icing calls for his defensemen. But Plante's greatest contribution to the art of goaltending was his willingness to roam from the crease, a strategy that he first devised when he was playing in the Quebec junior league during its expansion from 4 to 11 teams in 1947. "They needed all the players they could get," he explained. "We had four defensemen. One couldn't skate backwards. One couldn't turn to his left. The others were slow. It was a case of me having to go and get the puck when it was shot into our end because our defense couldn't get there fast enough. The more I did it, the farther I went. It seemed to be the best thing to do, so I did it, and it worked."

Plante was just as adventurous when he joined the NHL, and his success with the powerhouse Canadiens of the 1950s undoubtedly contributed to the adoption of his method by the goalies who followed him. The great goaltender Chuck Rayner was also wandering from his crease at about the same time, but because he toiled for the lowly New York Rangers, it did not garner him the same attention.

Eventually, Plante wore out his welcome in Montreal.

The Canadiens faltered three times after five consecutive Stanley Cups, and in 1963, Plante was sent to the Rangers in a trade for Gump Worsley. He bragged that he'd win his seventh Vezina Trophy in New York, but playing for such a weak club seemed to cause him to lose heart. Suffering a demotion to the minors, he retired, demoralized, in 1965.

In 1968, however, the St. Louis Blues lured him back to split goaltending duties with Glenn Hall, and the two veterans shared the Vezina Trophy in 1968-69. The rejuvenated Plante played well into his forties. Sold to Toronto in 1970, he was dealt to Boston near the end of the 1972-73 campaign, his last in the NHL. Plante had one final stint with Edmonton in the WHA in 1974-75 before retiring for good. He succumbed to cancer in 1986.

Jacques Plante, above, clears the puck out of harm's way as Toronto's Ron Stewart rushes in. Plante ended a three-year retirement in 1968 to join the St. Louis Blues. Facing page: Plante makes a smooth kick-save, depriving former teammate Jean Beliveau of the rebound.

Patrick Roy

Nine-goals-against in half a game is a goaltender's nightmare, but that ordeal is one of the defining moments of Patrick Roy's career. On December 2, 1995, on their way to an NHL record for wins in a season, the powerhouse Detroit Red Wings sent a relentless barrage of shots at Roy as the over-matched Montreal Canadiens put in a particularly hapless effort. Mario Tremblay, Montreal's rookie coach, let Roy twist in the wind in front of a mocking Montreal Forum crowd for far too long. The score was 9–1 before Tremblay gave Roy a merciful hook.

Humiliated and enraged, Roy stormed over to Canadiens president Ronald Corey, seated in the first row behind the Montreal players' bench, and vehemently declared that he'd played his last game for Montreal. Despite the circumstances, such a public display of insubordination made a trade inevitable. Four days later, Roy was dealt to the Colorado Avalanche, formerly the archrival Quebec Nordiques, which had been transplanted to Denver that season.

Roy, who grew up cheering for the Nordiques, quickly jelled with his new team. And when the Avalanche faced the Canadiens a few weeks later, Roy was at his best, stopping 37 of 39 shots for a 5–2 victory. The win itself wasn't enough for Roy, though, and he added a final insult by flipping the puck at Tremblay when the game ended. "It made me feel so good. It was a mistake, but I don't regret it," Roy told the media after the game. "I'm an emotional person. I let my emotions go. I know sometimes it gets me in trouble, but I know it sometimes helps me to play better too."

While his trade to the Colorado Avalanche was all about "pride" for Roy, it was about winning the Stanley Cup for the Avalanche. Although the team included superstars Joe Sakic and Peter Forsberg, Colorado coach Marc Crawford credited Roy's presence as the critical element that pushed the Avalanche to the top.

The Canadiens were eliminated in the first playoff round that season, but Roy backstopped his team to the Stanley Cup finals. The Avalanche won the first two games against the surprising Florida Panthers—Roy let in only a single goal in each game. The Panthers potted two quick goals early in the third game, however, and Roy suffered a barrage of plastic rats from the Florida fans each time. This celebratory gesture got so out of hand that the NHL later strengthened the rules against throwing items on the ice.

Unlike the other opposing goalies who had faced a similar rain of rodents during the Panthers' run to the Cup, Roy refused to creep back into his net for protection. He skated in small circles, with the dignity of a zoo tiger having marshmallows tossed at him. As the rats were being scooped up by the maintenance crew, Roy skated over to the Colorado bench. "No more rats," he quietly told his teammates. He did not let in another goal in the series, helping the Avalanche complete a sweep with a triple-overtime shutout in game four.

Overtime hockey was nothing new to Roy, who was in goal for the Montreal Canadiens' record-breaking run of 10 consecutive overtime wins in their 1993 Stanley Cup triumph. Those playoff victories cemented Roy's reputation as one of the greatest pressure goalies of all time. In such a "zone" during the final series against the Los Angeles Kings, he even had the effrontery to give a sly wink to Tomas Sandstrom, after continually stymieing the Finnish sniper. "I knew he wasn't going to beat me," said Roy.

Rather than enflaming the opposition, Roy's cocky gesture just seemed to underline the obvious. The Habs won the series 4–1, and Roy was awarded the Conn Smythe Trophy for the second time. It was a feat that he first accomplished as a 20-year-old rookie in 1985, the youngest winner ever. "I haven't seen goaltending like that in 14 years," said Larry Robinson at the time, alluding to Ken Dryden's amazing debut.

Although many goalies are known for their eccentricities, Roy has more quirks than most. His superstitions include not stepping on the red or blue lines on the ice, and he has been called "The Goose" for his habitual neck flexing, a technique he uses to stay loose. Roy's use of visualization, initially reported as "talking to his goalposts," is another celebrated aspect of his game. While his confidence borders on arrogance, it is as much a calculated strategy as a personality trait. "A goalie has to show he's confident, to his teammates as well as himself," he explained. "You are the last guy before that special red line. You make yourself confident. You make yourself hard to beat."

Roy's 1985 brilliance as a rookie caught most observers by surprise, but in the ensuing years, he has consistently been among the NHL's goaltending elite. His style has evolved from stand-up to butterfly, best suited to getting his large frame in the way of pucks he can't even see. His manner of going down to cover the bottom half of the net has become standard practice among young goalies, and who could question their choice of role model? Roy already holds the goaltending record for most playoff victories, a statistic he is certain to pad before his retirement.

Patrick Roy, right, was a relative newcomer when he backstopped the Colorado Avalanche to the 1996 Stanley Cup. Facing page: A two-time Stanley Cup champion with the Montreal Canadiens, Roy fires the puck up-ice to a waiting teammate.

Terry Sawchuk

Terry Sawchuk's triumphs as a goaltender serve as a counterpoint to his life off the ice. Even his boyhood success was tinged by sadness. His brother died of a heart attack at the age of 17, and 10-year-old Terry inherited his goalie equipment. "The pads were always around the house," Sawchuk explained, "and I fell into them." He was such a natural that he was playing junior hockey within five years and signed his first pro contract with Omaha, in the Detroit Red Wings organization, a few years later.

Sawchuk became the starting goalie for the defending Stanley Cup champions in Detroit in the autumn of 1950 and won the Calder Trophy and First All-Star Team honors that season. He played all 70 games and had 11 shutouts. He followed up with an even better season, earning a dozen shutouts and whittling his goals-against average down to a measly 1.90 to win the Vezina Trophy. But he saved the best for last: Detroit swept both playoff series in 1951-52, and Sawchuk let in only five goals over the eight games for a 0.63 average.

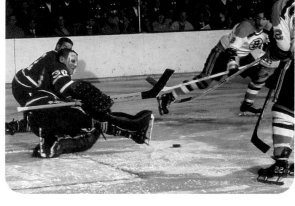

Sawchuk got his name on the Stanley Cup two more times in the following three years. "We could always count on him to come up with the big save," recalled Hall of Fame defenseman Bob Goldham. "When I look back on those Stanley Cup series [of 1954 and 1955], what I remember is 'Ukey' making one big save after another. He was the greatest goaltender who ever lived."

"I try to concentrate on the puck," said Sawchuk, in trying to describe his style. "I'm not a holler guy. I have a very low crouching style; my reflexes are that way, I guess. I can see better through the legs than over some tall guy's shoulder." His vulnerability in placing his face so close to the action wasn't lost on him. "I'm scared every time they get near me," he admitted, and the injuries he sustained over the years—ranging from facial gouges to bone fractures and ruptured spinal disks—are almost incredible. He once quipped, "We are the people who make health insurance popular."

But Sawchuk was loath to miss a game, not wanting anyone else to have a chance to shine. His first game in the NHL came when he was called up from Indianapolis to fill in for Detroit's injured goaltender Harry Lumley. Sawchuk sparkled over a seven-game stint, earning his first of a record 103 career shutouts, and the veteran Lumley was traded. Sawchuk's fears about missing a game were valid. After Glenn Hall filled in for him for two games in the 1954-55 season and showed plenty of poise, Sawchuk was deemed expendable and traded to the Boston Bruins for the 1955-56 and 1956-57 seasons.

Sawchuk had battled a weight problem over the years, tipping the scales at a portly 230 pounds in the fall of 1951 before eventually dropping to a gaunt 170 pounds. His fluttery nerves were typical of those in his profession, but the move to Boston only added to his problems. Hospitalized for two weeks with mononucleosis midway through his second season in Beantown, Sawchuk was unable to regain his All-Star form. He quit the game briefly after suffering a nervous collapse. It took a trade back to Detroit in 1957 to get him on track again.

Sawchuk earned Second All-Star Team honors twice more in Detroit before being placed on the trading block once again. He joined the Toronto Maple Leafs in 1964, sharing duties with Johnny Bower for three seasons before stepping into the limelight one last time in 1967. Sawchuk, occasionally spelled by Bower, was outstanding in Toronto's upset Stanley Cup victory over Chicago and Montreal. "I'd like to leave hockey like that," said Sawchuk after a particularly splendid game, "in good style."

It did not happen. "As soon as I go into the net, I bend down and take a sideways peek at the goalposts," Sawchuk once said. "If they look close, I know I'm going to have a good night. Some nights, those damn posts look a mile away." Sawchuk showed only flashes of his former glory during the 1967-68 season with the Los Angeles Kings, had a disappointing season with Detroit and spent his final year in the NHL used sparingly by the New York Rangers. But a calamity followed. After engaging in a postseason tussle with teammate Ron Stewart, Sawchuk died in hospital of internal injuries in May 1970. His induction into the Hockey Hall of Fame in 1971 marked the postscript to a brilliant but tragic career.

Terry Sawchuk, above, posted his one-hundredth shutout in the 1966-67 season while playing for the Toronto Maple Leafs. His record of 103 still stands. Facing page: Sawchuk shows the physically reckless style that anchored three Stanley Cup wins for the Detroit Red Wings in the 1950s.

Billy Smith

"I will match them insult for insult," Billy Smith once said, after giving the finger to New York Rangers' fans. "I was just waving them on." One of hockey's greatest playoff goalies, "Battlin' Billy" provoked his opponents and their supporters alike. A fierce competitor, he was sometimes known to skip the traditional handshake after losing a playoff series.

"I never saw a goalie so willing to crack people across the ankles with his stick," said Gump Worsley in 1975, "but he calmed down a bit last season, which helped his game."

Smith was admittedly overly preoccupied with clearing his crease of enemy forwards, but at the time, rules to protect the goaltender were less stringent than they are today and the crease was considerably smaller. "I don't bother people unless they're bothering me," he maintained in 1982. "I just try to give myself a little working room. But if a guy bothers me, then I retaliate." Smith slashed, brawled and did whatever he felt was needed, but in 1986, he stepped over the line. After breaking the jaw and cheekbone of Chicago's Curt Fraser, he sat out a six-game suspension.

Smith had been drafted by the Los Angeles Kings in 1970. Sent immediately to the minors, he helped the Springfield Kings win the Calder Trophy in the American Hockey League. Despite being named his team's most valuable player, he got only a five-game tryout with Los Angeles in 1971-72. Smith's future brightened considerably, however, when he was picked up in the 1972 expansion draft by the New York Islanders. They needed all the help they could get.

Despite playing for a last-place club and allowing an average of more than four goals per game, Smith was awarded NHL rookie-of-the-year honors for his strong efforts. While he was routinely shelled, he shaved more than a full goal off his goals-against average in year two. The team was getting stronger, and life became even better for Smith when Glenn "Chico" Resch became his netminding partner. The two soon formed one of the NHL's strongest duos, a relationship that lasted for almost seven years. Nervous about extending himself and getting injured, Smith was content to watch about half of the games from the bench. For the same reason, he avoided on-ice practice as much as possible, concentrating on tennis to enhance his footwork and pioneering the use of

computer games and simulations in training to improve his hand-eye coordination.

Smith became the first NHL goalie to score a goal when he made a save against the Colorado Rockies in 1979. With the goaltender pulled during a delayed-penalty call, Colorado defenseman Rob Ramage sent an errant pass into his own net. Smith, the last Islander to have touched the puck, was credited with the goal.

Only once did Smith post a better regular-season average than Resch. "But when it came to the playoffs," said Smith, "I always seemed to get on a roll. There was more pressure, which helped my concentration, and the game seemed a little easier." After several promising seasons, the Islanders won the Stanley Cup for four consecutive years starting in 1980, with Smith in the cage for 20 of the 21 playoff games.

"They call [baseball slugger] Reggie Jackson Mr. October," noted Islanders coach Al Arbour. " 'Smitty' is our Mr. April and Mr. May."

Smith's strong play eventually made Resch expendable. And with rookie Roland Melanson as his partner in 1981-82, Smith had his best season. He was selected to the First All-Star Team and received the Vezina Trophy, the first time the NHL's general managers voted for the league's best goalie.

Many wondered whether the Islanders would crumble before the Edmonton Oilers' offensive juggernaut in the 1983 Stanley Cup finals. Not only did Smith meet the Oilers with "probably the finest game I ever played," shutting them out 2–0 in the series opener, but he also denied Wayne Gretzky a single goal in a four-game sweep. Smith was acknowledged as the playoffs' most valuable player with the Conn Smythe Trophy.

The Oilers succeeded in knocking the Islanders off in the next season's final series, and Smith's team went into a rebuilding phase. By then the last of the original Islanders, Smith continued to play well until his retirement in 1989. The Islanders retired his jersey number 31 in 1993, the year Smith was inducted into the Hockey Hall of Fame.

Billy Smith, above, shows the aggressiveness that characterized his play, especially when it came to defending his crease and the area around the net. Facing page: His ability to focus was key to the New York Islanders' success in the early 1980s; Smith was the 1983 Conn Smythe winner.

TOP 15 GOALTENDERS

Vladislav Tretiak

NHL fans, especially in Canada, waited with glee for the beginning of the 1972 Summit Series. Canada's professionals would finally prove their vast superiority over the Soviet Union, which had been dominating international hockey for a generation with its "amateurs."

While preparing for the first game in Canada, 20-year-old Soviet goaltender Vladislav Tretiak received a surprise visitor, who brought along his own translator. "He meticulously told me, as a goalie, how to play the big Canadian shooters," recalled Tretiak. "Then he shook my hand and left. I can't explain why he came to give me secrets against his own players. Maybe he felt pity that I was so inexperienced, pity for a boy he thought Phil Esposito was going to tear apart. I wish to thank Jacques Plante for his advice."

Team Canada's scouts had reported that Tretiak was the weakest part of his team, but the opposite was true. The Canadian goalies detected Plante's influence right away, but the acrobatic Tretiak brought more than insider information to the game. "If there is a comparison to an NHL goalie I would make for Tretiak," remarked Paul Henderson, whose last-minute heroics in the final game gave Canada the narrowest of victories, "it would be Terry Sawchuk."

The Canadians were shocked to lose the opening game 7–3, but the Soviets had been honing their club for the match. "Canadians were amazed that we were not intimidated by their rough play," noted Tretiak in 1979, revealing a secret for the first time. "The Central [Red] Army sports center spent the summer preparing us for rough play. We even took boxing lessons."

Tretiak was the backbone of his team's success. Over the course of his career, he won 10 World Championship gold medals, three Olympic golds and one Olympic silver. Although he didn't play his first hockey game until he was 11 years old, he was "appointed" to the dominant Central Red Army team at age 17. He was on a record 13 Soviet league championship teams, selected Soviet player of the year five times and was winner of the Gold Stick three times as the season's outstanding European player. These are tremendous achievements, but it was his play against the NHL pros that elevated him to mythic status in North America.

Many still remember the game played in the Montreal Forum on New Year's Eve 1976. Tretiak's Red Army went head-to-head against the Montreal Canadiens' dynastic club, backstopped by Ken Dryden. Outshot 38–13, the Soviets earned a 3–3 draw due almost solely to Tretiak's superb play. He was in net when the Soviets beat the NHL All-Stars in the 1979 Challenge Cup, a three-game tournament in Madison Square Garden. In the 1981 Canada Cup tournament, he led his team to victory, allowing only eight goals in six games. "He had better concentration," remarked Wayne Gretzky, "than any goalie I've ever seen."

Tretiak's single-mindedness had developed under the watchful eye of Anatoly Tarasov, an innovative coach but a ruthless disciplinarian. "He ensured that wherever I was, I had to toss and catch a tennis ball continuously," said Tretiak, reminiscing about a reprimand he once received from Tarasov for not having a ball with him while relaxing in the ocean. "Do you think he was joking? I had to sew special pockets into my swimming trunks to hold a tennis ball." But Tretiak credited Tarasov for much of his success. "Some may think this was too much," he speculated, "but who knows?"

After picking up clues that Tretiak might be interested in joining them, the Montreal Canadiens selected him in the 1983 NHL entry draft. The Soviet Ice Hockey Federation forbade Tretiak to leave. The party line was: "We are not a farm system for the NHL." And in the Soviet era, it was not even possible for Tretiak to acknowledge that he had asked for permission. "I would have loved to play in Montreal," he admitted in later years, but the dissolution of the Soviet Union came too late for him.

It has been noted that the Soviet Union was able to prepare its national team to peak at short tournaments, while

NHL players underwent a constantly grueling season. But after 15 seasons of playing almost every game for the national team and his own club, Tretiak was burned out. "I reached a point where I got tired of the hockey uniform," he admitted, "and didn't want to put it on anymore." In 1972, he had been given Jacques Plante's book on goaltending. "It seemed to me at the time that he spent too much time on the psychological strains experienced by goalies," said Tretiak. "Now I know how right he was."

Tretiak retired in 1984 and eventually took a job as goaltender coach for the Blackhawks, a position he still holds. In the 1999 Stanley Cup finals, the two opposing goalies were former students: Buffalo's Dominik Hasek and Ed Belfour of the Dallas Stars, wearing number 20 in tribute to Tretiak.

Soviet Union netminder Vladislav Tretiak, above, forces Team Canada sniper Yvan Cournoyer to shoot wide during the 1972 Summit Series. Facing page: Tretiak foils his 1972 nemesis Paul Henderson during the 1974 series between the Soviets and the Canadian stars of the WHA.

Lorne 'Gump' Worsley

"If you want to be a good goaltender," claimed Lorne "Gump" Worsley, "it helps to be a little crazy."

Worsley had a wry wit, and his round face and pudgy physique added another dimension to his humorous persona. A boyhood friend in Montreal had named him after the comic-strip character Andy Gump, and Worsley was so short that for his own safety, he wasn't allowed to play any position other than goal. But there was nothing funny about Worsley's work in net.

"Chuck Rayner taught me how to cut down the shooters' angles and how to position myself in the net on breakaways," said Worsley, describing the help the soon-to-retire veteran goalie gave him in his 1952-53 rookie year with the New York Rangers. "Hell, he taught me everything he knew—and that was a lot. Without his guidance and encouragement, I'd probably never have made the grade."

Despite playing for a last-place club, Worsley won rookie-of-the-year honors, but the Rangers responded to his request for a raise by bringing in Johnny Bower to replace him. Worsley spent a season back in the minors, but he replaced Bower in turn the following year.

The Rangers fluctuated between NHL mediocrity and inferiority, and Worsley later admitted that he sometimes used the bottle "to chase all those bad games and bad goals away." But he retained his sense of humor. His response to a reporter's question of which team gave him the most trouble—"The Rangers"—remains one of hockey's best quips. Rangers coach Phil Watson once accused Worsley of having a beer belly. "Beer is the poor man's champagne," Worsley retorted. "I'm strictly a VO [rye whiskey] man."

While facing a barrage of shots every night—50 to 60 was not uncommon—Worsley posted a decent goals-against average of 3.10 over 10 seasons with the Rangers. But he saw his trade to Montreal in the summer of 1963 as a chance to "get out of the Rangers' jailhouse." But Worsley had difficulty establishing his place in Montreal. In his eighth game with the Habs, he pulled a hamstring muscle. A week later, he was sent to the minors to get in shape, and he didn't make it back until almost a year and a half later.

Facing the possibility that his NHL career was over, Worsley worked hard to reestablish himself as Montreal's number-one netminder. "The Gumper" tasted his first Stanley Cup champagne that spring. "Nothing has ever matched that thrill," he said. Voted Second All-Star Team goaltender, Worsley shared the Vezina Trophy with Charlie Hodge and won the Cup again the following season.

At the age of 39, Worsley played what was arguably his best hockey during the 1967-68 season. He shared the Vezina Trophy with Rogie Vachon and took First All-Star Team honors, and Montreal won the Cup again. His only frustration was seeing St. Louis netminder Glenn Hall awarded the Conn Smythe Trophy. While he liked and admired Hall—the two had swapped "trade secrets" about shooters on other teams over the years— Worsley had helped take his team to the Stanley Cup for the second time only to see the other goaltender receive the award for most valuable playoff performer. Detroit's Roger Crozier had won it in 1966.

"The abuse we goaltenders are forced to accept sometimes becomes intolerable," said Worsley. "That's why so many of us suffer nervous breakdowns." Claude Ruel—Montreal's new coach—didn't allow his aging goalie the latitude in practice that former coach Toe Blake had permitted, and the frequent air travel due to league expansion was wearing on Worsley, who was a white-knuckle flyer. He suffered an emotional collapse during the 1968-69 season but came back and helped Montreal to another championship in 1969, his fourth. Early in the next season, Vachon was doing most of the goaltending, and Worsley was sent to the minors. He went home instead.

Wren Blair of the Minnesota North Stars persuaded him to play the rest of the season for him, and Worsley stayed for five years. He found the perfect goaltending partner in lanky Cesare Maniago, and the two veterans were soon likened to the comic-strip characters "Mutt and Jeff." Worsley let his brush-cut hair grow longer and had another rebirth at the age of 42. Only Chicago goalie Tony Esposito finished with a lower average in the 1971-72 season.

"Gump Worsley really showed me something," said Phil Esposito after the Bruins fired 67 shots at Worsley in one game. "For an old man, he did one hell of a job."

Worsley retired in 1974, shortly before turning 45, and entered the Hockey Hall of Fame in 1980.

Gump Worsley, above, snaps the puck from behind the Montreal
net ahead of Toronto Maple Leaf Paul Henderson and Montreal
defenseman Terry Harper. Facing page: Worsley, shown here
thwarting Toronto's Dave Keon, weathered 10 seasons with the
New York Rangers.

Martin Brodeur

"I need a goal now," New Jersey netminder Martin Brodeur said in 1995. "I'm looking for the chance all the time. If I get it and it doesn't jeopardize my team, I'm going for it." While he came close several times to fulfilling his dream of scoring, it didn't happen until a playoff game on April 17, 1997.

Down two goals late in the Eastern Conference quarter-final series opener, the Montreal Canadiens pulled goaltender Jocelyn Thibault for an extra attacker. Brodeur quickly snagged a Habs dump-in and fired the puck the length of the ice into the vacant net. The New Jersey crowd celebrated as wildly as did Brodeur, who leapt with joy.

Brodeur grew up idolizing Patrick Roy and had little difficulty observing his hero up close, since Brodeur's father Denis, a former goalie who had won a bronze medal with Canada's 1956 Olympic team, was the official photographer for the Montreal Canadiens. Like Roy, Brodeur developed a rather conservative stand-up style that has evolved over time.

Brodeur may be the NHL's strongest goalie technically, always squarely in position and playing the angles impeccably, but he can sprawl with the best of them when he's down. Goal scoring aside, his stick work and crisp passes force teams to try to keep him from handling the puck. A teammate only half-jokingly suggested that despite the encumbrance of today's huge goalie gloves, Brodeur could play point on the New Jersey power play because of the strength of his shot.

In the 1991-92 season, with both New Jersey goaltenders injured, Brodeur got a brief emergency NHL call-up from the Quebec junior league. After another year of seasoning with Utica in the American Hockey League, he was fully prepared for the big time. He won NHL rookie-of-the-year honors in 1993-94, assisted to a degree by coach Jacques Lemaire's system of team defense. Although he often saw little action that season, Brodeur was never bored. "I don't mind," he once said. "I just keep my eye on the puck. Hockey is a good game to watch, you know."

In the 1995-96 season, veteran Grant Fuhr set the NHL record for most starts, with 79 for the St. Louis Blues, but his coach Mike "Captain Hook" Keenan pulled him out of many games. Brodeur, on the other hand, set the NHL mark for minutes played by a goaltender the same year, with 4,443 minutes over 76 games. He made his All-Star Game debut in midseason and turned aside every one of the 12 shots he faced during his first-period stint as the Eastern Conference starter. Brodeur has played in every All-Star Game since.

Brodeur's 1.88 goals-against average in 1996-97 was the NHL's lowest since Tony Esposito hit 1.77 in 1971-72, and Brodeur became only the third goalie in league history to post consecutive seasons under the magical 2.00 mark the following year. His concurrent back-to-back seasons with 10 or more shutouts were the first since Bernie Parent's Vezina Trophy-winning seasons in the mid-1970s. Unfortunately for Brodeur, Dominik Hasek was simultaneously locking up most of the top NHL awards with his netminding wizardry for the Buffalo Sabres.

The two had had their first serious head-to-head confrontation during the 1994 playoffs. While Brodeur stopped 49 of 50 shots in a four-overtime-period marathon in game six of the opening round, Hasek posted a shutout to get his team a seventh game. But rookie Brodeur and the New Jersey Devils prevailed in the end and went on to eliminate the Bruins in the second round before finally succumbing to Mark Messier and the New York Rangers in the Eastern Conference finals. The experience proved invaluable the following season.

Brodeur posted three shutouts in backing the Devils to a Stanley Cup championship in 1995. Yet he was the lowest-paid player in the league, prorated over the lockout-shortened season to just $80,000. The Devils gave him a retroactive raise of $710,000 the following year, but money is not a motivator for Brodeur. He signed a multiple-year contract extension in December 1997 that pays him about $4 million a season. "Money is really important in the sport right now, there's no doubt," says Brodeur, "but it's not everything. I don't have any shame in being the fifth highest-paid goalie in this league. I'd rather have a chance to win another Cup than just get the money and struggle for the rest of my career."

When Robbie Ftorek became the New Jersey coach in the fall of 1998, he introduced a strategy of more offense that has paid dividends for the Devils. But the decrease in defense has not helped Brodeur's personal statistics. "It does bother me a little bit," admits Brodeur, "but I'm having fun. The team is doing well, and it's not as much pressure. I know my team is going to score goals."

Asked whether he measures himself against goalies such as Hasek, Brodeur replies, "I think you'd be crazy not to look at other players. But I'm only 26 years old, so it's really tough for me not to compare myself to the guys that are over 30. Sometimes I get caught up in that, but, hey, I've got time."

Martin Brodeur, right, is about to launch the puck with the same fierce snap that allowed him to score a goal during the 1997 Stanley Cup playoffs. Facing page: Brodeur already holds every New Jersey franchise record of consequence for goaltenders, both seasonal and career.

Byron Dafoe

Byron Dafoe fans didn't have a chance to vote him a spot at the 1999 NHL All-Star Game. Despite the stellar season that Dafoe had had the year before, his name didn't even appear on the millions of preprinted ballots.

Perhaps the slight came through confusion about which team he was eligible for—the North American Team or the World Team. Born in Sussex, England, Dafoe moved to Canada at 3 months of age with his British mother and Canadian father. Even then, there was a commotion about his nationality, and Canadian immigration authorities held Mrs. Dafoe with her baby for questioning. "I don't know exactly what it was, but some of the paperwork wasn't right; there was some delay," says Dafoe, relating an old family story. "Finally, the guy just let her through, and no lie, this is what he said: 'Aw, go ahead. We'll let him in. He looks like a hockey player.' "

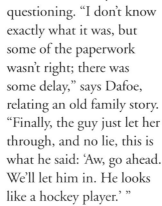

Drafted by the Washington Capitals in 1989, Dafoe spent most of three seasons in the American Hockey League before sharing the league's low-average award with Olaf Kolzig as a member of the Calder Cup-winning Portland Pirates in 1993-94. Two brief call-ups to Washington brought little more than frustration, though. Dafoe spent most of the 1994-95 NHL lockout with Phoenix in the International Hockey League, convinced that once the NHL dispute was over, he'd have a job with the Capitals.

Unfortunately, instead of battling with Kolzig for the number-one spot on the Washington team, Dafoe watched 20-year-old Jim Carey take over. Dafoe refused his demotion to Portland and was suspended for two weeks before he finally acquiesced. "In some ways, though, it was a blessing in disguise," he says, "because it forced their hand a little in the off-season to trade me [to the Los Angeles Kings].

"I never had the feeling in L.A. that I wasn't at least a legitimate backup," Dafoe recalls, splitting the Kings' netminding duties with Kelly Hrudey in 1995-96 and Stephane Fiset the following season. "I liked L.A. It was really my first full-time work." Backing a weak team gave Dafoe opportunities to shine.

"He had one of the greatest games I've ever seen," said Felix Potvin when Dafoe stopped 56 of 58 shots in a 2–2 tie against the Toronto Maple Leafs on October 28, 1995.

"For the first time, I was comfortable, very comfortable," says Dafoe, looking back on his two seasons in Los Angeles. "I'd been in a situation in Washington where I felt I had no chance. I'd play well and then go back down; it didn't matter how I played. So when the trade to Boston came, it really threw me for a loop."

Dafoe was sent to the Boston Bruins late in the summer of 1997, ironically faced with the prospect of dislodging his old nemesis Carey for the starting position. "I knew I had my work cut out for me, but I had a good training camp as well as a good start to the season. [Boston coach] Pat Burns went with me 10 games into the year."

Hockey reporters felt that Burns gave the starting position to Dafoe before he'd earned it, but "Lord Byron" made his coach look like a genius. "I owe a lot to him," says Dafoe, "because he gave me the opportunity to play night in and night out. As my confidence grew, my game improved, and it carried right through the whole year."

"Stopping the puck is the name of the game for him," explains Burns. "He's very aggressive."

Dafoe also showed the maturity of a man who's paid his dues. He backstopped Boston into the playoffs before he ran into his old friend Kolzig, who took his Washington Capitals past the Bruins to the Stanley Cup finals. Despite their on-ice competition, each still served as best man at the other's wedding over the summer of 1998. Not surprising, then, was their behavior during an on-ice melee in a Boston-Washington matchup in November of the same year. Both Kolzig and Dafoe were ejected for leaving their creases and pairing off in what looked like a tussle, except both players were laughing.

"I don't only want to be a good number-one goalie," says Dafoe, "I want to be an elite goalie. I feel last year [1997-98] was my breakthrough season. When we have a game now with [Curtis] Joseph or [Dominik] Hasek in the other net, I feel I'm on a par with those guys. I doubt my skill level has changed much in years, but my mental game, I'd say, has grown in leaps and bounds."

With 10 shutouts, Byron Dafoe, above left, led all NHL goalies in the 1998-99 season and was a Vezina Trophy finalist for the first time. Facing page: Dafoe's strong play has been a big reason for the reemergence of the Boston Bruins as a contending team in the late 1990s.

Nikolai Khabibulin

Nikolai Khabibulin was 14 years old when he read a book about Soviet goaltender Vladislav Tretiak that changed the course of his life. Inspired by Tretiak's example, Khabibulin began to work his way up through the Soviet hockey system. Within five years, Khabibulin was a backup goaltender for Russia at the 1992 Olympics.

Unfortunately, the experience was not a positive one. Because Khabibulin saw no game action, his coach kept the gold medal that should have been his. When the Russians came calling for the 1998 Olympics, they found that the bit-

ter Olympic experience and a disappointing 1996 World Cup had left the nation's best goaltender uninterested in playing for his country again. "The reasons are the same as I've told you a thousand times," he responded. "It was the style we played, the way we were treated and the way we were coached. It was terrible."

Khabibulin had been allowed to keep the gold medal he won with the Soviet Union in the 1992 World Junior Championships, and that summer, the Winnipeg Jets selected him in the ninth round of the NHL entry draft. Khabibulin earned a regular spot on the famed Central Red Army team in Moscow, though, and spent two seasons strengthening his game before coming to North America in the summer of 1994.

After half a season with Springfield in the American Hockey League, Khabibulin played his first game for Winnipeg in January 1995. He was named team rookie of the year at season's end and was voted Winnipeg's most valuable player for his second NHL season, yet his exciting play might have been the NHL's best-kept secret outside of Manitoba. That all changed when the Jets made the playoffs the following season and faced the league-leading Detroit Red Wings.

Over the 1995-96 regular season, the Red Wings finished 53 points ahead of the Winnipeg Jets, who also faced the distraction of playing out their last season in Canada before being transformed into the Phoenix Coyotes. All signs pointed to a

lopsided defeat. In the first game of the playoffs, though, Detroit was kept off the score sheet until the third period; still, the Jets lost the first two games in Detroit before Khabibulin posted his first playoff win. He allowed only one goal and was named the game's first star. He repeated the feat in game five, stopping 51 of 52 Detroit shots. In the end, Detroit proved too powerful for Winnipeg, but Khabibulin had shone under pressure in a spectacular way. "The Bulin Wall" had arrived.

Khabibulin, a Phoenix Coyote since the franchise was transferred in 1996, has been thrilled to play for the World Team at both the 1998 and 1999 NHL All-Star Games. "Goalies take it more seriously than everybody else," he says. "You just don't want to get embarrassed." He played the third period both times and allowed only three goals in total, but chumming with starter Dominik Hasek was also a highlight.

"We had fun Saturday and Sunday," said Hasek 48 hours after the 1999 All-Star tilt. "Today, it was a different story. We are not friends when we face each other."

In January 1999, the Phoenix Coyotes and Buffalo Sabres battled to a 1–1 tie, and the goaltenders were the story of the day. "Nikki got us the point," said Phoenix captain Keith Tkachuk. "We're relying on him too much. If not for him, we'd get blown out." That has become almost as common a refrain for the Coyotes as it has been for the Sabres about Hasek in recent years. Khabibulin has emerged as a premier netminder.

In 1996-97, Khabibulin had set franchise records with seven shutouts and 72 game appearances. He loved the heavy workload, maintaining a happy-go-lucky temperament through highs and lows. Khabibulin was hesitant to shed his workhorse image, but being spelled off more frequently in the 1998-99 season helped him play a more consistent game. He also dropped an old habit of poring over statistics and comparing himself with others. "When you don't know your stats," he says, "you think less. I don't know if it was hurting too much, but it obviously wasn't helping."

The Coyotes led the league for weeks, surprising many observers. "They just hung on there at the end," griped Calgary's Theo Fleury after a game. "That's the way it is every night. If they don't get a big effort from Khabibulin, they don't win." More often than not, however, with "The Bulin Wall" in place, the Coyotes *do* win.

Nikolai Khabibulin, above left, stones Vancouver's Mark Messier from in close with a sprawling save. Facing page: Khabibulin has matured with the Phoenix Coyotes into one of the NHL's elite netminders. He played in the annual All-Star Game in both 1998 and 1999.

Chris Osgood

"I was always confident before," Chris Osgood said at the outset of the 1998-99 season, "but now I have this supreme confidence, like I can beat anybody on any night." Two Stanley Cup rings will do that for you. "I don't care if I play two games, six games or however many games," he laughed in the Red Wings' locker room, "just as long as I'm standing here with a championship shirt on and holding the Cup."

Although Osgood had played the majority of regular-season games, Detroit coach Scotty Bowman had given the nod to veteran Mike Vernon in the 1997 playoffs. Osgood was unfazed. It took the un-

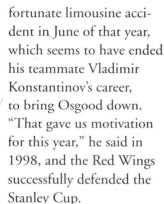

fortunate limousine accident in June of that year, which seems to have ended his teammate Vladimir Konstantinov's career, to bring Osgood down. "That gave us motivation for this year," he said in 1998, and the Red Wings successfully defended the Stanley Cup.

"Maybe I have some things to prove," Osgood said midway through the 1998 Western Conference finals against the Dallas Stars. "But if we win, next year you'll have to ask me different questions." Looking shaky on occasion, especially on some long-distance shots, Osgood showed an uncommon ability to bounce back strongly each time. After letting in Jamie Langenbrunner's overtime shoot-in, he was greeted before game six with chants of "Ozzie! Ozzie! Ozzie!" by the Detroit faithful. With an inspired effort, he shut out the Stars to help his team to the Stanley Cup finals, where he sparkled in a four-game sweep.

"I knew, come the playoffs, I had to prove I could play—for myself, for my teammates, for Vlady and for the fans," said Osgood. "I think I've done that. It's gratifying. I thrived off criticism more than anything. To have lived it and played it is a lot different than just watching. Steve Yzerman gave me the Stanley Cup right after Vlady. To me, when [Steve] says things, that means more than anyone else talking. He was always behind me in these playoffs and was always saying good things about me."

Yzerman wasn't the only one. "Even though Ozzie was a member of the first Stanley Cup-winning team," said Detroit teammate Brendan Shanahan, "he probably was still one of the few guys who felt he had to prove he could win one because Vernie got all the starts. While we believed in him, it was nice to see him carry a team on his own."

Osgood grew up in Alberta and idolized Grant Fuhr of the Edmonton Oilers. He played three years of junior hockey in the Western Hockey League, primarily for Medicine Hat. Drafted in 1991 by the Detroit Red Wings, Osgood finished out his junior eligibility and spent 1992-93 seasoning in the AHL before graduating to the NHL for the 1993-94 season.

"He doesn't look like the paperboy," said Detroit's general manager Bryan Murray. "He looks like the paperboy's little brother." Osgood's boyish looks are enhanced by the huge goalie paraphernalia that makes him look even smaller than his 160-pound five-foot-ten.

After two decent seasons, Osgood was rock-solid during the 1995-96 campaign and shared the William M. Jennings Trophy for team goals-against average with Mike Vernon. He even scored a goal against Hartford, launching a shot the length of the ice when the Whalers pulled their goalie for an extra attacker—a feat he'd also accomplished with Medicine Hat in 1991. Osgood finished second behind Washington's Jim Carey in Vezina Trophy voting, a competition he dearly wants to win.

"Winning [the Cup] gets you a certain respect that other things you accomplish don't bring you. But I want to be the best goalie this year," he said in the fall of 1998. "To do that, I have to have pretty much a flawless season, but that's something I want to accomplish. It's something that keeps me going, trying to win the best-goalie-in-the-league award."

There have been some hiccups along the way, though. "The Wizard of Oz" had his curtain pulled when he was benched by Red Wings coach Bowman for a few games midway through the 1998-99 season. "You know how mad I am?" Osgood asked the press. "I'm so mad, I almost swore to you guys. I mean, not at you, but to you. I don't know what he wants. I don't know what else I'm supposed to do. Put it

this way: It doesn't do anything good to a guy's confidence."

No one else in the club panicked, however. "Chris wants to be the best he can," said Detroit's assistant general manager Ken Holland at the time. "He'll seethe right now. He'll seethe until he gets in the net again."

Goaltending partner Kevin Hodson added, "Chris is a very humble guy. He doesn't like the spotlight. But he just oozes confidence."

By giving him something to prove once again, Bowman got the goaltender he wanted. Unfortunately, a knee injury knocked Osgood out of the first four games of the second-round 1999 playoffs. Although unable to right a careening ship, Osgood at least had the pleasure of hearing everyone who was cheering for Detroit clamoring for his return.

Detroit's Chris Osgood, above, utilizes his strong glove hand to snag the puck out of the air. Facing page: Showing the calm focus that has been his trademark, Osgood readies himself for a shot. The young goalie was a key to Detroit's 1998 defense of the Stanley Cup.

Felix Potvin

There was only a hint of a silver lining in the dark cloud that hung over Felix Potvin's 1998-99 season—he joined the team on which his childhood hero Billy Smith had starred. "This whole year has been a setback," admitted Potvin after aggravating a groin injury that knocked him out of the New York Islanders' lineup for a month. "This season has been one long bad break."

It all started back in July 1998. In a surprise move, the Toronto Maple Leafs signed free-agent goaltender Curtis Joseph to a four-year $24 million contract. Leafs management intended to deal

Potvin simultaneously, but that plan fell through. In a role he hadn't played for six years, Potvin began the season as backup while awaiting a trade that the Leafs publicly acknowledged was coming. Although Potvin had cultivated an image of almost implacable coolness under pressure, the waiting almost caused him to snap.

"As a member of the Toronto Maple Leafs organization for the past eight years," he announced on December 3, 1998, "I have given my maximum effort each day and have always been proud to be a member of this great city's hockey club. Today, however, it is with great regret that I have chosen to leave the organization." Although Potvin was immediately suspended without pay, he believed his walkout was necessary.

"I was miserable," he explained. "After practice, I would go home in a bad mood, and I didn't want to be around my family. So I felt the best thing to do was eliminate going to the rink."

Maple Leafs general manager Mike Smith was sympathetic. "I think he's reached the breaking point," he observed. "He's a real warrior, but what we've asked of him is extremely difficult." Still, it took Smith until January 9, 1999, to send Potvin to the New York Islanders in exchange for defenseman Bryan Berard.

"I can't afford to take too long to get it going," said Potvin, after losing his first game in the Islanders' net. "We

want to stay in the playoff hunt here." But things went from bad to worse. Potvin looked rusty in posting only one win and a tie in his first eight games before going on the injured list with a pulled groin muscle. "I wonder what my season would have been like," he speculated, "had the deal happened when it should have—at the start of the year." But he refused to criticize the Leafs too harshly. "There is definitely a little bitterness," he admitted, "but I'd rather look at the first six years I spent in a Leafs uniform than the past year."

Potvin certainly had some great times in Toronto. Drafted by the Leafs in 1990, he was voted Canada's Junior Goaltender of the Year the following season. A year of apprenticeship in St. John's, Newfoundland, saw Potvin win both the American Hockey League rookie-of-the-year award and the Baz Bastien Trophy as the league's top goalie. A four-game call-up went well, but the Leafs were adamant that they were going to bring their prospect along slowly. When both Toronto netminders went down with injuries at the start of the 1992-93 season, though, Potvin stepped into the breach.

Despite his stellar play, Potvin was sent back to St. John's briefly in December when Grant Fuhr returned to the lineup, but he was recalled less than a month later. Fuhr shared tips he had gathered over 11 years in the league, but Potvin already showed sufficient poise and proficiency that the Leafs soon dealt Fuhr to the Buffalo Sabres.

Potvin's 2.50 goals-against average that season led the league, he came third in Vezina Trophy voting, and he made the NHL All-Rookie Team. Yet he saved his best play for the playoffs. The emergence of "Felix the Cat" highlighted Toronto's best season in a generation. He outdueled Curtis Joseph, then playing for the St. Louis Blues, by allowing only 11 goals in the seven-game 1993 conference semifinals, and he appeared 21 times in the playoffs—more than fans saw of any other goaltender that spring. Only Wayne Gretzky's heroics in the Leafs' seventh game against Los Angeles stopped Potvin from going to the Stanley Cup finals as a freshman.

Fans voted Potvin into the starting position for the 1994 NHL All-Star Game, and he was spectacular in a first-round playoff defeat of the Chicago Blackhawks, notching three 1–0 shutouts. Although he backed his team to the conference finals for the second year in a row, Potvin was held partially to blame whenever the Leafs faltered in the next few years. "Fans in Toronto have become accustomed to the superlative from him," said Cliff Fletcher, then Maple Leafs general manager. "But if we're going to start doubting Felix, who aren't we going to doubt?"

Given the team's rise and fall, Potvin's numbers were surprisingly consistent in Toronto, creeping over a three-goals-per-game average only during the 1996-97 season, when he faced an NHL record number of 2,438 shots in 74 games with a solid .908 save percentage.

Yet Potvin is a Leaf no more. When he was traded to the Islanders in 1999, he had to forgo wearing his familiar number 29, since former Leafs teammate Kenny Jonsson— now the team's best defense-man—was already wearing it. Islanders' fans are hoping that Potvin, too, will be a key addition from the Leafs.

Felix Potvin, right, is ready to make the save for the Toronto Maple Leafs. Facing page: Despite posting his second-best goals-against average in 1997-98, Potvin was traded to the New York Islanders in January 1999, and only near the end of the 1998-99 season did he fully recover his form.

Statistics

Abbreviations

1st All-Star and 2nd All-Star: A First and Second All-Star Team, each comprising a center, a right-winger, a left-winger, two defensemen and a goaltender, are selected at the end of every season by the Professional Hockey Writers' Association.

Calder: The Calder Memorial Trophy is an annual award presented to "the player selected as the most proficient in his first year of competition in the NHL," as chosen by the Professional Hockey Writers' Association.

Ross: The Art Ross Trophy is presented annually to "the player who leads the league in scoring points at the end of the regular season."

Hart: The Hart Memorial Trophy is an annual award presented to "the player adjudged to be the most valuable to his team," as selected by the Professional Hockey Writers' Association.

Byng: The Lady Byng Memorial Trophy is an annual award presented to "the player adjudged to have exhibited the best type of sportsmanship and gentlemanly conduct combined with a high standard of playing ability," as selected by the Professional Hockey Writers' Association.

Norris: The James Norris Memorial Trophy is an annual award presented to "the defense player who demonstrates throughout the season the greatest all-round ability in the position," as selected by the Professional Hockey Writers' Association.

Richard: The Maurice "Rocket" Richard Trophy is presented annually to "the player who leads the league in goals scored at the end of the regular season."

Masterton: The Bill Masterton Memorial Trophy is an annual award presented to "the player who best exemplifies the qualities of perseverance, sportsmanship and dedication to hockey," as selected by the Professional Hockey Writers' Association.

Clancy: The King Clancy Memorial Trophy is an annual award presented to "the player who best exemplifies leadership qualities on and off the ice and has made a noteworthy humanitarian contribution in his community," as selected by the Professional Hockey Writers' Association.

Jennings: The William M. Jennings Trophy is an annual award presented "to the goalkeeper(s) having played a minimum of 25 games for the team with the fewest goals scored against it." (This was the criteria for the Vezina Trophy before the 1981-82 season.)

Vezina: The Vezina Trophy is an annual award presented to "the goalkeeper adjudged to be the best at his position," as selected by the general managers of each NHL club. Until the 1981-82 season, the Vezina Trophy was awarded to "the goalkeeper(s) of the team with the fewest goals scored against it."

Pearson: The Lester B. Pearson Award is an annual award presented to the NHL's outstanding player, as selected by the National Hockey League Players' Association.

Smythe: The Conn Smythe Trophy is an annual award presented to "the most valuable player for his team in the playoffs," as selected by the Professional Hockey Writers' Association.

HOF: Honored member of the Hockey Hall of Fame. The year of induction follows.

rs: regular season
po: playoffs
For forwards and defensemen:
gp: games played; **g:** goals; **a:** assists; **tp:** total points; **pim:** penalties in minutes
For goaltenders:
gp: games played; **m:** minutes; **ga:** goals against; **so:** shutouts; **ave:** goals against per game average

Top 15 Centers

Charles Joseph Sylvanus Apps

Paris, Ontario
January 18, 1915–December 24, 1998
NHL Career: 1936-43, 1945-48
Toronto

	gp	g	a	tp	pim
rs	423	201	231	432	56
po	69	25	28	53	16

1st All-Star (2), 2nd All-Star (3), Calder, Stanley Cup (3), HOF 1961

Jean Arthur Beliveau

Trois-Rivières, Quebec
August 31, 1931–
NHL Career: 1953-71
Montreal

	gp	g	a	tp	pim
rs	1125	507	712	1219	1029
po	162	79	97	176	211

1st All-Star (6), 2nd All-Star (4), Ross, Hart (2), Smythe, Stanley Cup (10), HOF 1972

Robert Earl Clarke

Flin Flon, Manitoba
August 13, 1949–
NHL Career: 1969-84
Philadelphia

	gp	g	a	tp	pim
rs	1144	358	852	1210	1433
po	136	42	77	119	152

1st All-Star (2), 2nd All-Star (2), Hart (3), Pearson, Masterton, Stanley Cup (2), HOF 1987

Marcel Elphege Dionne

Drummondville, Quebec
August 3, 1951–
NHL Career: 1971-89
Detroit, Los Angeles, NY Rangers

	gp	g	a	tp	pim
rs	1384	731	1040	1771	600
po	49	21	24	45	17

1st All-Star (2), 2nd All-Star (2), Ross, Byng (2), Pearson (2), HOF 1992

Philip Anthony Esposito

Sault Ste Marie, Ontario
February 20, 1942–
NHL Career: 1964-81
Chicago, Boston, NY Rangers

	gp	g	a	tp	pim
rs	1282	717	873	1590	910
po	130	61	76	137	137

1st All-Star (6), 2nd All-Star, Ross (5), Hart (2), Pearson (2), Stanley Cup (2), HOF 1984

Wayne Douglas Gretzky

Brantford, Ontario
January 26, 1961–
NHL Career: 1979-99
Edmonton, Los Angeles, St. Louis, NY Rangers

	gp	g	a	tp	pim
rs	1487	894	1963	2857	577
po	208	122	260	382	66

1st All-Star (8), 2nd All-Star (7), Ross (10), Hart (9), Byng (5), Pearson (5), Smythe (2), Stanley Cup (4), HOF 1999

Roger Mario Lemieux

Montreal, Quebec
October 5, 1965–
NHL Career: 1984-97
Pittsburgh

	gp	g	a	tp	pim
rs	745	613	881	1494	737
po	89	70	85	155	83

1st All-Star (5), 2nd All-Star (3), Calder, Ross (6), Hart (3), Masterton, Pearson (4), Smythe (2), Stanley Cup (2), HOF 1997

Mark Douglas Messier

Edmonton, Alberta
January 18, 1961–
NHL Career: 1979-
Edmonton, NY Rangers, Vancouver

	gp	g	a	tp	pim
rs	1463	610	1050	1660	1687
po	236	109	186	295	244

1st All-Star (4), 2nd All-Star, Hart (2), Pearson (2), Smythe, Stanley Cup (6)

Stanley Mikita

Sokolce, Czechoslovakia
May 20, 1940–
NHL Career: 1958-80
Chicago

	gp	g	a	tp	pim
rs	1394	541	926	1467	1270
po	155	59	91	150	169

1st All-Star (6), 2nd All-Star (2), Ross (4), Hart (2), Byng (2), Stanley Cup, HOF 1983

Howarth William Morenz

Mitchell, Ontario
September 21, 1902–March 8, 1937
NHL Career: 1923-37
Montreal, Chicago, NY Rangers

	gp	g	a	tp	pim
rs	550	270	197	467	531
po	47	21	11	32	68

1st All-Star (2), 2nd All-Star, Ross (2), Hart (3), Stanley Cup (3), HOF 1945

Joseph Henri Richard

Montreal, Quebec
February 29, 1936–
NHL Career: 1955-75
Montreal

	gp	g	a	tp	pim
rs	1256	358	688	1046	928
po	180	49	80	129	181

1st All-Star, 2nd All-Star (3), Masterton, Stanley Cup (11), HOF 1979

Milton Conrad Schmidt

Kitchener, Ontario
March 5, 1918–
NHL Career: 1936-42, 1945-55
Boston

	gp	g	a	tp	pim
rs	778	229	346	575	466
po	86	24	25	49	60

1st All-Star (3), 2nd All-Star, Ross, Hart, Stanley Cup (2), HOF 1961

Nelson Robert Stewart

Montreal, Quebec
December 29, 1902–August 21, 1957
NHL Career: 1925-40
Montreal Maroons, Boston, NY Americans

	gp	g	a	tp	pim
rs	651	324	191	515	943
po	54	15	13	28	61

Ross, Hart (2), Stanley Cup, HOF 1962

Bryan John Trottier

Val Marie, Saskatchewan
July 17, 1956–
NHL Career: 1975-92, 1993-94
NY Islanders, Pittsburgh

	gp	g	a	tp	pim
rs	1279	524	901	1425	912
po	221	71	113	184	277

1st All-Star (2), 2nd All-Star (2), Calder, Ross, Hart, Clancy, Smythe, Stanley Cup

Stephen Gregory Yzerman

Cranbrook, British Columbia
May 9, 1965–
NHL Career: 1983-
Detroit

	gp	g	a	tp	pim
rs	1178	592	891	1483	782
po	145	61	87	148	68

Pearson, Smythe, Stanley Cup (2)

5 Young Centers

Peter Mattias Forsberg

Örnsköldsvik, Sweden
July 20, 1973–
NHL Career: 1995-
Quebec, Colorado

	gp	g	a	tp	pim
rs	344	128	312	440	338
po	68	31	48	79	75

1st All-Star (2), Calder, Stanley Cup

Eric Bryan Lindros

London, Ontario
February 28, 1973–
NHL Career: 1992-
Philadelphia

	gp	g	a	tp	pim
rs	431	263	337	600	863
po	48	23	33	56	118

1st All-Star, 2nd All-Star, Hart, Pearson

Michael Thomas Modano

Livonia, Michigan
June 7, 1970–
NHL Career: 1989-
Minnesota, Dallas

	gp	g	a	tp	pim
rs	710	311	424	735	496
po	95	32	47	79	76

Stanley Cup

Mats Johan Sundin

Bromma, Sweden
February 13, 1971–
NHL Career: 1990-
Quebec, Toronto

	gp	g	a	tp	pim
rs	693	296	419	715	543
po	36	19	14	33	30

Alexei Yashin

Sverdlovsk, U.S.S.R.
November 5, 1973–
NHL Career: 1993-
Ottawa

	gp	g	a	tp	pim
rs	422	173	225	403	192
po	22	6	8	14	20

2nd All-Star

Top 15 Wingers

Michael Dean Bossy

Montreal, Quebec
January 22, 1957–
NHL Career: 1977-87
NY Islanders

	gp	g	a	tp	pim
rs	752	573	553	1126	210
po	129	85	75	160	38

1st All-Star (5), 2nd All-Star (3), Calder, Byng (3), Smythe, Stanley Cup (4), HOF 1991

John Paul Bucyk

Edmonton, Alberta
May 12, 1935–
NHL Career: 1955-78
Detroit, Boston

	gp	g	a	tp	pim
rs	1540	556	813	1369	497
po	124	41	62	103	42

1st All-Star, 2nd All-Star, Byng (2), Smythe, Stanley Cup (2), HOF 1981

Charles William Conacher

Toronto, Ontario
December 20, 1909–December 30, 1967
NHL Career: 1929-41
Toronto, Detroit, NY Americans

	gp	g	a	tp	pim
rs	460	225	173	398	523
po	49	17	18	35	53

1st All-Star (3), 2nd All-Star (2), Ross (2), Stanley Cup, HOF 1961

Michael Alfred Gartner

Ottawa, Ontario
October 29, 1959–
NHL Career: 1979-98
Washington, Minnesota, NY Rangers, Toronto, Phoenix

	gp	g	a	tp	pim
rs	1432	708	627	1335	1159
po	122	43	50	93	125

Joseph Andre Bernard Geoffrion

Montreal, Quebec
February 14, 1931–
NHL Career: 1951-64, 1966-68
Montreal, NY Rangers

	gp	g	a	tp	pim
rs	883	393	429	822	689
po	132	58	60	118	88

1st All-Star, 2nd All-Star (2), Calder, Ross (2), Hart, Stanley Cup (6), HOF 1972

Statistics

Gordon Howe

Floral, Saskatchewan
March 31, 1928–
NHL Career: 1946-71, 1979-80
Detroit, Hartford

	gp	g	a	tp	pim
rs	1767	801	1049	1850	1685
po	157	68	92	160	220

1st All-Star (12), 2nd All-Star (9), Ross (6), Hart (6), Stanley Cup (4), HOF 1972

Robert Marvin Hull

Pointe Anne, Ontario
January 3, 1939–
NHL Career: 1957-72, 1979-80
Chicago, Winnipeg, Hartford

	gp	g	a	tp	pim
rs	1063	610	560	1170	640
po	119	62	67	129	102

1st All-Star (10), 2nd All-Star (2), Ross (3), Hart (2), Byng, Stanley Cup, HOF 1983

Brett Hull

Belleville, Ontario
August 9, 1964–
NHL Career: 1986-
Calgary, St. Louis, Dallas

	gp	g	a	tp	pim
rs	861	586	459	1045	328
po	130	77	58	135	55

1st All-Star (3), Hart, Byng, Pearson, Stanley Cup

Jaromir Jagr

Kladno, Czechoslovakia
February 15, 1972–
NHL Career: 1990-
Pittsburgh

	gp	g	a	tp	pim
rs	662	345	517	862	501
po	113	55	64	119	97

1st All-Star (4), 2nd All-Star, Ross (3), Hart, Pearson, Stanley Cup (2)

Jari Pekka Kurri

Helsinki, Finland
May 18, 1960–
NHL Career: 1980-98
Edmonton, Los Angeles, NY Rangers, Anaheim, Colorado

	gp	g	a	tp	pim
rs	1251	601	797	1398	545
po	200	106	127	233	123

1st All-Star (2), 2nd All-Star (3), Byng, Stanley Cup (5)

Guy Damien Lafleur

Thurso, Quebec
September 20, 1951–
NHL Career: 1971-85, 1988-91
Montreal, NY Rangers, Quebec

	gp	g	a	tp	pim
rs	1126	560	793	1353	399
po	128	58	76	134	67

1st All-Star (6), Ross (3), Hart (2), Pearson (3), Smythe, Stanley Cup (5), HOF 1988

Robert Blake Theodore Lindsay

Renfrew, Ontario
July 29, 1925–
NHL Career: 1944-60, 1964-65
Detroit, Chicago

	gp	g	a	tp	pim
rs	1068	379	472	851	1808
po	133	47	49	96	194

1st All-Star (8), 2nd All-Star, Ross, Stanley Cup (4), HOF 1966

Francis William Mahovlich

Timmins, Ontario
January 10, 1938–
NHL Career: 1956-74
Toronto, Detroit, Montreal

	gp	g	a	tp	pim
rs	1181	533	570	1103	1056
po	137	51	67	118	163

1st All-Star (3), 2nd All-Star (6), Calder, Stanley Cup (6), HOF 1981

Richard Winston Moore

Montreal, Quebec
January 6, 1931–
NHL Career: 1951-63, 1964-65, 1967-68
Montreal, Toronto, St. Louis

	gp	g	a	tp	pim
rs	719	261	347	608	652
po	135	46	64	110	122

1st All-Star (2), 2nd All-Star, Ross (2), Stanley Cup (6), HOF 1974

Joseph Henri Maurice Richard

Montreal, Quebec
August 4, 1921–
NHL Career: 1942-60
Montreal

	gp	g	a	tp	pim
rs	978	544	421	965	1285
po	133	82	44	126	188

1st All-Star (8), 2nd All-Star (6), Hart, Stanley Cup (8), HOF 1961

5 Young Wingers

Pavel Bure

Moscow, U.S.S.R.
March 31, 1971–
NHL Career: 1991-
Vancouver, Florida

	gp	g	a	tp	pim
rs	439	267	227	494	332
po	60	34	32	66	72

1st All-Star, Calder

Paul Tetsuhiko Kariya

Vancouver, British Columbia
October 16, 1974–
NHL Career: 1994-
Anaheim

	gp	g	a	tp	pim
rs	302	168	210	378	93
po	14	8	9	17	4

1st All-Star (3), Byng (2)

Zigmund Palffy

Skalica, Czechoslovakia
May 5, 1972–
NHL Career: 1994-
NY Islanders, Los Angeles

	gp	g	a	tp	pim
rs	331	168	163	331	173
po	0	0	0	0	0

Teemu Ilmari Selanne

Helsinki, Finland
July 3, 1970–
NHL Career: 1992-
Winnipeg, Anaheim

	gp	g	a	tp	pim
rs	485	313	331	644	185
po	21	13	7	20	8

1st All-Star (2), 2nd All-Star (2), Calder, Richard

Keith Matthew Tkachuk

Melrose, Massachusetts
March 28, 1972–
NHL Career: 1992-
Winnipeg, Phoenix

	gp	g	a	tp	pim
rs	526	272	237	509	1318
po	39	18	8	26	96

2nd All-Star (2)

Top 15 Defensemen

Raymond Jean Bourque
Montreal, Quebec
December 28, 1960–
NHL Career: 1979-
Boston

	gp	g	a	tp	pim
rs	1453	385	1083	1468	1067
po	180	36	125	161	151

1st All-Star (12), 2nd All-Star (6), Calder,
Norris (5), Clancy

Christos K. Chelios
Chicago, Illinois
January 25, 1962–
NHL Career: 1984-
Montreal, Chicago, Detroit

	gp	g	a	tp	pim
rs	1076	165	633	798	2282
po	173	28	92	120	333

1st All-Star (4), 2nd All-Star (2), Norris (3),
Stanley Cup

Francis Michael Clancy
Ottawa, Ontario
February 25, 1903–November 10, 1986
NHL Career: 1921-37
Ottawa, Toronto

	gp	g	a	tp	pim
rs	592	137	143	280	904
po	61	9	8	17	92

1st All-Star (2), 2nd All-Star (2),
Stanley Cup (3), HOF 1958

Aubrey Victor Clapper
Newmarket, Ontario
February 9, 1907–January 21, 1978
NHL Career: 1927-46
Toronto

	gp	g	a	tp	pim
rs	833	228	246	474	462
po	86	13	17	30	50

1st All-Star (3), 2nd All-Star (3),
Stanley Cup (3), HOF 1947

Paul Douglas Coffey
Weston, Ontario
June 1, 1961–
NHL Career: 1980-
Edmonton, Pittsburgh, Los Angeles, Detroit,
Hartford, Philadelphia, Chicago, Carolina

	gp	g	a	tp	pim
rs	1322	385	1102	1487	1732
po	193	59	137	196	264

1st All-Star (4), 2nd All-Star (4), Norris (3),
Stanley Cup (4)

Douglas Norman Harvey
Montreal, Quebec
December 19, 1924–December 26, 1989
NHL Career: 1947-64, 1966-69
Montreal, NY Rangers, Detroit, St. Louis

	gp	g	a	tp	pim
rs	1113	88	452	540	1216
po	137	8	64	72	152

1st All-Star (10), 2nd All-Star, Norris (7),
Stanley Cup (6), HOF 1973

Myles Gilbert Horton
Cochrane, Ontario
January 12, 1930–February 21, 1974
NHL Career: 1952-74
Toronto, NY Rangers, Pittsburgh, Buffalo

	gp	g	a	tp	pim
rs	1446	115	403	518	1611
po	126	11	39	50	183

1st All-Star (3), 2nd All-Star (3),
Stanley Cup (4), HOF 1977

Leonard Patrick Kelly
Simcoe, Ontario
July 9, 1927–
NHL Career: 1947-67
Detroit, Toronto

	gp	g	a	tp	pim
rs	1316	281	542	823	327
po	164	33	59	92	51

1st All-Star (6), 2nd All-Star (2), Norris,
Byng (4), Stanley Cup (8), HOF 1969

Robert Gordon Orr
Parry Sound, Ontario
March 20, 1948–
NHL Career: 1966-78
Boston, Chicago

	gp	g	a	tp	pim
rs	657	270	645	915	953
po	74	26	66	92	107

1st All-Star (8), 2nd All-Star, Calder,
Hart (3), Ross (2), Norris (8), Smythe (2),
Stanley Cup (2), HOF 1979

Douglas Bradford Park
Toronto, Ontario
July 6, 1948–
NHL Career: 1968-85
NY Rangers, Boston, Detroit

	gp	g	a	tp	pim
rs	1113	213	683	896	1429
po	161	35	90	125	217

1st All-Star (5), 2nd All-Star (2), Masterton,
HOF 1988

Pierre Paul Pilote
Kénogami, Quebec
December 11, 1931–
NHL Career: 1955-69
Chicago, Toronto

	gp	g	a	tp	pim
rs	890	80	418	498	1251
po	86	8	53	61	102

1st All-Star (5), 2nd All-Star (3), Norris (3),
Stanley Cup, HOF 1975

Denis Charles Potvin
Ottawa, Ontario
October 29, 1953–
NHL Career: 1973-88
NY Islanders

	gp	g	a	tp	pim
rs	1060	310	742	1052	1354
po	185	56	108	164	253

1st All-Star (5), 2nd All-Star (2), Calder,
Norris (3), Stanley Cup (4), HOF 1991

Laurence Clark Robinson
Winchester, Ontario
June 2, 1951–
NHL Career: 1972-92
Montreal, Los Angeles

	gp	g	a	tp	pim
rs	1384	208	750	958	793
po	227	28	116	144	211

1st All-Star (3), 2nd All-Star (3), Norris (2),
Smythe, Stanley Cup (6), HOF 1995

Serge A. Savard
Montreal, Quebec
January 22, 1946–
NHL Career: 1967-83
Montreal, Winnipeg

	gp	g	a	tp	pim
rs	1040	106	333	439	592
po	130	19	49	68	88

2nd All-Star, Smythe, Masterton,
Stanley Cup (7), HOF 1986

Edward William Shore
Fort Qu'Appelle, Saskatchewan
November 25, 1902–March 17, 1985
NHL Career: 1926-40
Boston, NY Americans

	gp	g	a	tp	pim
rs	550	105	179	284	1037
po	55	6	13	19	179

1st All-Star (7), 2nd All-Star, Hart (4),
Stanley Cup (2), HOF 1947

Statistics

5 Young Defensemen

Bryan William Berard

Woonsocket, Rhode Island
March 5, 1977–
NHL Career: 1996-
NY Islanders, Toronto

	gp	g	a	tp	pim
rs	226	31	97	128	193
po	17	1	8	9	8

Calder

Nicklas Lidstrom

Västerås, Sweden
April 28, 1970–
NHL Career: 1991-
Detroit

	gp	g	a	tp	pim
rs	612	101	322	423	164
po	114	24	53	77	32

1st All-Star (2), Stanley Cup (2)

Robert Scott Niedermayer

Edmonton, Alberta
August 31, 1973–
NHL Career: 1992-
New Jersey

	gp	g	a	tp	pim
rs	526	63	214	277	272
po	68	9	21	30	48

2nd All-Star, Stanley Cup

Sandis Ozolinsh

Riga, Latvia
August 3, 1972–
NHL Career: 1992-
San Jose, Colorado

	gp	g	a	tp	pim
rs	424	99	218	317	323
po	90	16	54	70	90

1st All-Star, Stanley Cup

Chris Robert Pronger

Dryden, Ontario
October 10, 1974–
NHL Career: 1993-
Hartford, St. Louis

	gp	g	a	tp	pim
rs	429	50	136	186	713
po	42	4	19	23	92

2nd All-Star

Top 15 Goaltenders

John William Bower

Prince Albert, Saskatchewan
November 8, 1924–
NHL Career: 1953-54, 1958-70
NY Rangers, Toronto

	gp	m	ga	so	ave
rs	552	32077	1347	37	2.52
po	74	4350	184	5	2.54

1st All-Star, Vezina (2), Stanley Cup (4),
HOF 1976

Francis Charles Brimsek

Eveleth, Minnesota
September 26, 1915–November 11, 1998
NHL Career: 1938-43, 1945-50
Boston, Chicago

	gp	m	ga	so	ave
rs	514	31210	1404	40	2.70
po	68	4365	186	2	2.56

1st All-Star (2), 2nd All-Star (6), Calder,
Vezina (2), Stanley Cup (2), HOF 1966

Walter Edward Broda

Brandon, Manitoba
May 15, 1914–October 17, 1972
NHL Career: 1936-43, 1945-52
Toronto

	gp	m	ga	so	ave
rs	629	38167	1609	62	2.53
po	101	6406	211	12	1.98

1st All-Star (2), 2nd All-Star, Vezina (2),
Stanley Cup (5), HOF 1967

Kenneth Wayne Dryden

Hamilton, Ontario
August 8, 1947–
NHL Career: 1971-73, 1974-79
Montreal

	gp	m	ga	so	ave
rs	397	23352	870	46	2.24
po	112	6846	274	10	2.40

1st All-Star (5), 2nd All-Star, Vezina (5),
Stanley Cup (6), HOF 1983

William Ronald Durnan

Toronto, Ontario
January 22, 1916–October 31, 1972
NHL Career: 1943-50
Montreal

	gp	m	ga	so	ave
rs	383	22945	901	34	2.36
po	45	2871	99	2	2.07

1st All-Star (6), Vezina (6), Stanley Cup (2),
HOF 1964

Grant Fuhr

Spruce Grove, Alberta
September 28, 1962–
NHL Career: 1981-
Edmonton, Toronto, Buffalo, Los Angeles,
St. Louis

	gp	m	ga	so	ave
rs	845	47678	2679	25	3.37
po	150	8819	430	6	2.93

1st All-Star, 2nd All-Star, Jennings, Vezina,
Stanley Cup (5)

Glenn Henry Hall

Humboldt, Saskatchewan
October 3, 1931–
NHL Career: 1955-71
Detroit, Chicago, St. Louis

	gp	m	ga	so	ave
rs	906	53464	2239	84	2.51
po	115	6899	321	6	2.79

1st All-Star (7), 2nd All-Star (4), Calder,
Vezina (3), Smythe, Stanley Cup, HOF 1975

Dominik Hasek

Pardubice, Czechoslovakia
January 29, 1965–
NHL Career: 1990-
Chicago, Buffalo

	gp	m	ga	so	ave
rs	414	23902	901	42	2.26
po	56	3382	116	5	2.06

1st All-Star (5), Hart (2), Pearson (2), Jennings,
Vezina (5)

Bernard Marcel Parent

Montreal, Quebec
April 3, 1945–
NHL Career: 1965-72, 1973-79
Boston, Philadelphia, Toronto

	gp	m	ga	so	ave
rs	608	35136	1493	55	2.55
po	71	4302	174	6	2.43

1st All-Star (2), Vezina (2), Smythe (2),
Stanley Cup (2), HOF 1984

Joseph Jacques Plante

Mont-Carmel, Quebec
January 17, 1929–February 27, 1986
NHL Career: 1952-65, 1968-73
Montreal, NY Rangers, St. Louis, Toronto,
Boston

	gp	m	ga	so	ave
rs	837	49533	1965	82	2.38
po	112	6651	241	15	2.17

All-Star (3), 2nd All-Star (4), Hart, Vezina (7),
Stanley Cup (6), HOF 1978

Patrick Roy

Quebec City, Quebec
October 5, 1965–
NHL Career: 1985-
Montreal, Colorado

	gp	m	ga	so	ave
rs	778	45397	2014	46	2.66
po	179	11052	444	12	2.41

1st All-Star (3), 2nd All-Star (2), Vezina (3),
Jennings (4), Smythe (2), Stanley Cup (3)

Terrance Gordon Sawchuk

Winnipeg, Manitoba
December 28, 1929–May 31, 1970
NHL Career: 1950-70
Detroit, Boston, Toronto, Los Angeles,
NY Rangers

	gp	m	ga	so	ave
rs	971	57114	2401	103	2.52
po	104	6311	267	12	2.54

1st All-Star (3), 2nd All-Star (4), Calder,
Vezina (4), Stanley Cup (4), HOF 1971

William John Smith

Perth, Ontario
December 12, 1950–
NHL Career: 1971-89
Los Angeles, NY Islanders

	gp	m	ga	so	ave
rs	680	38431	2031	22	3.17
po	132	7645	348	5	2.73

1st All-Star, Jennings, Vezina, Smythe,
Stanley Cup (4), HOF 1993

Vladislav Aleksandrovich Tretiak

Dmitrov, U.S.S.R.
April 25, 1952–
No NHL experience
HOF 1989

Lorne John Worsley

Montreal, Quebec
May 14, 1929–
NHL Career: 1952-53, 1954-74
NY Rangers, Montreal, Minnesota

	gp	m	ga	so	ave
rs	862	50232	2432	43	2.90
po	70	4080	192	5	2.82

1st All-Star, 2nd All-Star, Calder, Vezina (2),
Stanley Cup (4), HOF 1980

5 Young Goaltenders

Martin Pierre Brodeur

Montreal, Quebec
May 6, 1972–
NHL Career: 1992-
New Jersey

	gp	m	ga	so	ave
rs	375	21627	789	36	2.19
po	61	3874	126	6	1.95

2nd All-Star (2), Calder, Jennings (2),
Stanley Cup

Byron Jaromir Dafoe

Sussex, England
February 25 1971-
NHL Career: 1994–
Washington, Los Angeles, Boston

	gp	m	ga	so	ave
rs	230	12941	579	17	2.68
po	21	1328	46	3	2.08

2nd All-Star

Nikolai Khabibulin

Sverdlovsk, U.S.S.R.
January 13 1973–
NHL Career: 1994-
Winnipeg, Phoenix

	gp	m	ga	so	ave
rs	284	16026	735	21	2.75
po	24	1419	65	1	2.75

Christopher John Osgood

Peace River, Alberta
November 26, 1972–
NHL Career: 1993-
Detroit

	gp	m	ga	so	ave
rs	284	16491	647	23	2.35
po	53	3077	111	6	2.16

2nd All-Star, Jennings, Stanley Cup (2)

Felix Potvin

Anjou, Quebec
June 23, 1971–
NHL Career: 1992-
Toronto, NY Islanders

	gp	m	ga	so	ave
rs	360	22067	1063	12	2.89
po	52	3205	147	5	2.75

Bibliography

The books listed here were of immeasurable assistance, but several other sources were equally useful. The archived newspaper and magazine clippings at the Hockey Hall of Fame in Toronto as well as the Hall Website (www.hhof.com) provided a wealth of material. Other Internet sites I frequently visited were: Slam! Sports Hockey (www.canoe.com/Hockey/home.html), operated by the *Sun* newspaper chain; (ESPNET.SportsZone.com/nhl), run by ESPN; and *LCS Guide to Hockey* (www.lcshockey.com), written by Joe Pelletier and Pat Houda. Although too numerous to mention, dozens of other Websites—run primarily by fans out of an enthusiastic loyalty to the game and to particular players—were of some practical use. Many newspaper Websites, especially those of *The Boston Globe*, *The St. Louis Post-Dispatch*, *The London Free Press*, *The Toronto Star* and *The Globe and Mail*, were also helpful.

Dozens of issues of *The Hockey News* were used as sources, and their many writers and editors deserve credit, not only from me but for the fine work they do for the sport of hockey. Articles in *Sports Illustrated* also served as a source for quotes. Several volumes of the annual *National Hockey League Official Guide and Record Book* were indispensable for their statistical information, as were a large assortment of individual clubs' 1998-99 NHL media guides.

Benedict, Michael, and D'Arcy Jenish (eds.). *Canada on Ice: Fifty Years of Great Hockey*. The Penguin Group, Toronto, 1998.

Brewitt, Ross. *Last Minute of Play: Tales of Hockey Grit and Glory*. Stoddart Publishing Co. Ltd., Toronto, 1993.

Coleman, Jim, et al. *Legends of Hockey*. Viking/Opus Productions, Toronto, 1996.

Dryden, Steve (ed.). *The Top 100: NHL Players of All Time*. McClelland & Stewart Inc., Toronto, 1998.

Fischler, Stan. *Bad Boys: The Legends of Hockey's Toughest, Meanest, Most-Feared Players*. McGraw-Hill Ryerson Ltd., Whitby, 1991.

———. *Bobby Orr and the Big, Bad Bruins*. Dell Publishing Co., Inc., New York, 1969.

———. *Golden Ice: The Greatest Teams in Hockey History*. McGraw-Hill Ryerson Ltd., Scarborough, 1990.

———. *The Greatest Maple Leafs: 1946-51*. Warwick Publishing Inc., Toronto, 1995.

——— and Shirley Fischler. *Heroes & History: Voices from the NHL's Past*. McGraw-Hill Ryerson Ltd., Whitby, 1994.

———. *The Rivalry: Canadiens vs. Leafs*. McGraw-Hill Ryerson Ltd., Whitby, 1991.

Forrest, Brett. *Men's Journal*. Wenner Media Inc., New York, May 1998.

Goyens, Chris, and Allan Turowetz. *Lions in Winter*. Prentice-Hall Canada Inc., Scarborough, 1986.

Houston, William. *Pride & Glory: 100 Years of the Stanley Cup*. McGraw-Hill Ryerson Ltd., Whitby, 1992.

Hughes, Morgan. *Best of Hockey*. Publications International, Inc., Chicago, 1998.

———. *Hockey Legends of All Time*. Publications International, Inc., Chicago, 1996.

Hunter, Douglas. *A Breed Apart: An Illustrated History of Goaltending*. Viking, Toronto, 1995.

———. *Champions: The Illustrated History of Hockey's Greatest Dynasties*. Penguin Studio, Toronto, 1997.

———. *Open Ice: The Tim Horton Story*. Viking, Toronto, 1997.

Irvin, Dick. *The Habs: An Oral History of the Montreal Canadiens, 1940-1980*. McClelland & Stewart Inc., Toronto, 1991.

Klein, Jeff Z., and Karl-Eric Reif. *The Coolest Guys on Ice*. Turner Publishing, Inc., Atlanta, 1996.

Leonetti, Mike. *Hockey's Golden Era: Stars of the Original Six*. Macmillan of Canada, Toronto, 1993.

Liebman, Glenn. *Hockey Shorts: 1,001 of the Game's Funniest One-Liners*. Contemporary Books, Chicago, 1996.

MacGregor, Roy. *The Home Team: Fathers, Sons & Hockey*. Viking, Toronto, 1995.

MacKinnon, John. *NHL Hockey: The Official Fans' Guide*. Raincoast Books, Vancouver, 1996.

McDonell, Chris. *For the Love of Hockey: Hockey Stars' Personal Stories*. Firefly Books Ltd., Willowdale, 1997.

McKinley, Michael. *Hockey Hall of Fame Legends*. Viking/Opus Productions, Toronto, 1993.

O'Brien, Andy, and Frank Pagnucco. *Heroes: Stars of Hockey's Golden Era*. Prentice-Hall Canada Inc., Scarborough, 1985.

Potvin, Denis, with Stan Fischler. *Power on Ice*. Harper & Row, New York, 1977.

Robinson, Dean. *Howie Morenz: Hockey's First Superstar*. The Boston Mills Press, Erin, 1982.

Robinson, Larry, and Chris Goyens. *Robinson for the Defence*. McGraw-Hill Ryerson Ltd., Scarborough, 1988.

Romain, Joseph, and James Duplacey. *Hockey Superstars*. Smithbooks in Canada, Toronto, 1994.

Ross, Sherry. *Hockey Scouting Report 1998-1999*. Greystone Books, Vancouver, 1998.

Roxborough, Henry. *The Stanley Cup Story*. The Ryerson Press, Toronto, 1964.

Weekes, Don. *Old-Time Hockey Trivia*. Greystone Books, Vancouver, 1995.

Worsley, Lorne, with Tim Moriarty. *They Call Me Gump*. Dodd, Mead & Company, New York, 1975.

Acknowledgments

I could not do what I do without the support and encourage-ment of Sue Gordon. I did not thank her enough during the process of writing this book, but I am grateful for all that she gives me. Our children—Quinn, Tara and Isaac—have been patient and tolerant of the time I have spent writing. Their curiosity, enthusiasm and growing willingness to voice both shared and contrary hockey opinions have made this project even more enjoyable.

The idea behind *Hockey's Greatest Stars: Legends and Young Lions* evolved from conversations with Lionel Koffler and Michael Worek of Firefly Books. I am deeply appreciative for their vision and for all their efforts in making this book a reality. Many others have also played an essential part. In addition to analyzing written opinion, I consulted a variety of hockey experts. I promised anonymity, but you know who you are—thank you for making a difficult job a little easier.

Various NHL media and communications personnel have also been of assistance, answering myriad questions and pointing me in the right direction, particularly Pat Park of the Toronto Maple Leafs.

Craig Campbell at the Hockey Hall of Fame entered the breach with me once more and sourced another outstanding collection of images with patience and good humor. Other staff members—Jane Rodney and Phil Pritchard, in particular—also made my visits to the Hall more productive and pleasant.

Larry Scanlan offered his editorial overview again, with an attentive look at making sure that I gave each player his due, an effort for which I am thankful. My pages were always returned speckled with small, cryptic notes that were immensely helpful. Tracy Read and Susan Dickinson of Bookmakers Press and Andrew McLachlan of Kroma Design took the words and pictures to the next level and sculpted them with the highest standards of accuracy and clarity and beauty. I am very pleased with the result and glad to have had the chance to work with such good people again.

My parents, Alanson and Nora McDonell, have been behind me all the way, as have my siblings. Anne McDonell and John Travaglini, Marjorie and Larry MacIsaac, Janet and Mike Palmer and my brother Kevin McDonell have been generous in concrete ways and have provided moral support, which has also come from my sisters Carolyn McDonell and her husband Ross Perrault, across the continent in Los Angeles, and my sister Barbara Vincent and her husband Ryan, across the world in Australia. My in-laws Randy and Nancy Gordon have given generously in words and deeds, and other members of the Gordon clan—particularly Karen with our children; Eric and Eileen in Utah; and Mary in Victoria, British Columbia—have also been encouraging. My thanks to you all.

The London Waldorf School community has been a gift that Sue and I have valued. Older friends from farther afield have likewise been a blessing. Last, but not least, I'd like to thank all the hockey players of my youth in the St. Timothy schoolyard, especially Ted Moriarty, Leonard Crichton and Pete Mariani. The passion for hockey that defined so much of our lives then pulses through me still. If not for the purity of that experience, *Hockey's Greatest Stars* would not have been written.

—Chris McDonell

Index

Photo Credits

Brian Babineau/Hockey Hall of Fame
71, 72, 101, 172, 173

Steve Babineau/Hockey Hall of Fame
29, 91, 97, 99, 151, 178

John Cordes/Hockey Hall of Fame
88

Graphic Artists/Hockey Hall of Fame
23, 54, 59, 68, 80, 110, 111, 114, 117,
118, 119, 141, 166, 167, 168, 169

Hockey Hall of Fame
33, 39, 104, 105, 127

Imperial Oil-Turofsky/Hockey Hall of Fame
10, 14, 15, 34, 36, 37, 60, 61, 64, 65, 67, 78, 79, 82,
83, 84, 85, 96, 102, 103, 109, 112, 113, 126, 138, 140,
142, 143, 144, 145, 148, 149, 152, 159, 163

Fred Kennan/Hockey Hall of Fame
115

London Life-Portnoy/Hockey Hall of Fame
18, 20, 21, 22, 28, 31, 41, 58, 66, 77, 81, 116, 120,
121, 123, 124, 125, 156, 157, 164, 165

Doug MacLellan/Hockey Hall of Fame
8, 26, 27, 40, 48, 50, 62, 63, 74, 86, 94, 95, 100, 107,
122, 132, 133, 135, 136, 160, 171, 175, 176

Craig Melvin/Hockey Hall of Fame
55

Mike Nadal/Hockey Hall of Fame
56

O-Pee-Chee/Hockey Hall of Fame
19, 23, 25, 57, 75, 98, 106

Frank Prazak/Hockey Hall of Fame
11, 13, 16, 17, 30, 35, 69, 76,
108, 146, 147, 153, 158, 162

James Rice/Hockey Hall of Fame
32, 38

Dave Sandford/Hockey Hall of Fame
6, 9, 12, 24, 42, 43, 44, 45, 46, 47, 49, 51, 52, 53,
70, 73, 87, 89, 90, 92, 93, 128, 129, 130, 131, 134,
137, 139, 150, 154, 155, 161, 170, 174, 177, 179

Front cover photograph:
© Graphic Artists/Hockey Hall of Fame

Back cover photograph:
© Dave Sandford/Hockey Hall of Fame